Chaos and Violence

Chaos and Violence

What Globalization, Failed States, and Terrorism Mean for U.S. Foreign Policy

Stanley Hoffmann

ROWMAN & LITTLEFIELD PUBLISHERS, INC.
Lanham • Boulder • New York • Toronto • Plymouth, UK

ROWMAN & LITTLEFIELD PUBLISHERS, INC.

Published in the United States of America
by Rowman & Littlefield Publishers, Inc.
A wholly owned subsidiary of The Rowman & Littlefield Publishing Group, Inc.
4501 Forbes Boulevard, Suite 200, Lanham, Maryland 20706
www.rowmanlittlefield.com

Estover Road, Plymouth PL6 7PY, United Kingdom

Distributed by NATIONAL BOOK NETWORK

Copyright © 2006 by Rowman & Littlefield Publishers, Inc.

British Library Cataloguing in Publication Information Available

Library of Congress Cataloging-in-Publication Data

Hoffmann, Stanley.
    Chaos and violence : what globalization, failed states, and terrorism mean for U.S.
foreign policy / Stanley Hoffmann.
        p.   cm.
    Includes bibliographical references and index.
    ISBN-13: 978-0-7425-4071-2 (cloth : alk. paper)
    ISBN-10: 0-7425-4071-5 (cloth : alk. paper)
        1. United States—Foreign relations—2001–   2. United States—Foreign relations—
1993–2001.   3. World politics—1995–2005.   4. Intervention (International law)
5. Security, International.   6. Iraq War, 2003–   7. War on Terrorism, 2001–   I. Title.
JZ1480.H64   2006
327.73—dc22

                                                                        2006014085

Printed in the United States of America

∞ ™ The paper used in this publication meets the minimum requirements of American
National Standard for Information Sciences—Permanence of Paper for Printed Library
Materials, ANSI/NISO Z39.48-1992.

For Pierre Hassner,

my friend for fifty years—and my model as an essayist who
spreads the light of knowledge, wisdom, and reason over the
tormented landscape of international affairs

Contents

viii   *Contents*

· 1 ·

Introduction: The State of the World and the State of the Discipline

I.

In the fifty years I have been observing and writing on international affairs, never has the world seemed so disordered. This is my fifth collection of essays on international affairs in forty years. It consists of pieces written in the past six years. The previous collection was called *World Disorders*. These disorders have taken a turn for the worse; to all the previous problems, new ones have been added: the development of terrorism on a world scale, even if most destructive forms of it are those linked to Islamic fundamentalism, and the "revolution" of American foreign policy under George W. Bush. Many of the essays that follow deal with those two changes. Insofar as terrorism is concerned, it is important to note the multiplicity of its causes and, in the case of Islamic fundamentalism, of its grievances, such as the various forms of American presence in the Islamic world, the revival of a militant Islam that is sharply critical of many aspects of Western culture and of Christian faith, and the widespread discrimination that Muslims experience in Western countries, where they have become a considerable and uneasy presence. The main question is why all those grievances have turned to such violence, and here again there are many reasons: the role of religious schools and preachers who fan the flames of the sense of despair, humiliation, and resentment that animates the terrorists and leads many to accept their own death in order to cause the deaths of others. It is not in any way a form of apology or a condoning of terrorism to try to explain it, if only because we need to address the serious problems that are behind it.

Many of the terrorists come from areas where ethnic groups struggle for their autonomy, such as Palestine or Chechnya, and most come from countries in which democracy, as the West understands it, does not exist—hence the American drive, a little belatedly, to spread democracy in the Middle East

1

and indeed in all the other parts of the world that do not benefit from it. But we have to be triply cautious. First, not everything that looks democratic on paper is necessarily democratic in effect. What we ought to be concerned with is the spread of liberal democracy, the kind that Tocqueville and John Stuart Mill endorsed. Many countries give themselves constitutions (or rather are given constitutions by their leaders) that seem admirably democratic but turn out to be empty shells. It is not just free elections that matter. What matters is how open they are and what they lead to. It is perfectly possible to imagine a Middle East that, in appearance, would have partly yielded to the American effort to bring it Western forms of government but that, in effect, would be dangerously illiberal, with often xenophobic regimes. This would not be much of a progress. Second, building democracy is a very slow process. One of the great merits of Tocqueville was to show how much, in America, the institutions of the independent United States owed to the mores and practices that had developed over time and had been, in large part, imported from Britain. Those practices, "habits of the heart," and institutions (local self-government, a free press, a free judiciary, good schooling systems, and so on could not be set up overnight, and when they are imported from abroad, it usually takes time for them to find new roots. The establishment of democratic regimes from outside is successful only in exceptional cases, such as those of Germany and Japan at the end of the most devastating war the world has ever known and at a moment when the destruction had created a tabula rasa in Germany and Japan. For all these reasons, we need to remember the words that the late and great George Kennan wrote many years ago about foreign policy being more a form of gardening than a kind of engineering; but engineering is the American mode of action.

I consider one of the most important of the essays that follow to be the first one, on the state of the world today; it summarizes my reading of the multiple currents that change, pervert, and disturb it and primarily the forms and effects of globalization, and it examines how the world of globalization interacts with the traditional nature of interstate relations, which persist with problems old and new. Among the latter, nuclear proliferation is certainly one of the most serious. I want to underline here a point that is present, directly or indirectly, in many of the essays: the need for stronger institutions in a world in which so many problems can be treated only at the global or regional level and in which so many states are facades behind which chaos and violence are manifest. The frequent weakness of national institutions makes even more deplorable that of regional and international organizations, which depend for their consolidation and for the enforcement of their policies on the help of states, many of which oppose it or are too frail to be very constructive. This is a world that harbors not only the traditional games of states that they continue to play even as their sovereignty (i.e., their capacity to control events) is eroding but also a kind of global society that is both civil and uncivil. As a result, there are, so to speak, two states of nature to contend with: that of the states still devoid of any effective central power above them and of any consensus on many issues and that of an incipient global society that is wracked by glaring inequalities, injustices, and forms of violence and rather poorly regulated by the states and by multinational agencies. It is not a pretty picture, and it lacks the relative simplicity of periods in which two sets of forces confronted each other all over the globe, as was the case during the age of totalitarianism (there are many similarities between secular totalitarismisms and Islamic fundamentalism, but they are sufficiently different for us not to assimilate them completely). Fanaticism has certainly not disappeared, and the proliferation of militant and extreme forms of religious faith—Christian, Muslim, and Judaic—is a major factor of chaos and violence. This has often been the case in history: Christianity has meant both Jesus and the Inquisition. One attempt by states to provide themselves with a central, common power—the European Union—is currently in trouble; the reader will find it discussed in the last chapter.

As for the "revolution" in American foreign policy, it is the subject of several of these essays as well as of my book *Gulliver Unbound* (2004). As I stated in its conclusion, I am struck by the consensus of the American establishment on the virtues of unipolarity and of American hegemony. The Democrats seem to believe that if we stopped mishandling friends and allies, sent delegations to them, and so on, they'd be willing again to follow us as the only superpower. After Iraq, how many of our friends in the world will still see us as a power that "sees farther" and is wiser than anyone else? As long as we not only exert leadership but also interpret it as a right or even a duty to set (after consultation, to be sure) policies for the world that others will be glad to endorse, we shall be frustrated, and we'll discover that the desire "to exert more influence and hold American power in check" will persist. We need to understand that our task ought to be to contribute to the definition of *common* policies, especially in all the areas where we can't operate without the consent and participation of others, even if this means compromises and the sharing of initiatives (in other words, acting in a way that has not marked either our policy in the case of the Israeli–Palestinian "road map" or our attitude toward the European Union's attempts at shaping a common EU security policy). It is not up to us to decide what is or is not "central to the self-interest" of others.

I believe that it is actually in America's own interest to allow groupings of foreign powers—in Europe, Africa, Asia, and Latin America—to increase their power and means of action. I also believe that the United States should reconsider the way it envisages the battle against global terrorism, an approach that would emphasize struggles rather than war, distinguish between kinds of terrorism, and thus make international cooperation easier.

The Middle East peace process should certainly be among the highest priorities. But it also requires a clear direction: a return to negotiations between Israeli and Palestinian officials, a repudiation of unilateral measures that aggravate the prospects for peace (the opposite from our quasi-unconditional endorsement of a West Bank wall that annexes de facto parts of Palestine), and a willingness to deal quickly with fundamental issues, such as the creation of a viable Palestinian state.

Much more needs to be said about the distribution of U.S. resources for foreign affairs. The protection of our security does not require a budget of over $400 billion, much of which will go to the production of fancy new weapons in a world that is not currently faced with an imminent battle of Titans. The absolutely vital tasks of economic development and state building need to be undertaken on a vastly grander scale than until now, and taking these tasks seriously would contribute greatly to the struggle against terrorism.

Finally, a new policy toward our Middle East friends (or in some cases "friends") will require a new willingness to push more ardently toward a degree of democratization, but peacefully and skillfully, and to put more distance between us and authoritarian leaders on whom we have relied. This will require a new oil policy at home as well as serious thought about how to support forces of modernization and democratization abroad without turning them into clients and dependents.

II.

The discipline of international relations should help us better understand a world traversed by so many conflicting trends and actors. But it often does not. One of the troubles is that the discipline remains an American social science, as I suggested many years ago. With the single exception of the "British school," founded on a notion of the international system that takes into account political philosophy, history, and normative concerns and which integrates elements of realism and Grotian liberalism, the discipline remains imbued with American scientism. This has many aspects, such as the perennial search for certainty, which leads to a desire to distinguish it from history, often ignored or neglected by the desire for greater rigor, consistency in propositions, predictive power, and modelization. This kind of "economics envy" is understandable, but it tends to treat historical processes as bundles of separable data. In addition, it leads to a frequently slanted view of the world. This view is horizontal rather than vertical and doesn't take sufficiently into account phenomena of inequality. It doesn't pay enough attention to the diversity and occasional perversity of perceptions shaped by diverse historical experiences, cultural perspectives, and geographical situations. There is an implicit assumption that all the actors are basically alike. There are traces of this even in philosophies as powerful and important as those of John Rawls and Michael Walzer, not to mention, of course, American foreign policy. And there is myopia about the American role in the world, including in the world economy. This ranges from underestimating the degree to which globalization is not merely a kind of international relations distinguished by its novelty and originality—a view that is fashionable both in theoretical and in empirical analysis—but also an American policy that serves American preponderance.

Officially, everybody agrees that the purpose of the discipline is a systematic understanding of the world, but this conceals one important tension. Is understanding the world an end in itself, or do we try to understand it in order better to build theory? If it is the former, theory is very useful for focusing on important variables and correlations and for developing hypotheses that need to be tested, but these are mainly tools for research that will allow, of course, for theoretical refinement. If its purpose is the latter, there are many dangers. Often there is insufficient testing, or the squeezing of reality into conceptual boxes, causing oversimplification and what might be called causal monomania. There are important areas in which theorizing is deemed to be either too complex or unnecessary, such as foreign policy studies, which are neglected; case studies, often the best studies we have at our disposal, are discarded or discounted because they are not susceptible to generalization. The need for theoretical pluralism is also frequently discarded, and explanation occurs at the expense of evaluation. Thus, methodological battles have continued, partly because of the hegemonic behavior of the proponents of rational choice. Rational choice is a perfectly useful and sensible method in much of international economic analysis. Just as in domestic economics, the assumption of a multitude of rational actors seeking gain is essential, but in many other fields of international relations, rational choice models are often based on unstated assumptions or on assumptions that are explicit but highly debatable, such as the notion that every leader seeks only to maintain himself in power. Among the fundamental assumptions, that of the unitary actor is often quite wrong: this complicates, of course, the assessment of preferences. In addition, what is rational remains an exceedingly complex question. International politics, like all politics, is driven by ends, and the empirical findings of the ends of the actors cannot be adequately replaced by incorrect or oversimplified assumptions. Many of the miscalculations that occur in international affairs result from a wrong analysis of one's opponents' goals. It is not very satisfying to declare rational any means that assumes to lead to whatever end an actor has in mind. There are cases when an actor uses means that conflict with his ends, such as the case of the conflict analyzed by Scott Sagan between the Japanese desire, in 1941, to use force so as to prod the United States into a change of its policy of hostility to Japanese expansion and the decision to destroy the American fleet at Pearl Harbor, which was bound to lead to total war instead. In addition, can one really call rational policies that use a means such as the systematic killing of innocents? In other words, are policies of terrorism rational? Maybe, but only if one completely separates rationality from morality. The main problems with rational choice are a discounting of uncertainty that can always disrupt the best calculations or make very different means to an end appear equally rational and the fitting of what is not rational into its mold. This happens when one tries to provide an account of nationalism and ethnicity in rational choice terms. One of the possible effects of rational choice hegemony is a waste of effort and money on attempts to quantify phenomena that are either almost impossible to measure or perfectly obvious, such as unipolarity. Some foreign policies pursued by Nazism or communism cannot be understood if one fails to take into account the distortions introduced by ideology (anti-Semitism, say, or the centrality of the class struggle) on the choice of means toward ends.

All the different theories of international relations are open to criticism. Realism has some formidable names in its heritage, such as Thucydides, Morgenthau, and Aron. It remains relevant insofar as it is based on the idea of the centrality of war, hence on the necessity of actors to calculate their forces in a universe of threats. But this does not account for all of international affairs. Also debatable is the assumption that political regimes, while they certainly can aggravate matters (Morgenthau was not blind to the effects of Nazism or communism in international affairs) are ultimately trumped by geopolitics. This has led realist theorists to remain very skeptical about the theory of the democratic peace. Realism also suffers from some inner uncertainties—are alignments determined by the balance of power or by the balance of threats?—and by some oversimplifications in its way of looking at the game of power as being dominated by "hard" power. Realism's assumption that the choice of states is between balancing and bandwagoning is certainly parsimonious, but it is also a bit miserly. There are other choices and periods in history where balancing mechanisms did not operate. In its neorealist or "structural" realist form, the theory discards domestic factors and transnational phenomena, makes little or insufficient room for the role of ideas, and displays a certain poverty in its conceptions of change.

Liberalism, on the political front, shows a profound faith in the peace-making capacity of democracy, but the verdict is not fully in. There is no evidence that democratic countries in their relations with undemocratic ones do much to curb violence, there is no consensus on what constitutes a democracy, and in the relations among democratic states we have too few examples to be sure that if a clash of vital interests occurred between two of them, the outcome would always be accommodation. (Would a democratic Pakistan and a democratic India have been invariably peaceful in their conflict over Kashmir? Will a democratic Palestine reduced to a few Bantustans try to resolve its differences with Israel only by peaceful means?) The other assumption of liberalism has been that there wasn't any need for a world government and that there would be sufficient harmony among states if they were democratic; but does this apply even in an age in which the management of globalization and that of nuclear proliferation becomes the dominant issue? On the economic front, liberalism's faith is in markets and interests. This leads it to neglect the disruptive effects of markets among and inside the states and to pay insufficient attention to the role of the state in selecting and aggregating interests. Indeed, it sometimes understates the political foundations of the private market. Experience has shown that progress both in interstate political society and in the world economy is quite reversible.

Institutionalism has developed as an amendment to liberalism. It assumes that the liberal objectives of peace and justice can be promoted even in a world where many states are not democracies and where the global system of states remains anarchical but where institutions facilitate cooperation and affect the way in which the actors define their interests. This neglects somewhat the bewildering diversity of institutions. Some are mere alliances, others are very weak, and very few are endowed with considerable powers of enforcement. The hypothesis according to which strong institutions affect positively the definition of the national interest needs to be verified; it has been the case in Europe (but even there not always).

Finally, constructivism strikes me less as a theory than as a critique of the flaws of existing theories. It has some good points: the emphasis on the importance of perceptions, ideas, beliefs, ideologies, and precedents and also on the symbolic dimension of international relations, such as the importance of status for states and the importance of norms. But constructivism tends to underplay what other theories may overplay: the imperatives of power and the pressure of interests. The game of power has more discontinuities than constructivists suggest.

My own position is an eclectic one. Fundamentally, I am a realist in analyzing the strategic and diplomatic scene, and I also recognize the weight of interests, private and public, in the economic sphere. But, because I believe that there is an important normative dimension to politics, which shapes the choices actors make, and gives to evaluation a role as important as description and causal analysis, I tend to emphasize the actors' choices more than I try to predict them. Normatively, I favor a combination of liberalism and institutionalism as an approach to a better future, and, like the constructivists, I pay attention to what goes on in the actors' minds and guts. Unlike the neorealists, I do not believe that the units are interchangeable. Domestic factors are of crucial importance. Nor do I believe that it is possible to reduce the events of world affairs to single causes or to objective laws of permanent validity. Like all politics, it is a domain marked by a multiplicity of causal theories, by a multiplicity of actors with very different logics and objectives, by the possibility of changes of paradigm. Think of the changes in Europe, from a "state of war" to a cooperative and peaceful coalition. Economic development has been shaped by a series of fashions. All this leads me to remain very skeptical of predictions and proclamations of inevitability. I am fully aware of the flaws of eclecticism, but I prefer them to those of clashing dogmatisms.

·*2*·

A View of the World

A NEW PARADIGM?

$\mathcal{W}$hat is the state of international relations today? In the 1990s, specialists concentrated on the partial disintegration of the global order's traditional foundations: states. During that decade, many countries, often those born of decolonization, revealed themselves to be no more than pseudostates, without solid institutions, internal cohesion, or national consciousness. The end of communist coercion in the former Soviet Union and in the former Yugoslavia also revealed long-hidden ethnic tensions. Minorities that were or considered themselves oppressed demanded independence. In Iraq, Sudan, Afghanistan, and Haiti, rulers waged open warfare against their subjects. These wars increased the importance of humanitarian interventions, which came at the expense of the hallowed principles of national sovereignty and nonintervention. Thus, the dominant tension of the decade was the clash between the fragmentation of states (and the state system) and the progress of economic, cultural, and political integration—in other words, globalization.

Everybody has understood the events of September 11 as the beginning of a new era. But what does this break mean? In the conventional approach to international relations, war took place among states. But in September, poorly armed individuals suddenly challenged, surprised, and wounded the world's dominant superpower. The attacks also showed that, for all its accomplishments, globalization makes an awful form of violence easily accessible to hopeless fanatics. Terrorism is the bloody link between interstate relations and global society. As countless individuals and groups are becoming global actors along with states, insecurity and vulnerability are rising. To assess today's bleak state of affairs, therefore, several questions are necessary. What concepts help explain the new global order? What is the condition of the interstate part of international relations? And what does the emerging global civil society contribute to world order?

9

SOUND AND FURY

Two models made a great deal of noise in the 1990s. The first one—Francis Fukuyama's "End of History" thesis—was not vindicated by events. To be sure, his argument predicted the end of ideological conflicts, not history itself, and the triumph of political and economic liberalism. That point is correct in a narrow sense: the "secular religions" that fought each other so bloodily in the last century are now dead. But Fukuyama failed to note that nationalism remains very much alive. Moreover, he ignored the explosive potential of religious wars that has extended to a large part of the Islamic world.

Fukuyama's academic mentor, the political scientist Samuel Huntington, provided a few years later a gloomier account that saw a very different world. Huntington predicted that violence resulting from international anarchy and the absence of common values and institutions would erupt among civilizations rather than among states or ideologies. But Huntington's conception of what constitutes a civilization was hazy. He failed to take into account sufficiently conflicts within each so-called civilization, and he overestimated the importance of religion in the behavior of non-Western elites, who are often secularized and westernized. Hence, he could not clearly define the link between a civilization and the foreign policies of its member states.

Other, less sensational models still have adherents. The "realist" orthodoxy insists that nothing has changed in international relations since Thucydides and Machiavelli: a state's military and economic power determines its fate, interdependence and international institutions are secondary and fragile phenomena, and states' objectives are imposed by threats to their survival or security. Such is the world described by Henry Kissinger. Unfortunately, this venerable model has trouble integrating change, especially globalization and the rise of nonstate actors. Moreover, it overlooks the need for international cooperation that results from natural disasters, epidemics, and famines and from such new threats as the proliferation of weapons of mass destruction (WMD). And it ignores what the scholar Raymond Aron called the "germ of a universal consciousness": the liberal, pro-market norms that developed states have come to hold in common.

Taking Aron's point, many scholars today interpret the world in terms of a triumphant globalization that submerges borders through new means of information and communication. In this "flat" universe, a state choosing to stay closed invariably faces decline and growing discontent among its subjects, who are eager for material progress. But if it opens up, it must accept a reduced role that is limited mainly to social protection, physical protection against aggression or civil war, and maintaining national identity. The champion of this epic without heroes is *New York Times* columnist Thomas Friedman. He contrasts barriers with open vistas, obsolescence with modernity, and state control with free markets. He sees in globalization the light of dawn, the "golden straitjacket" that will force contentious publics to understand that the logic of globalization is that of peace (since war would interrupt globalization and therefore progress), democracy (because new technologies increase individual autonomy and encourage initiative), and prosperity (through unencumbered trade and investments).

BACK TO REALITY

Let us therefore leave models behind and start from realities. We begin with what is traditionally meant by international affairs: the anarchic system described by the realists, the world of states, alliances, wars and arms races, and rivalries for power and prestige, a world where, as Thucydides said, trouble comes from the fear that the rise of some actors provokes among the others, a world of often inexpiable conflict fostered by rival claims on the same territory, in Palestine or Kashmir or over the future of Taiwan, and so on. (Whether outsiders try to resolve such conflicts is not a matter of waiting for them to "ripen" but of how awful and dangerous they are.) Four remarks come to mind.

First, rivalries among great powers (and the capacity of smaller states to exploit such tensions) have most certainly not disappeared. For a while now, however, the existence of nuclear weapons has produced a certain degree of prudence among the powers that have them. The risk of destruction that these weapons hold has moderated the game and turned nuclear arms into weapons of last resort. But the game could heat up as more states seek other WMD as a way of narrowing the gap between the nuclear club and the other powers. The sale of such weapons thus becomes a hugely contentious issue, and efforts to slow down the spread of all WMD, especially to dangerous "rogue" states, can paradoxically become new causes of violence.

Second, if wars between states are becoming less common, wars within them are on the rise—as seen in the former Yugoslavia, Iraq, much of Africa, and Sri Lanka. Uninvolved states first tend to hesitate to get engaged in these complex conflicts, but they then (sometimes) intervene to prevent these conflicts from turning into regional catastrophes. The interveners, in turn, seek the help of the United Nations or regional organizations to rebuild these states, promote stability, and prevent future fragmentation and misery.

Third, states' foreign policies are shaped not only by realist geopolitical factors such as economics and military power but also by domestic politics. Even in undemocratic regimes, forces such as xenophobic passions, economic grievances, and transnational ethnic solidarity can make policymaking far more complex and less predictable. Many states—especially the United States—have to grapple with the frequent interplay of competing government branches. And the importance of individual leaders and their personalities is often underestimated in the study of international affairs.

Finally, new forms of violence result from the marriage between the system of states and the actors of global society. States hire mercenaries to fight predatory wars aimed at gaining power and grabbing resources in weak or disintegrating neighbors. Terrorist gangs like al-Qaeda rely on the active support or passive tolerance of states that harbor them.

For realists, then, transnational terrorism creates a formidable dilemma. If a state is the victim of private actors such as terrorists, it will try to eliminate these groups by depriving them of sanctuaries and punishing the states that harbor them. The national interest of the attacked state will therefore require either armed interventions against governments supporting terrorists or a course of prudence and discreet pressure on other governments to bring these terrorists to justice. Either option requires a questioning of sovereignty—the holy concept of realist theories. The classical realist universe of Hans Morgenthau and Aron may therefore still be very much alive in a world of states, but it has increasingly hazy contours and offers only difficult choices when it faces the threat of terrorism.

At the same time, the real universe of globalization does not resemble the one that Friedman celebrates. In fact, globalization has three forms, each with its own problems. First is economic globalization, which results from recent revolutions in technology, information, trade, foreign investment, and international business. The main actors are companies, investors, banks, and private services industries as well as states and international organizations. This present form of capitalism, ironically foreseen by Karl Marx and Friedrich Engels, poses a central dilemma between efficiency and fairness. The specialization and integration of firms make it possible to increase aggregate wealth, but the logic of pure capitalism does not favor social justice. Economic globalization has thus become a formidable cause of inequality among and within states, and the concern for global competitiveness limits the aptitude of states and other actors to address this problem. As a result, domestic "losers," victims of economic dislocations, often become bitter opponents of globalization.

Next comes cultural globalization. It stems from the technological revolution and economic globalization, which together foster the flow of cultural goods. Here the key choice is between uniformization (often termed "Americanization") and diversity. The result is both a "disenchantment of the world" (in Max Weber's words) and a reaction against uniformity. The latter takes form in a renaissance of local cultures and languages as well as assaults against Western culture, which is denounced as an arrogant bearer of a secular, revolutionary ideology and a mask for U.S. hegemony.

Finally, there is political globalization, a product of the other two. It is characterized by the preponderance of the United States and its political institutions and by a vast array of international and regional organizations and transgovernmental networks (specializing in areas such as policing or migration or justice). It is also marked by private institutions that are neither governmental nor purely national—say, Doctors Without Borders or Amnesty International. But many of these agencies lack democratic accountability and are weak in scope, power, and authority. Furthermore, much uncertainty hangs over the fate of American hegemony, which faces significant resistance abroad and is affected by America's own oscillation between the temptations of domination and isolation.

The benefits of globalization are undeniable. But Friedman-like optimism rests on very fragile foundations. For one thing, globalization is neither inevitable nor irresistible. Rather, it is largely an American creation, rooted in the period after World War II and based on U.S. economic might. By extension, then, a deep and protracted economic crisis in the United States could have as devastating an effect on globalization as did the Great Depression.

Second, globalization's reach remains limited because it excludes many poor countries, and the states that it does transform react in different ways. This fact stems from the diversity of economic and social conditions at home as well as from partisan politics. The world is far away from a perfect integration of markets, services, and factors of production. Sometimes the simple existence of borders slows down and can even paralyze this integration; at other times it gives integration the flavors and colors of the dominant state (as in the case of the Internet).

Third, international civil society remains embryonic. Many nongovernmental organizations (NGOs) reflect only a tiny segment of the populations of their members' states. They largely represent only modernized countries or those in which the weight of the state is not too heavy. Often, NGOs have little independence from governments.

Fourth, the individual emancipation so dear to Friedman does not quickly succeed in democratizing regimes, as one can see today in China. Nor does emancipation prevent public institutions such as the International Monetary Fund, the World Bank, or the World Trade Organization from remaining opaque in their activities and often arbitrary and unfair in their rulings.

Fifth, the attractive idea of improving the human condition through the abolition of barriers is dubious. Globalization is in fact only a sum of techniques (audio- and videocassettes, the Internet, instantaneous communications) that are at the disposal of states or private actors. Self-interest, passions, and ideology, not humanitarian reasons, are what drive these actors. Their behavior is quite different from the vision of globalization as an Enlightenment-based utopia that is simultaneously scientific, rational, and universal. For many reasons—misery, injustice, humiliation, attachment to traditions, aspiration to more than just a better standard of living—this "Enlightenment" stereotype of globalization thus provokes revolt and dissatisfaction.

Another contradiction is also at work. On the one hand, international and transnational cooperation is necessary to ensure that globalization will not be undermined by the inequalities resulting from market fluctuations, weak state-sponsored protections, and the incapacity of many states to improve their fates by themselves. On the other hand, cooperation presupposes that many states and rich private players operate altruistically—which is certainly not the essence of international relations—or practice a remarkably generous conception of their long-term interests. But the fact remains that most rich states still refuse to provide sufficient development aid or to intervene in crisis situations such as the genocide in Rwanda and the atrocities in Darfur. That reluctance compares poorly with the American enthusiasm to pursue the fight against al-Qaeda and the Taliban. What is wrong here is not patriotic enthusiasm as such but the weakness of the humanitarian impulse when the national interest in saving non-American victims is not self-evident.

GLOBALIZATION AND INTERNATIONAL POLITICS

Among the many effects of globalization on international politics, three hold particular importance. The first concerns institutions. Contrary to realist predictions, most states are not perpetually at war with each other. Many regions and countries live in peace; in other cases, violence is internal rather than state to state. And since no government can do everything by itself, interstate organisms have emerged. The result, which can be termed "global society," seeks to reduce the potentially destructive effects of national regulations on the forces of integration. But it also seeks to ensure fairness in the world market and create international regulatory regimes in such areas as trade, communications, human rights, migration, and refugees. The main obstacle to this effort is the reluctance of states to accept global directives that might constrain the market or further reduce their sovereignty. Thus, the powers of the United Nations remain limited and sometimes only purely theoretical. International criminal justice is still only a spotty and contested last resort. In the world economy—where the market, not global governance, has been the main beneficiary of the state's retreat—the network of global institutions is fragmented and incomplete. Foreign investment remains ruled by bilateral agreements. Environmental protection is badly ensured, and issues such as migration and population growth are largely ignored. Institutional networks are not powerful enough to address unfettered short-term capital movements, the lack of international regulation on bankruptcy and competition, and primitive coordination among rich countries. In turn, the global "governance" that does exist is partial and weak at a time when economic globalization deprives many states of independent monetary and fiscal policies, or it obliges them to make cruel choices between economic competitiveness and the preservation of social safety nets. All the while, the United States displays an increasing impatience toward institutions that weigh on American freedom of action. Movement toward a world state looks increasingly unlikely. The more state sovereignty crumbles under the blows of globalization or such recent developments as humanitarian intervention and the fight against terrorism, the more states cling to what is left to them.

Second, globalization has not profoundly challenged the enduring national nature of citizenship. Economic life takes place on a global scale, but human identity remains national—hence the strong resistance to cultural homogenization. Over the centuries, increasingly centralized states have expanded their functions and tried to forge a sense of common identity for their subjects. But no central power in the world can do the same thing today, even in the European Union. There, a single currency and advanced economic coordination have not yet produced a unified economy or strong central institutions endowed with legal autonomy, nor have they resulted in a sense of postnational citizenship. The march from national identity to one that would be both national and European has only just begun. A world very partially unified by technology still has no collective consciousness or collective solidarity. What states are unwilling to do the world market cannot do all by itself, especially in engendering a sense of world citizenship.

Third, there is the relationship between globalization and violence. The world, integrated through capitalism, remains the theater of multiple fragmentations, all dangerous, often explosive. There is the gap between rich and poor states, which development policies have not filled. There is another map that overlaps with that of the rich and the poor state: that of functioning states and of purely nominal ones that have been left chaotic by the failures of "nation building." There is the worm in the fruit of national identity and integration: there are few homogeneous nation-states, based on either ethnicity (such as Japan) or an effective melting pot (the United States). Far more are mosaics or tense arrangements between the dominant national group and foreign residents.

Of course, the traditional state of war, even if it is limited in scope, still persists. There are high risks of regional explosions in the Middle East and in East Asia, and these could seriously affect relations between the major powers. Because of this threat and because modern arms are increasingly costly, the "anarchical society" of states lacks the resources to correct some of globalization's most flagrant flaws. These very costs, combined with the classic distrust among international actors who prefer to try to preserve their security alone or through traditional alliances, prevent a more satisfactory institutionalization of world politics—for example, an increase of the powers of the United Nations. This step could happen if global society were provided with sufficient forces to prevent a conflict or restore peace—but it is not. In this world, transnational forces and linkages are of two kinds. The integrative one—the universe of business, of many NGOs, and of efforts such as the European enterprise—is founded on a mix of common interests and of altruistic passions. But other transnational linkages are violent and destructive. They bring together, across borders, either those who are losers and outsiders in their own societies or those who, having emigrated in a search for a better life in more prosperous or freer countries, feel that they have remained second-class subjects amidst their hosts, resent the exclusions and discriminations they experience, and try to find a solidarity across borders through a fundamentalist interpretation of Islam. Like the secular ideologies of the nineteenth and twentieth centuries, it offers to the outsiders, the humiliated, and the resentful a brew of bloody revenge and a promise of reward after death.

Globalization, far from spreading peace, thus seems to foster conflicts and resentments. The lowering of various barriers celebrated by Friedman, especially the spread of global media, makes it possible for the most deprived or oppressed to compare their fate with that of the free and well-off. These dispossessed then ask for help from others with common resentments, ethnic origin, or religious faith. Insofar as globalization enriches some and uproots many, those who are both poor and uprooted may seek revenge and self-esteem in terrorism and in a faith of unforgiving fury. Those who, in the nineteenth century, resented the poverty and hierarchy to which capitalism condemned them often turned to an ideology of nonreligious revolutionary salvation and yet were gradually integrated into their nations through the schools and the armies. Their conflicting solidarities—socialism and nationalism—were both open. Today's resentful—the humiliated, the disgusted, and the disoriented—when they turn to action, are clandestine.

GLOBALIZATION AND TERROR

Terrorism is the poisoned fruit of several forces. It can be the weapon of the weak in a classic conflict among states or within a state, as in Kashmir or the Palestinian territories. But it can also be seen as a product of globalization. Transnational terrorism is made possible by the vast array of communication tools. Islamic terrorism, for example, is not only based on support for the Palestinian struggle and opposition to an invasive American presence. It is also fueled by a resistance to "unjust" economic globalization and to a Western culture deemed threatening to local religions and cultures.

If globalization often facilitates terrorist violence, the fight against this war without borders is potentially disastrous both for national integration and for economic development and globalization. Antiterrorist measures may lead to what Pierre Hassner has called the "barbarization of the Bourgeois." In addition, they restrict mobility and financial flows, while new terrorist attacks could lead the way for an antiglobalist reaction comparable to the chauvinistic paroxysms of the 1930s. Global terrorism is not the simple extension of war among states to nonstates. It is the subversion of traditional ways of war because it does not care about the sovereignty of either its enemies or the allies who shelter them. It provokes its victims to take measures that, in the name of legitimate defense, violate knowingly the sovereignty of those states accused of encouraging terror. (After all, it was not the Taliban's infamous domestic violations of human rights that led the United States into Afghanistan; it was the Taliban's support of Osama bin Laden.)

But all those trespasses against the sacred principles of sovereignty do not constitute progress toward global society, which has yet to agree on a common definition of terrorism or on a common policy against it. Indeed, the beneficiaries of the antiterrorist "war" have been the illiberal, poorer states that have lost so much of their sovereignty of late. Now the crackdown on terror allows them to tighten their controls on their own people, products, and money. They can give themselves new reasons to violate individual rights in the name of common defense against insecurity—and thus stop the slow, hesitant march toward international criminal justice.

Another main beneficiary will be the United States, the only actor capable of carrying the war against terrorism into all corners of the world. Despite its power, however, America cannot fully protect itself against future terrorist acts, nor can it fully overcome its ambivalence toward forms of interstate cooperation that might restrict U.S. freedom of action. Thus, terrorism is a global phenomenon that ultimately reinforces the enemy—the state—at the same time that it tries to destroy it. The states that are its targets have no interest in applying the laws of war to their fight against terrorists; they have every interest in treating terrorists as outlaws and pariahs. The champions of globalization have sometimes glimpsed the "jungle" aspects of economic globalization, but few observers foresaw similar aspects in global terrorist and antiterrorist violence.

Finally, the unique position of the United States raises a serious question over the future of world affairs. In the realm of interstate problems, American behavior will determine whether the nonsuperpowers and weak states will continue to look at the United States as a friendly power (or at least a tolerable hegemon) or whether they are provoked by Washington's hubris into coalescing against American preponderance. America may be a hegemon, but combining rhetorical overkill and ill-defined designs is full of risks. Washington has yet to understand that nothing is more dangerous for a "hyperpower" than the temptation of unilateralism. It may well believe that the constraints of international agreements and organizations are not necessary since U.S. values and power are all that is needed for world order. But in reality, those same international constraints provide far better opportunities for leadership than arrogant demonstrations of contempt for others' views, and they offer useful ways of restraining unilateralist behavior in other states. A hegemon concerned with prolonging its rule should be especially interested in using internationalist methods and institutions, for the gain in influence far exceeds the loss in freedom of action.

In the realm of global society, much will depend on whether the United States will overcome its frequent indifference to the costs that globalization imposes on poorer countries. For now, Washington is too reluctant to make resources available for economic development, and it remains hostile to agencies that monitor and regulate the global market. All too often, the right-leaning tendencies of the American political system push U.S. diplomacy toward an excessive reliance on America's greatest asset—military strength—as well as an excessive reliance on market capitalism and a "sovereigntism" that offends and alienates. That the mighty United States is so afraid of the world's imposing its "inferior" values on Americans is often a source of ridicule and indignation abroad.

ODD MAN OUT

For all these tensions, it is still possible that the American war on terrorism will be contained by prudence and that other governments will give priority to the many internal problems created by interstate rivalries and the flaws of globalization. But the world risks being squeezed between a new Scylla and Charybdis. The Charybdis is universal intervention, unilaterally decided by

American leaders who are convinced that they have found a global mission provided by a colossal threat. Presentable as an epic contest between good and evil, this struggle offers the best way of rallying the population and overcoming domestic divisions. The Scylla is resignation to universal chaos in the form of new attacks by future bin Ladens, fresh humanitarian disasters, or regional wars that risk escalation. Only through wise judgment can the path between them be charted.

We can analyze the present, but we cannot predict the future. We live in a world where a society of uneven and often virtual states overlaps with a global society burdened by weak public institutions and underdeveloped civil society. Domestic civil societies all have their uncivil side: criminals, or the multiple victims of anomie, the unschooled, the uncared-for. But—not always, alas—there are domestic means of coping, from the police and courts to hospitals and charitable agencies. Violence and anomie in the world system are not so susceptible of containment and correction, given the weakness of common institutions and the absence of a common consensus. To be sure, a single power dominates, but its economy could become unmanageable or disrupted by future terrorist attacks. Thus, to predict the future confidently would be highly incautious or naive. The world has survived many crises, but it has done so at a very high price, even in times when WMD were not available.

Precisely because the future is neither decipherable nor determined, students of international relations face two missions. They must try to understand what goes on by taking an inventory of current goods and disentangling the threads of current networks. But the fear of confusing the empirical with the normative should not prevent them from writing as political philosophers at a time when many philosophers are extending their conceptions of just society to international relations. How can one make the global house more livable? The answer presupposes a political philosophy that would be both just and acceptable even to those whose values have differing foundations. As the late philosopher Judith Shklar did, we can take as a point of departure and as a guiding thread the fate of the victims of violence, oppression, and misery; as a goal, we should seek material and moral emancipation. While taking into account the formidable constraints of the world as it is, it is possible to loosen them.

NOTE

An earlier version of this essay appeared under the title "Clash of Globalizations," *Foreign Affairs* 81, no. 4 (July–August 2002).

·3·

Lost Illusions

$\mathcal{R}$aymond Aron had two disciples who spent most of their lives studying international relations and took him, as Pierre Hassner has written, as "their master in international relations and in intellectual hygiene."[1] In these last years of my career, I want to tell Pierre how much I have owed him during the forty-nine years of our friendship and in particular how much his thoughts about the present state of the world have stimulated mine.

I.

Hassner writes about violence. I prefer to use the word "war" in order to distinguish it from the "ordinary" forms of violence within states. In the twentieth century and in the beginning of the twenty-first, war has taken every imaginable form. Two world wars have ravaged the world, redrawn its map, and given rise to the ideologies and regimes of fascism and communism. Multipolar international systems so scorned by Wilson and by American political science had ensured a kind of peace between the fall of Napoleon and the crisis of summer 1914. No such system revived between the Versailles Treaty and Munich. The withdrawal of the new American superpower after 1918, the isolationism of the new Soviet Union, and the distrust that Moscow provoked outside its borders left the game to tired European actors who haggled with each other and to the Germans electrified by Hitler. At the end of World War II, atomic war made its atrocious and blinding appearance, the Cold War began quickly, and almost all international relations experts spent more than forty years on the theory of a nuclear war between the two superpowers. Fortunately, we didn't get to practice it, and there is a lesson here: the enormous importance of internal factors, that is, the liberal optimism of the Americans, persuaded that history had more chances than war in eroding communism; the Marxist-Leninist optimism, which promised the inevitable

21

final triumph of communism over capitalism; the economic bankruptcy of the Soviet regime; and the success of an American economy that consumed Keynesian recipes despite the ideology of the free market. This period, which was so often nerve-wracking—at the time of the coup d'état in Prague, of the Korean War, of the Cuban crisis, and of the missile crisis of 1983—appears today so far away that the American commentators, in this country, whose memory is short, now describe the Cold War as a confrontation between two conservative powers. As if a frenzied arms race had not wasted precious resources in a world that was largely miserable and as if the need for nuclear prudence, the certain risk of nuclear retaliation in the case of a massive conventional confrontation, had not heavily weighed on daily life. Expelled from the realm of direct shocks between blocs armed to excess, war during those years shifted toward armed interventions without excessive risk: the United States in Central America and sometimes in the Middle East and the Soviets in order to maintain order in their empire and to intervene in Africa and Afghanistan. While the great powers discovered both the necessity of limits and that of arms control, the huge movement of decolonization produced two eight-year-long wars (Indochina and Algeria) after having killed hundreds of thousands of people at the time of India's partition; it left the former Belgian Congo in chaos and resulted in a cascade of wars between Arabs and Israelis.

After the collapse of the Soviet Union, one was able to believe, during the period of a new war in the Middle East about Kuwait, that the model on which the United Nations had been built and that the Cold War had paralyzed—a world united against aggression under the leadership of the "big five" Security Council powers—was finally going to be realized. We know what happened instead. The alliance against Saddam Hussein left him in place, and we entered in a new phase about which Hassner and I have written a great deal, that of the failed states or pseudostates that were disintegrating, of ethnic conflict where people who had been obliged to coexist within the same borders rediscovered a hatred that many of them hadn't been aware of and manifested a passion for independence or revenge with extraordinary savagery. The 1990s in Yugoslavia, in central and East Africa, and in many parts of Asia were years of civil war (which Thucydides had already described in paragraphs saturated with emotion as particularly horrible) and so-called humanitarian interventions or, indeed, calculated noninterventions as in Rwanda. The lessons are stark. The worst violence often occurs within legally sovereign states that happen to be fragile or artificial, and only force coming from the outside can reestablish an often fragile and artificial peace; but collective interventions occurring on behalf of humanitarian and nonegoistic interests meet strong opposition in a world where the national interest remains defined in narrowly self-interested terms. The responsibility that the interveners inherit doesn't suit them very well, and they usually try to escape from it as soon as the battle stops or else by abstaining from action altogether.

At the beginning of the new century, in 2001, one could have thought that in the previous century, all conceivable kinds of atrocities, genocides, and collective crimes had been in evidence. We had continued to reason in terms of states and of peoples aspiring to have their state, in other words, in the classical terms of international relations. The eleventh of September 2001 has revolutionized our perspective. We knew that modern weapons made security behind borders impossible to preserve. We now know that nonstate actors, private groups, or gangs, armed with weapons as unexpected as hijacked civilian aircraft, could settle almost anywhere and strike deliberately, civilians above all, and spread terror. Terrorism is not new, but it had mainly been an internal phenomenon except when the terrorists were serving a state that wanted to strike far from its borders. Now we can talk about a universal war that knows no borders, which makes the idea of victory perfectly unrealistic. From the New York towers to the discotheques of Bali and the transport system of London, nothing is safe. The connection between state conflicts or ambitions and private terrorists deserves extensive study. The war against Iraq has provoked, even without any initiative from Saddam Hussein, terrorist movements of solidarity and new recruits for a Muslim fundamentalism very different from the lay skepticism of Saddam.

Thus, in less than a hundred years, our poor planet will have known a devaluation of borders and a multiplication of actors in the realm of violence. We have taken many steps toward the "one world" of the idealists, but this single world has all the aspects of a jungle. The state, national or not, lives in a perfectly paradoxical situation. It is in fact open to all forms of insecurity coming from the outside, and its attempts to overcome these, by controlling access or by extensive surveillance of potential suspects, risk delivering it to various polices and to professional antiliberals, as well as creating citizens with limited rights and immigrants under suspicion, without, however, ever reaching the famous "homeland security" about which so much is said.

II.

In the history of theories that try to give us concept for understanding international relations and means of affecting them, there are two that matter most: realism and its variations, idealism and its variations (i.e., the different schools of liberalism). Realism guarantees a permanent "state of war," more or less moderate; idealism assures us that peace is possible. Both deserve the same bad grade. Neither one is of much help in the world as it is now.

The vast body of realism extends from Thucydides (who in any case is too subtle and deep to let himself be encased in a single "conceptual" framework) to the present-day so-called neorealists (for whom a state's foreign policy is determined by the distribution of power in the world). It has, indeed, many merits. Interstate relations often resemble the realists' universe: the quest for power, state goals of security and domination, the preeminence of military power, profound differences between the big and the other actors, balancing and coalition exercises, and so on. These are indeed tunes. Hans Morgenthau devoted a hymn to them, Aron a symphony of Mahlerian complexity, and Kenneth Waltz, the leading neorealist, a monody as simple as the music of Eric Satie. But the problems are numerous. The hypothesis according to which the combination of human nature and international anarchy obliges all the actors to pursue the same objectives—survival and security—is false insofar as states aim at more than survival and security and make their own choices about everything else. Moreover, they also choose different kinds of security and different strategies of survival, depending on their geographical situation, their historical experiences, their means, and their regimes. The most intelligent of the realists, such as the Swiss Arnold Wolfers and the Frenchman Raymond Aron, knew this extremely well. The years of humanitarian interventions have confirmed it. Furthermore, with some exceptions, the realists have underestimated the role of ideals (political or religious) of ideologies, of purely or primarily internal factors in the making of foreign policy (Thucydides knew this well: the democracy of Alcibiades was not that of Pericles). The realists have overestimated hard power—military and economic—and underestimated what Joseph Nye is calling soft power,[2] the power to influence and persuade through one's culture and one's skills. Finally, just as realism has devoted too little attention to internal civil and political society, it has not paid any more attention to transnational networks and flows, it has remained excessively skeptical of the effects of economic globalization, and it has discounted what Aron called the germs of universal consciousness, for instance, insofar as human rights are concerned. Realist thought is not false, but it is poor.

The problems of idealism do not always consist in a refusal to take into account the truths of realism: the description by Kant of the international "state of war" is very close to what Hobbes had said about it. But Kant's purpose is to leave this reality behind, and he has two powerful arguments. In his project on perpetual peace, he counts on the moral sense of human beings (which he describes as still dormant); in his essay on universal history, he counts on the meaning and direction of history, which will lead to peace both through the intolerable exacerbation of violence and through trade and other benefits of enlightenment. Moral imperatives, in the purely normative version, and the cunning of nature, analyzed in the essay on history, lead to the creation of representative regimes inside the states and to interstate peace guaranteed by a sort of confederation in international affairs. Kant inspired Woodrow Wilson and, more recently, John Rawls's philosophy.

In the eighteenth century, Rousseau had, in advance, rejected Kant's philosophy of history. War breeds only war, trade breeds only rivalries and conflicts, and peace can occur only in a world of very small states ruled by the principles of the social contract and concentrated on themselves—a world without the hostilities, envies, and temptations characteristic of interstate relations. And yet Kant was partly right. Trade, already celebrated by Montesquieu, is the motor of globalization today, and it often softens or sweetens the relations among states; this is one of the factors that led to the Cold War's end as it is today in the improvement of relations between the capitalist world and China. The possession by several countries of an "absolute" bomb has so far deterred its possessors from using it. However, representative democracy has not become the universal regime, and thus Rawls was obliged in his ideal theory to leave room for so-called decent but not democratic regimes. In the absence of such a universal domestic regime, representative democracies continue to make war against undemocratic regimes—we have seen this in and since 2001—and interstate organizations, the modern version of Kant's confederation, do not have the means to create peace in the world. Moreover, Kant and the idealists who, as good liberals, know the importance of civil society and of the "social capital" that animates it leave much to be desired when the issues they have to face are the development of poor countries and the very complex effects of this global society that they conceive simplistically as predominantly a good thing. Universal terror is an effect more visible than the peace, democracy, and individual emancipation that the champions of globalization expected from it. The call for a solidarity of human beings and states is not enough to remove, in a state or among states, the disruptions, inequalities, injustices, and exploitations that feed fanaticism and terrorist violence.

The most ambitious attempt at building an idealist philosophy of international relations at the end of the twentieth century and of his life was that of Rawls, but it is disappointing.[3] He leaves "nonideal" philosophy to deal with many of the real problems of international relations, such as secession, refugees, and migrations. The famous "difference principle," which within a "well-ordered" society allows only those inequalities that aim at improving the fate of the least favored, is not, according to Rawls, applicable among states. In his conception of "the law of peoples," he does not define what constitutes a people, and he limits human rights to what "decent" societies are willing to accept. Finally, the principles that democratic states and decent states should agree on are strictly interstate norms: there is very little on the regulation of global civil society, and we remain in the universe of the Westphalian treaties of the seventeenth century. This reminds us that the last word of liberal thought has always been the separation between a private, transnational society that is largely commercial and financial and an interstate society whose mode of regulation is cooperation among states but not a real supranational cosmopolitan power.

III.

When one thinks of the future of this fragmented as well as "globalized" world, one should remember the most disquieting of realists, Hobbes. He had the most somber conception of human nature and the most radical conception of the only way in which man can be saved from the annihilation that the war of all against all makes likely. The establishment of an absolute central power (although limited in scope) is the solution of the problem of insecurity in a community of human beings seeking survival. Hobbes considered that the international state of nature was less catastrophic than the state of nature within a group of men and women and that one could therefore stay at the stage of competing states, but the reasons he was giving for this difference are no longer valid. His main concern was the survival of individuals. The state today is not capable any longer of softening, for its citizens, the effect of interstate wars and of saving them from violent death. The potential of destruction of human lives both by the states' weapons and by terrorist forces has increased dramatically. The same logic that made the internal Leviathan necessary—the necessity to survive—should now push toward a worldwide Leviathan.

The least one can say is that it is unlikely. Individuals eager to survive, weak by nature, and relatively equal in their weakness have an interest in signing a social contract in order to create a strong and protective power. States that are very unevenly powerful and a heterogeneous mass of interests capable of ignoring borders do not have the same reasons to precipitate themselves in the arms of a world government. Many will believe, like terrorist groups, that they are best capable of surviving in a world that is both open and anarchical. The strongest states prefer to ensure their own security by traditional means, including alliances, even if these means are insufficient, rather than giving up their ambitions and transferring their powers to a world Leviathan that risks oscillating between global tyranny and the kind of inefficiency of which the UN system gives a rather unappetizing idea.

In this decidedly unideal world, the substitute for a world Leviathan established by agreement is a global imperial power. Today it would be the American empire, which a large part of current American elites considers as the least bad of solutions, either, of course, from the viewpoint of the imperial power or, in Wilson's homeland, from the viewpoint of everybody's real interest all over in the world. But it is easy to see that this solution is not any more satisfactory. An empire "by invitation" and not by conquest, a world under the protection but not the direct control of the American "hyperpower," risks being constantly in a state of turbulence, like so many historical empires that were too large. It would be contested from within and rejected outside by all those who do not wish to submit. Moreover, the American empire lacks imperialists at home. The American people do not desire to be the international gendarme; they do not have the enthusiasm or endurance necessary to ensure either human rights or, what is even better and more difficult, democracy elsewhere; nor do they have the altruism indispensable to guarantee lasting and fair development, which would have to be less inegalitarian than the present kind and therefore accompanied by much regulation rather than left to pure free-trade liberalism. Nor does it have the altruism necessary to preserve the cultural identity of the satellites and the clients without which they risk rebelling.

To paraphrase Aron: empire is unlikely; peace is impossible. We are at the bottom of an abyss (one can alas always go even more deeply, and I cannot but think about the war against Iraq, perhaps more murderous than the Vietnam War but with external political and economic effects that could be much worse). Let me repeat: the state of war across borders affects both states and individuals or organized groups. Transnational society is made up in part of unrealized promises—concerning the environment, health, and also human rights (except in the limited world of real democracy) and international justice—against which the single superpower is waging both war and blackmail. For the rest, this society often appears like a sum, not of benefits as Thomas Friedman seems to believe[4] but of evils: in the economic realm, free trade and the freedom of financial flows, which are promoted by the hyperpower and by the international agencies it dominates, create as many woes among the weak as they create benefits for the strong; in the political realm, the evils are called forced migrations, mafias, and terrorism.

How can we climb out of this abyss? There is no single recipe. There is much room for the joint efforts of international organizations (despite their meager means, their few powers, and their lack of autonomous military forces), of the states (despite the constant tension between long-term interests, which often argue for risky political interventions and for "sacrifices" to help the poor, and egoistic interests), and of nongovernmental organizations (NGOs) whose efficiency is often inferior to their goodwill. The ultimate objective should be a point of agreement between Hobbes and a renovated idealism: the gradual establishment of a world Leviathan that would be able to complement the efforts of the other actors and to deal with the problems that those actors cannot solve either by themselves or by the usual methods of cooperation. The unfortunately slow and shaky European Union could be an example if not a model. For humanitarian and security reasons, the grievances that are often at the root of terrorist actions should be seriously examined and dealt with. In a world in which democracy and hideous regimes, honest and corrupt ones, continue to coexist, the road to this global Leviathan will be neither easy nor swift, but it is evident that it passes through a reinforcement, also gradual, of international organizations that need financial and military resources of their own. The current hostility of imperial America to the United Nations, its conviction that the "only superpower" can do without it and keep its hands free, makes such a reinforcement impossible, but the interconnection of danger points in the world—the unwanted presence of foreign forces, the existence of tyrannical regimes often supported from the outside, the misery of millions of human beings, the degradation of the environment, the multiplicity of terrorisms, and the spread of weapons of mass destruction—is such that it is more and more perilous to allow important conflicts to rot and to inject destructive passions into the hearts of people, as is the case of the conflict between the Israelis and the Palestinians or that between India and Pakistan.

In a world full of axes and forces of evil, where most politicians think only of their own survival, it is more than ever necessary to remind oneself that the goddess Reason celebrated by the revolutionaries at the end of the century of Enlightenment has many weaknesses of her own. On the one hand, she will always find it difficult to rule a world of human beings, in other words, of emotions and passions that often put reason at their service and that reason only occasionally succeeds in mastering. There are, of course, positive emotions and passions, but they rarely govern statesmen in international relations. The NGOs that try to improve these relations usually lack the necessary means to repress the ethnic and ideological passions that take the Enemy or the Other as their target. As for religious passions, they have often fostered violence rather than the love that religion celebrates, hence the precariousness of philosophies that put too much trust in the possibility and durability of fundamental agreement or consensus among allegedly rational human beings, such as the theories of Rawls and Habermas. On the other hand, one should not confuse instrumental and calculating reason, which can be deployed toward any kind of objective including genocide, conquest of territory, or forcible collectivism, and Reason considered as the expression of a moral will as Kant had proposed in his *Metaphysical Foundations of Ethics* (a confusion between the two notions frequently afflicts the theory of rational choice). Realists who are pessimistic about human nature and about the nature of states but concerned about the survival, the welfare, and the freedoms or capabilities of human beings, idealists who are appalled by the huge gaps that separate ideal theory from reality, could meet around the nonmetaphysical liberalism that Judith Shklar had called the liberalism of fear: a philosophy and ethics centered on the fight against and prevention of cruelty, oppression, fear, misery, and injustice—evils experienced by most human beings.[5] The realists will continue to think that it would engender only limited and temporary gains, the idealists would continue to be tormented by all the obstacles, but they should be capable of following that same road, even if they do not know how far they will be able to go.

Such a journey requires guides and leaders. The present American administration, with its unilateralist instincts and lack of diplomatic skills, is, alas, not wise enough to guide and is too much addicted to bullying to serve as a wise leader. Let us hope that this is just a temporary divagation and not one more lost illusion.

NOTES

Chapter 3 is a revised version of "Les illusions perdues," published in Anne-Marie Le Gloannec et Alexsander Smolnar, *Entre Kant et Kosovo* (études offertes à Pierre Hassner). (Paris: Presses de Sciences politiques, 2003). I translated it, and it appeared in Robert Fatton Jr. and R. K. Ramazani, eds., *The Future of Liberal Democracy: Thomas Jefferson and the Contemporary World* (New York: Palgrave Macmillan, 2004). It is further revised here.

1. *La violence et la paix* (Paris: Editions Esprit, 1995), 20.
2. See his *Paradox of American Power* (Oxford: Oxford University Press, 2002).
3. See his *Law of Peoples* (Cambridge, Mass.: Harvard University Press, 1999).
4. See his *The Lexus and the Olive Tree* (New York: Farrar, Straus and Giroux, 2000).
5. See her essay "The Liberalism of Fear," which first appeared in Nancy Rosenblum, ed., *Liberalism and the Moral Life* (Cambridge, Mass.: Harvard University Press, 1989).

· 4 ·

Thoughts on Fear in Global Society

I.

$\mathscr{I}$n a world of competing states, fear is a constant cause and effect of their contest. "What made [the Peloponnesian] war inevitable was the growth of Athenian power and the fear which this caused in Sparta."[1] Hobbes, who translated Thucydides, saw in the relations among "kings and persons of sovereign authority" a concrete example of what the state of nature would be in a world of individuals without superior power: the life of man in this state is "solitary, poor, nasty, brutish and short"; fear of death is the first of the reasons he gives of the "passions that encline men to peace." When war prevails, in the absence of common power, there is no law, there is neither justice nor injustice, no property, "no mine and thine distinct": the two cardinal virtues are Force and Fraud.[2] It is the domination of fear that drives men out of the state of nature into the Leviathan. But there is no global Leviathan.

If I may jump from the political thinkers to my own memories, it is in order to show that fear in the global state of nature is not only what grips abstractions such as Athens and Sparta or their rulers. I was born at the end of 1928; my mother, a pessimistic Austrian, moved to Nice, France, the following year. My first political memory is the assassination by the Nazis of the Austrian Chancellor Dollfuss in 1934; my mother read about it in a French newspaper while vacationing with me in a hotel near Nice—a place where Matisse's chapel was built ten years later. I remember her reaction: this means the end of Austria and a step toward a new war. Indeed, we saw her brothers flee from Vienna to France in the following years, full of fear about their present and their future. My second memory is also one of fear. This time, it was the spring of 1936; we had just moved to Paris, I was on the Champs-Elysées in a bus, and I saw huge headlines in the newspapers: "la guerre pour demain?" This was the fear provoked by the Rhineland crisis, by Hitler's destruction of the Versailles Treaty. In the next big crises, over the "Ansch-

31

luss" of Austria and the Sudentenland, fear took a very precise and unforget-
table form: the voice of Hitler on the radio, threatening his enemies,
screaming his grievances, mixing poisonous cocktails of savage warnings and
fake promises, the voice of a demonic *Erlkönig* that injected terror into the
minds and hearts of his listeners. The two voices that are still with me, in me,
are those of Hitler (I am forever grateful to Charlie Chaplin for having
defanged it by derision in *The Great Dictator*) and that of Charles de Gaulle,
which called for courage and resistance, promised a great future, and provided
hope without concealing the monumental difficulties ahead. Fear and hope,
the threat of horror and brutality, and the appeal to freedom and pride—this
was going to be the fundamental struggle between 1940 and 1945.

II.

There are many kinds of fears in the relations among peoples and states.
More (or more sharply) than in domestic politics, these relations are manifestations of either friendship or hostility. And the consequence of hostility in a
world without a central power is the state of war, which, as Hobbes put it
(and Rousseau and Kant after him), "consists not in battle only, or the act of
fighting, but in a tract of time wherein the will to contend by battle is sufficiently known, and therefore the notion of Time is to be considered in the
nature of war, as it is in the nature of weather. . . . So the nature of war
consists not in actual fighting, but in the known disposition thereto, during
all the time there is no assurance to the contrary. All other time is peace."
War, thus very broadly defined, is the domain of fear. There is the fear of
war, which was so prevalent in France, Britain, and an isolationist United
States in the 1930s: a revulsion from what had been, if not enthusiastically at
least wholeheartedly, accepted in 1914 and 1917. The fear of nuclear war,
during the Cold War, inspired strategies of deterrence rather than offense
and defense and was as salutary as the policies of appeasement of Hitler had
been disastrous. The behavior of both the United States and the Soviet Union
during the Cuban missile crisis showed that Khrushchev was right when he
said that no state would want to risk total destruction. But a state doctrine of
preventive war makes fear more pervasive and permanent.

There is also fear *in* war, which takes many forms. There is the fear of
the civilians exposed to invasion or to aerial warfare—a fear that drove ten
million people to the roads in western Europe in May–June 1940 (I was
among them, and it was the most traumatic experience of my life; when the
war began, in September 1939, hundreds of thousands of Parisians—I was
among them—had, much more comfortably, left Paris because they thought

of Guernica). There is the fear experienced by soldiers, those who were in the trenches of World War I and risked death whenever they were (mostly foolishly) ordered to run toward the enemy's positions (there is a great Italian film too few people know, Rosi's *Uomini contra*) or those soldiers who fight guerrillas in countries in which they cannot distinguish who is the friend, who is an innocent and terrified civilian, and who is an enemy, a situation that, as we know from Vietnam and now from Iraq, leads to atrocities. There are, in the Israeli–Palestinian tragedy, the combined fears of civilian Palestinians occupied by Israel and exposed to Israeli raids, destruction of houses, and multiple vexations and restrictions and of Israeli soldiers and civilians exposed to suicide bombings in buses or cafés—a situation that had been impressively described in *The Battle of Algiers*.

Fear can be fear of the known, when one is facing an enemy whose cruelties have been demonstrated before or whose intentions had been well publicized (think of Poland in 1939) or risking a war whose destructiveness had been demonstrated before (nuclear war, after Hiroshima and Nagasaki). But there is also fear of the unknown, so pervasive in guerrilla wars, or in a world where terrorists can strike, seemingly, any time and any place.

A French proverb tells us that "fear is a bad adviser." At the state level, it can lead to war (see the previous quote from Thucydides or evidence about Germany's fear before 1914 of the growing power of its enemies that led its leaders to adopt, in the summer of 1914, the stance that made war inevitable[3]). At the level of the soldier lost in hostile territory, it leads to My Lai. But violence is not the only effect. Fear can lead, as one saw in occupied Europe, to reprehensible and often criminal collaboration and to countless forms of "accommodation" that are easy to explain but morally dubious (I think of Mr. Papon). It can lead to excessive restrictions on public liberties or to harebrained schemes that waste the nation's money (I think of the internment of Japanese Americans in World War II and of Guantanamo today as well as of antiballistic missiles and of the latest surrealistic invention, a "virtual border" for tracking foreign visitors).

What interests me most is another set of categories. It is a distinction among three kinds of fears. The first I will call abstract or impersonal, the second concrete and localized, and the third concrete and global. Abstract fears, while characteristic of the monarchies of the seventeenth and eighteenth centuries, are in fact those of leaders through the ages. I refer to the fear of a potentially hostile and expansionist other power, capable of upsetting a more or less stable equilibrium and of pushing its way to domination. It animated Sparta as well as the much later British policy of balance or the anxious cold warriors in Washington from the late 1940s to the 1980s. There is also the fear of losing this intangible asset, credibility, or that of losing one's rank and one's glory—a frequent concern of modern France. What is behind all those fears of the statesmen is the internalized image of the competition, the view of interstate affairs as a never-ending race whose stakes are power, reputation, and perhaps survival.

Concrete fears correspond to the rise of democracy that fascinated Tocqueville—the entry of "the public" into the arena, with its passions, hopes, and envies and especially with its fears of other nations that could disrupt their lives, of immigrants who would come and threaten their identities, of alien cultures that could poison their own, of savages who might kill their missionaries or their merchants, or of ethnic or religious minorities in their midst whom they see as inassimilable and in need of extirpation so that their own society could become or remain integrated and cohesive. This adds a vast realm of fears to the abstract ones and a huge escalation of the category of the threatening other: not just a rival state but concrete groups of human beings whose humanity one often refuses to acknowledge. Abstract fears are based on calculations (of relative power or wealth) and on rational projections and extrapolations; concrete fears are often based on irrational or nonrational prejudices and phantasms (again, these are ideal types: the calculations of statesmen are not always rational [cf. the Bush invasion of Iraq], and the public's fears and passions often have roots in painful experiences). When abstract and concrete goals fuse, much of the world may turn into hell: think of the combination of anti-Semitic, anti-Slav, and eugenic fears with the revanchist goals of the Nazi leadership eager to regain lost territory and lost power and to return on a colossal scale to the old quest for preeminence that had fueled the competition with Britain and the fear of Russia at the beginning of the twentieth century. The traditional abstract fears were essentially aimed at other states. The concrete, "populist" ones often transgressed the border between hostilities among nations and civil wars, as in the twentieth-century Balkans from the beginning to the end as well as in Nazi-occupied Europe, where the lines of national fears and passions and those of ideological alignments interfered with each other, multiplied atrocities, and exacerbated desires for revenge.

We are now in a third universe of fears: universal, all-pervasive, and globalized. The progress of technology, the ease of communications, and the shrinking of distances result in fears not only of weapons of mass destruction that even small states can produce and export throughout the globe but also of world scourges such as epidemics, drug and arms trafficking, and of course terrorists. The latter signify the entry of "civil society" into the already vast domain of war making, hitherto reserved to states and their armies or to forces of resistance against invaders, that is, to actors with and within borders. "Private" terrorism used to be largely contained within borders and concerned with local causes, as in Ireland and the Basque province of Spain, in West Germany and Italy in the 1970s, and in the case of Palestinian suicide bombers now. Al-Qaeda, with its mix of Islamic fundamentalism and political hatred of the West, is something new under the sun.

As a result, global society resembles the state of nature that Hobbes described as a state of war of each against all, "where every man is enemy to every man." He had thought that the state of war among states was less lethal, even though most of them are in a "posture of war," because they are able to uphold thereby the industry of their subjects and thus save these from "that misery that accompanies the liberty of particular men."[4] This is clearly not a valid view anymore, in an age of both weapons of mass destruction at the service of states and of ubiquitous terrorism, traffics, and diseases. But the way of escaping from the fears of the state of nature—the establishment of a world Leviathan caused by both the passion to survive (or the fear of death and destruction) and human reason—is not a solution.

Partly this is because of one vast difference between the individuals in the state of nature and the states: individuals are equally weak and in "danger of violent death"; the bigger states are not, and their leaders still prefer to protect their own security rather than to entrust it to a world government that could be impotent or else tyrannical. Moreover, the multiple "private actors" that add to the miseries of the world have as few incentives to submit themselves to a macro-Leviathan as they do to give up their arms to various states' polices. Moreover—and most important—one of the major contributors to the universalization of fear is the very state that was supposed to protect the lives and industry of its subjects. The modern Leviathan, whether democratic or tyrannical, is fanning the flames and the fears. Instead of safeguarding its subjects, it acts as a frequent pyromaniac. The champions of the notion of the "democratic peace"—the "law" according to which liberal democracies do not fight each other—have adopted Kant's belief that in such nations the people will be reluctant to go to war and that the deliberations of the governing elites will ensure the triumph of reason. But one of the conclusions that evidence suggests is that the people are quite susceptible to the bellicose or chauvinistic arguments of some groups or of the media and that the governing elites can be brilliant at nourishing and manipulating prejudices and fears.

We all know about the manipulation of anti-Semitism by the Nazis, who exploited old resentments of Jews—Catholic as well as anticapitalist ones—and primitive fears of defilement and corruption of blood in a way that gave to irrational hatred a pseudoscientific cast.[5] The fear of Bolshevism was equally well manipulated by the Nazis and by governing conservatives in many parts of pre-1939 Europe. Alas, what we have been submitted to in this country by an administration that sees and proclaims itself in charge of bringing democracy to the whole world has been a cunning orchestration of the fear caused by September 11, 2001, a fear of invisible and untrackable terrorists destroying Americans' security. Instead of a leader who proclaims that "we have nothing to fear but fear itself," we have had a doctor who, instead of curing his charges of their fears or at least showing them ways of coping with these, has regularly injected an anxiety-inducing serum into them: different-colored terrorist threat alerts, the Patriot Act, ethnic profiling, and the amalgamation of Saddam Hussein, a barbaric possessor of weapons of mass destruction, with al-Qaeda, and so on. Far from working and standing for the public good, the contemporary Leviathans, from Mugabe to Sharon, from Saddam to the North Korean dynasty, from Pinochet to Milosevic, have exacerbated the fears of their subjects, and the United States has not been immune. The purpose of these manipulations has been double: to instill hostility, bellicosity, a fervor for revenge, and violent self-protection against external enemies (or "alien" ethnic, religious, or political groups at home) and to get citizens, properly scared, to accept, in the name of national and personal security, invasions of privacy and reductions of liberties they would not have tolerated if they had not been conditioned to fear. This is certainly not what Hobbes had in mind in describing the Leviathan or what theorists of liberal democracy expected from the restricted and representative state.

There has been another form of state-sponsored manipulation—this time not *of* fear but *against* the fear of war that animated pacifists or peace-oriented parts of the public at a time when war or its preparation was the policy the government deemed just or necessary. State propaganda came to the rescue of such a policy by exaggerating, so to speak, the perils of peace or of accommodation (Giraudoux's *Tiger at the Gates* is a fine satire of bellicism) or by celebrating on the heroic mode the glories of military valor. During the Cold War, the fear of communism and of Soviet expansionism was used at times by the American government to erase the bad effects that the fear of a nuclear war might have had among many citizens or to smother the protests of part of the public against American interventions in Latin America.

III.

Contemporary men and women are in a situation comparable to the beast in the burrow, immortalized in Kafka's short story. It hears ominous noises, knocks, and movements and runs from one place in the burrow to another in order to find where the threat is located—an exhausting life of fear. We know, today, that the threat can be almost anything: the acts of another state, the protests or uprisings of a religious or ethnic or political minority, domestic or foreign terrorists, or the repressive moves of one's own state. Given the means easily at the disposal of all the threateners, there isn't even safety in ignorance. As Judith Shklar put it, "Systematic fear is the condition that makes freedom impossible." What she wanted to diminish or, if at all possible, eliminate was the fear of systematic cruelty, "of pain inflicted by others to kill and maim us, not the natural and healthy fear that merely warns us of avoidable pain. And when we think politically, we are afraid not only for ourselves but for our fellow citizens as well. We fear a society of fearful people." The liberalism she called for required "the possibility of making the evil of cruelty and fear the basic norm of its political practices and prescriptions."[6] She was concerned primarily with domestic cruelty and evils and did not extensively apply her conception of liberalism to global society. Let us try here, however sketchily.

There is never any way, as she warned us, of eliminating fear ("to be alive is to be afraid and much to our advantage in many cases, since alarm often preserves us from danger"). We will never chase away the fear of death or disease or of the loss of those we love. Someone who fears nothing is all too likely to lack not only prudence but compassion—just as the current celebration of trust and of societies of trust forgets that a democracy requires a healthy dose of distrust of those who rule it, in politics, economics, and society. What needs to be reduced, if not eliminated, is the kind of fear that breeds hatred, dehumanization, and destruction.

For better or worse, I am a child of the Enlightenment, minus the illusion of continuous progress, as was my friend Shklar, and a product of the French Republican ideology that pervaded its educational system. I believe passionately that nothing is more important than the education of the democratic public, in two forms. One consists in providing each person with adequate information about the world in which we live and where this world comes from (since one cannot begin to understand it without some knowledge of its past—a point that American schools all too often seem to restrict to the history of the United States). The other form consists in training decent citizens, an even more difficult task: that of fighting, head-on, widespread or recurrent prejudices such as anti-Semitism, anti-Arab clichés, all forms of sexism, or prejudices against blacks or Latino-Americans. Those who, in this country, deem Mexicans or Cubans to be unassimilable and those who, in France or Germany, assert that Arabs or Turks cannot be integrated are people who do not want such integration or the institutional accommodation and social assistance needed to make it successful. This is, of course, a huge task and a Sisyphean one, but it is essential, and it requires special attention to resources for the training of teachers. With special reference to international affairs and history, patriotism must be made compatible with a cosmopolitanism that begins with empathy for the victims (whose point of view was that which both Simone Weil and Judith Shklar wanted us to adopt).

At the other extreme, so to speak, there is the need to address the two fears characteristic of—indeed inherent in—international relations and global society. One is the fear of anarchy—of a world without norms in which states are too weak to protect or are all too willing to terrorize their subjects and in which hard power is the only coin of exchanges and "games." The other is the fear of unfettered superior power, that is, of imperial domination presenting itself as the only alternative to chaos. Those who, today, celebrate the virtues of imperialism forget the cost of the kind of order it imposes; they are blind to the point of view of its victims and to the psychological sequels of submission and humiliation. Both chaos and imperialism breed violence and war (think of how many wars the imposition of an American empire would require and its preservation would dictate). And war, today, in all its forms—with or without weapons of mass destruction, war among states, or within pseudostates and repressive states or by private groups that resort to terror—is the greatest source of fear in global society.

There is no simple "remedy" against or cure for war or the "state of war." But there are ways of reducing the fears they provoke. States should respect the restrictions the UN Charter puts on the use and threat of force and be sanctioned if they do not. These restrictions are close to the conditions just-war theory puts on resort to the *jus ad bellum*. The *jus in bello*, both in that theory and many twentieth-century conventions, needs just as much to be observed in order to protect noncombatants as well as prisoners, the occupied, and the wounded. Above all, war needs to be treated as a last resort—unlike what the United States did in Iraq. The enforcement of these norms and restraints requires a revival (or resurrection) of those provisions of the UN Charter that aimed at allowing the Security Council to conduct military operations against aggressors and a realization of Brian Urquhart's project of a UN force at the disposal of the Security Council. An understanding among its permanent members defining the conditions in which they would use their right of veto in the realm of international security would have to be negotiated. A standing UN force would be essential both for peacemaking—getting the combatants to stop fighting—and for peacekeeping afterward. Also, in addition to the international conventions that aim at protecting the inhabitants of occupied territories, one needs an extensive codification of the measures that the occupier would not be authorized to take.

All these restrictions and regulations addressed to states would not be of much help in curbing the violence of nonstate actors, the fears they inspire, and the domestic repressive measures they provoke or "justify." The only way of dealing with terrorism—besides repression—is to address the many causes for its appearance and development. There are three evident categories. One is state collapse (or the collapse of pseudostates). This would require, under the aegis of the United Nations and of regional organizations, major resources for state building and in extreme cases temporary trusteeships. A second category is that of tyrannical states. As I have written elsewhere,[7] the United Nations has too many of them in its midst to be a likely engine of regime change, and unilateral change by great powers is unacceptable, yet the problem won't go away. For extreme cases (such as Saddam's Iraq), I have suggested an association of (real) democracies authorizing regime change when the United Nations is paralyzed, but only if there are plausible plans for the aftermath of the change (the United States had none in Iraq). In less acute cases, active support of democratic oppositions and sanctions against violations of human rights would be necessary. The third category is probably the biggest: massive social and political injustices that foster terrorist reactions in which despair and revenge are blended; I am thinking of Palestine and of Chechnya particularly. Sometimes these injustices are the result of governmental policies—in which case we are back in our second category. If they result from festering interstate conflicts (Palestine, Kashmir, and until recently Cyprus), energetic and persistent (not sputtering and desultory) mediation by the United Nations, regional agencies, and states needs to be organized and provided with incentives and penalties to be used toward a settlement. If they result from miserable economic circumstances, what one needs is a worldwide program of economic development aimed, in Shklarian fashion, at helping in priority the most miserable and disadvantaged. This would require nothing less than a revolutionary shift in state budgets: large cuts in military expenditures (what *can* the United States actually do with $500 billion for "defense" each year?) and huge increases for "development as freedom," the kind Amartya Sen has described. One of the major causes of terrorism is humiliation, particularly strong in the Muslim world and among the oppressed and those who see themselves as victims of globalization, attributed to the West and especially to the United States. There are no decisive institutional remedies, but there are politico-psychological ones that should be studied in another essay.

I recognize that all this is both too little—and too utopian. But a world Leviathan is neither plausible nor necessarily desirable. This world will remain one of states, with sovereignty limited both by the effects of globalization and—one hopes—by curbs on their capacity to make war and to mistreat their subjects and foreigners on their soil. It is also a world where a global, incomplete, imperfect civil society is desperately in need of both policing and regulation. This will have to be provided by the states and by international and regional organizations. The kinds of safeguards, habits, procedures, and citizen education Judith Shklar envisaged for liberation from fear within nations would also reduce fear in relations among them. The development, through education and by agreements among states, of a cosmopolitan spirit and of cosmopolitan practices and institutions would complement and extend the domestic agenda. It may sound too idealistic, but it is not merely a dream. For all its flaws (such as in the area of agricultural trade policies and immigration), the European Union is a remarkable achievement, even though many Americans, from Robert Kagan's criticism from the viewpoint of Mars to condescending media embedded in indifference and derision, do not like to recognize it. A zone of peace and common citizenship, with relatively democratic common institutions, a commitment to social justice, and institutions for the protection of human rights: what better way is there for reducing fear, for eliminating the international state of nature, and for replacing it with a Leviathan whose capacity for mischief is severely limited—too much so, in some respects, because of the European Union's minuscule budget?

IV.

Kant's reflections on perpetual peace and on the designs of history are, in some respects, quaint. The vision of a plan of nature bringing us all to peace through trade and enlightenment on the one hand and because wars would become increasingly destructive and unacceptable on the other is still appealing but obviously flawed (it leaves no room for fanatical prejudices and passions and for terrorists). The scheme of perpetual peace is rather timid—it is what Rawls would have called "ideal theory" since it requires a world of constitutional republics, and it offers us a world in which the links among states do not go very far or deep: a vaguely defined confederation, no recognition of the need for common forces, a rather strict insistence on nonintervention (which would permit more Rwandas), and a "cosmopolitan law . . . limited to conditions of universal hospitality," which means only "the right of a foreigner not to be treated with hostility when he arrives on the soil of another."[8] But the whole essay is pervaded by a notion that is as important today as it was in the eighteenth century: that of transparency and publicity. The regimes of fear are closed regimes (Saddam's, North Korea, Burma, much of post-Soviet Central Asia), regimes of censorship or strong and unfettered secret services, regimes that, in emergencies, remove suspects from legal protections and subject them to physical (Abu Ghraib prison) or mental (Guantanamo) torture. The freedom from fear requires, in interstate society, a network of inspections, especially in order to throw light on the development of terror weapons and on practices that violate human rights. In civil society, it requires courageous media whose members are willing to risk their lives, if necessary, to find the hidden in jail cages.

In the never-ending battle against fear, ignorance means doom; sharp light, transparency, and publicity mean hope for the victims, worries for the victimizers, and encouragement for oppositions that fight against state or private violence. This is not the place to attack head-on those who see in modern forms of tyrannies the distorted products of the Enlightenment (what did the Inquisition, Hitler, Stalin, or a Pinochet or a Saddam have to do with the Enlightenment?). When it comes to fear in global society, we can still find inspiration and guidance in philosophies that are the Enlightenment's descendants: liberalism, social democracy, and Christian democracy. We need, of course, to remember that after a plague, a new one would come some day to "awaken its rats and send them to their death in a happy city." But our duty remains to fight the bacillus "that never dies or disappears" (Camus) with as much lucidity and ardor as we can muster.

NOTES

Chapter 4 was published in the special issue "Fear," *Social Research* 71, no. 4 (winter 2004). I call global society the system constituted by interstate relations and by "private" transnational transactions undertaken by individuals and groups of the emerging world civil society. These are, of course, ideal types: many such people and groups serve, in fact, governments (think of private contractors in Iraq at present), and many states have little independence from powerful domestic pressure groups.

1. Thucydides, *The Peloponnesian War* (New York: Penguin, 1954), 49.
2. Hobbes, *Leviathan* (Everyman's Library, 1691), 64–65.
3. See David Fromkin, *Europe's Last War: Who Started the Great War in 1914?* (New York: Knopf, 2004).
4. Hobbes, *Leviathan*, 65.
5. See Claudia Koonz, *The Nazi Conscience* (Cambridge, Mass: Belknap Press, 2003).
6. Judith Shklar, "The Liberalism of Fear," in *Political Thought and Political Thinkers*, ed. Stanley Hoffmann (Chicago: University of Chicago Press, 1998), 12.
7. "America Goes Backward," *New York Review of Books*, June 12, 2003, 74–80.
8. C. J. Friedrich, ed., *Kant* (New York: Modern Library, 1949), 446.

·5·

World Governance: Goal or Mirage?

I. A WORLD OF COMPLEXITY

$\mathcal{T}$he very complexity of the present international scene makes a fair and effective system of world governance necessary, but it also makes it unlikely.

Traditionally, the distinctive feature of international politics has been its anarchic character. There is no superior power above the states. The absence of a super-Leviathan and the absence of a broad consensus on values or on procedures of conflict resolution mean that international politics is, in Rousseau's terms, a "state of war," real or potential. There can be truces, temporary remissions, and zones of peace. It wasn't before the nineteenth century that the main powers constituted a "Concert" to try to preserve the post-Napoleonic settlements, but it was primarily a mechanism of consultation, and it split over the issue of intervention in domestic affairs. After World War I, statesmen and citizens began to think of going beyond the sovereign nation-state. The League of Nations, which the victors created, seemed like a big step forward because of the Covenant's provisions against aggressive wars and its procedures for peaceful change. But it was a strictly international organization, its coercive powers depended on the willingness of the major states to put them into effect, and its strong connections with the territorial status quo established by the post-1918 treaties thwarted the application of the provisions on peaceful change.

The design of the United Nations, in 1945, appeared aimed at preventing a second fiasco of the League of Nations rather than at coping with the mess left by World War II. The Security Council was provided with far larger powers than the Council of the League. But within two years, the Cold War showed that these powers would remain on paper unless the major states were able to serve as a kind of directorate—which, during the Cold War, they could not. After the end of the Cold War and the collapse of the Soviet Union, hopes flourished again: the fundamental cause of the Security Council's paralysis was gone. But to the lesson of the League and of the United Nations before 1990—that these organizations could bring some order into the "anarchical society" only if its major powers provided reasonably united leadership—a new lesson was added: in a unipolar world, the global organization could function only insofar as it went in the direction set by the now single superpower.

Moreover, in the discordant universe of states, the attempt to maintain a separation between conflicts of power and interests among states and conflicts within borders—between issues of international peace and security and issues of domestic jurisdiction—proved untenable: during the Cold War, because one of the chief battlegrounds was the nature and composition of domestic regimes, and after the Cold War, because many of the states—especially in former colonized areas—disintegrated and their fragmentation incited external interventions. In addition, the new concern for human rights, a secondary issue when the UN Charter was established, contributed to erode the barrier between interstate and domestic affairs. The United Nations, as an organization, succeeded in extending its jurisdiction and in inventing new methods of peacekeeping. But it simply did not have the supranational powers and resources necessary to provide much more than band-aids or to force recalcitrant parties to solve hardy perennials such as conflicts in the Middle East, in Kashmir, or in Cyprus or between the two Koreas and between the two Chinas.

As if matters in the traditional domain of world politics—that in which the actors are the states—had not gotten complex enough, next to Thucydides's arena there developed a new realm of a very different sort: an emergent world society in which the role of force and conquest is far less significant and in which the actors are not just the states but a market that increasingly erodes borders—largely because the dominant power wants it so. Here the players are millions of private investors and speculators, thousands of nongovernmental organizations (NGOs) and multinational corporations, in addition to transnational alliances of specialized bureaucracies. Here, the leaps of information technology and means of communications are as much the driving force as the changing distribution of military might is the main determinant of power in the society of states. Here, too, the cacophony is deafening: the rich do not agree on how—indeed, on whether—to help the poor, the poor seem to have to choose between a more or less gilded dependence and an autarkic independence in misery, and the experts disagree (at any moment or over time) about the best formula for development. Environmental interests often clash with the demands for modernization, the concerns of labor with those of entrepreneurs, and so on. The champions of free markets—and of prosperity through the market—collide with those whom the inegalitarian trends of capitalism seem to loom or harm, and freedom of movement for persons has lagged far behind the movement of goods and services.

Thus, we live in a world where one crucial sector, that of security and survival, remains a zone of fragmentation while the domain of the world's economy and cultures is being progressively globalized, where the sweep of globalization gradually deprives the states of many of the instruments that used to be at their disposal (especially monetary and industrial policies) but where globalization, a new source of divisions and hostilities, is often limited to some sectors of society and is slowed down or stopped by vast remnants of state protectionism as well as skewed by the monopolistic and the corrupt forms the market often takes. In recent months, the two societies—that of the states and the global one—have been battered and bewildered by one phenomenon that affects and darkens them both. Terrorism uses the new means of technology, the open borders of the world economy, the many methods of information and misinformation, in order to demonstrate that violence on a very vast scale is no longer the preserve of states or would-be states. The troubles of the world economy, against which the various anti-globalization forces protest, risk being aggravated by the insufficiency of aid to development that the cost of the war on terrorism is making worse. We also discover that the so-often-lamented globalization and homogenization of culture are perhaps less regrettable than the clashes if not of civilizations then at least of fiercely opposed cultures, even within the same religion.

II. THE FLAWS OF WORLD GOVERNANCE

This does not mean that many steps haven't been taken in order to render this world less chaotic, violent, and unmanageable. In the society of states, two sets of advances have been noticeable—and, of course, controversial. We have witnessed a number of humanitarian interventions aimed at preventing mass killings for ethnic reasons, and the creation of new forms of international criminal justice has accompanied these efforts. But the defenders of national sovereignty have resisted both the internationalization of human rights and the assimilation of internal to international conflict. On each of these two paths, defeats have been as conspicuous as successes: think of Rwanda and of the American excommunication of the International Criminal Court. The vital issue of weapons of mass destruction remains a shaky mix of legal commitments with many holes and weak enforcement (such as the Nuclear Nonproliferation Treaty) and of traditional state pressures and inducements that often fail. The means of peacekeeping and peacemaking at the disposal of the United Nations and of regional organizations (both for internal and for interstate conflicts) remain pitifully insufficient in financial as well as military terms.

In the global society, governance is a crazy quilt. It is both fragmented and incomplete: it is fragmented into agencies that are specialized (and often contradictory in their policies) and provided with different powers (existing global institutions in such matters as the environment, population, and women are little more than talk shows); it is incomplete because of the strong opposition of interest groups and some powerful states to anything that could encumber the market with regulations and of their determination to eliminate all hurdles to a free market (for instance, in the domain of foreign investments or of short-term capital flows or as shown by the absence of an international bankruptcy code). This results from the preference of many states and domestic interests influential in them for having their national institutions provide economic and financial stability and "sound" policies to entrusting such powers to multinational agencies. Add to this the limited internationalism of the United States, reluctant to accept multinational constraints or forms of governance that would do more than liberate the markets from obstacles to trade or investments or the free circulation of currencies.

All these flaws and limitations have brought about a multidirectional onslaught against the present forms of governance. In the society of states, the main complaints are about the restrictions imposed on the United Nations (and on regional organizations) by the main powers, especially those endowed with a veto. The provisions of chapter VII of the UN Charter, aimed at giving military capabilities to the Security Council, for prevention and for action, have never been substantiated. A code defining the conditions in which humanitarian intervention could and should be undertaken has not been drafted (there is still disagreement on what constitutes genocide). The United States claims vociferously the right to act without UN endorsement when its security is at stake and has often resorted to unilateral sanctions without seeking external support. It has, more recently, pushed aside UN efforts in arms control.

As for the institutions of economic and social governance, they have been widely criticized as undemocratic, as obliging states to conform to the ideology of the free market and to obey the dictates of the International Monetary Fund (IMF) (i.e., of the United States)—thus weakening internal support for the state even though it remains the most legitimate and unspecialized institution. Many international agencies are denounced for being at the service of the United States, for operating at the expense of the poorer countries and of countries in crisis, for disregarding environmental or human rights standards, for acting in secret, and so on. Multinational corporations are attacked for usurping powers of governance: they are increasingly global in their control of resources, products, banking, and insurance; their connections with officials make them increasingly dominant (in trade negotiations, for instance), and their ability to shift their activities toward low-wage countries fosters a race to the bottom. They infiltrate into and occupy the vacuum between receding states and weak public international institutions.

III. IDEAL WORLD GOVERNANCE?

I will now try to sketch a scheme for world governance that would be an improvement over the present situation without being utopian; that is, it would be appropriate for the complex world described previously. This means that I reject a number of familiar schemes I deem inadequate. The first—chronologically—is Kant's confederation of representative democracies. On the one hand, its provisions for the abolition of war do not deal with such issues as humanitarian interventions (Kant is, fundamentally, a noninterventionist liberal) or terrorism. On the other hand, he limits global society to trade and to a right of individuals to hospitality abroad. This is too simple and sketchy for a world in which liberal regimes are relatively few, standing armies prosper, and armaments get ever more sophisticated and the world economy ever more inegalitarian and complex.

Another scheme, which had many proponents just after the end of World War II, is world government, usually advocated in the form of a global federation. It deals with a world of states but has little to say about the global society in which both states and a free market of individual actors and private groups and organizations operate, and its demand that the states give up their formal sovereignty is still "a bridge too far." Kant's critique of a world state remains valid: such a state would have to be imposed by force, or else it would be too weak to survive the daily crises and challenges of world and of internal affairs.

Nor do I find John Rawls's scheme in *The Law of Peoples* convincing.[1] He has little to say about governance, even though he realizes that in the world as it is—the world of "nonideal theory"—the states would have formidable tasks dealing with rogue and aggressive actors and with the "burdened societies" that need to be assisted. Paradoxically, in his ideal theory, his concern with the need for a consensus broader than that of liberal regimes leads him to a restricted conception of human rights that would have to be acceptable to what he calls "decent hierarchical" regimes, and the priority he gives to "the justice of societies" over the "welfare of individuals" raises important questions about the fate of the increasingly large number of individuals who do not fit into societies (migrants, refugees, and so on).

I will therefore leave (with some regret) the realm of utopia and describe briefly the kind of governance that would constitute a great improvement from the viewpoint of a rather traditional liberal with social-democratic leanings (in the sense that, à la Third Way, he recognizes the importance of economic growth and the merits of capitalism in this connection, but his allegiance is to the welfare and self-fulfillment of individuals; for that purpose, the blind rule of the market is often an evil and a broad variety of social safety nets an essential good).

In the society of states, two issues are central. The first is the protection of human rights. There are, in some parts of the world, such as Europe, strong agencies for their protection and possibilities for individuals to lodge complaints against state violations. But these institutions do not cover the globe, and the relevant UN agencies remain weak, politicized, and state centered. We need a world commission and a world court on human rights, on the European model, as well as the right of monitors and inspectors to operate at the service of such a commission. The latter would have the duty to report to—if necessary to ask for action from—the secretary-general and the political organs of the UN under chapter VII of the Charter if necessary. States, being the most frequent violators of human rights, should not be left in charge of initiating the enforcement of covenants they have either refrained from signing or, more usually, signed but disregarded.

The battle between sovereignty and human rights is still intense, although there has been a gradual shift away from the prevalence of the former. The battle between the nineteenth-century claim by states of a right to wage war, with limitations only on the means, and the return to a modern version of the old *jus ad bellum*, which bans aggression and recognizes as legal only wars of self-defense and of solidarity with the victims of aggression, has been won by the latter on paper, but it is a very shaky and patchy victory. A more satisfactory form of governance would require an enormous reinforcement of the powers of the United Nations. The secretary-general should be not merely allowed to bring dangerous cases to the Security Council: he should be obliged to activate the Council and the General Assembly when the legal limitations on the use of force among states have been or risk being violated and when grave violations of human rights risk being or have been committed internally (there needs to be a code describing such cases for valid humanitarian intervention). States that want to use force in self-defense, individual or collective, would need the authorization of the Security Council or of the General Assembly if the Council is paralyzed, and when the Assembly itself is for any reason blocked from expressing its approval or disapproval, the use of force as a last resort would have to be fully reported to the UN bodies. Above all, the Security Council would have to be provided with a standing force recruited from the states but placed under the jurisdiction of the Council and under a UN military command that would have a supranational character. This command would be put in charge of preventive or reactive operations licensed by the Security Council, and it would be supervised by a civilian board of collective military action composed of UN officials. These bodies would also have a right to inspect countries suspected of acquiring weapons of mass destruction and to call for sanctions by the Security Council if such weapons are indeed being acquired. The secretary-general should have the duty to be the chief negotiator for the United Nations in grave conflicts that threaten global or regional peace, either along with state efforts at good offices or instead of such efforts if they are blocked by states or if state efforts have failed. A permanent supranational arms control negotiating body would put pressure on states in dangerous zones to reduce their arsenals and to open their borders (and their arms acquisitions and sales) to inspections. In the case of humanitarian interventions—future Yugoslavias or Rwandas—the powers of the United Nations would go beyond restoring peace and extend to the kind of nation building or rebuilding that would be indispensable. Obviously, this would entail a vast increase of the UN budget and a substantial corps of international civil servants recruited by the UN secretariat. Against terrorism, an agency that would help coordinate the cooperation and responses of state police forces and that could submit its findings to the political and military agencies of the United Nations ought to be established. As in cases of inter- or intrastate wars, wars against terrorism and against states that foment or shelter it would have to be authorized by the Security Council and take place under the responsibility or with the participation of the UN military command.

If we now turn to the global society, just as nineteenth- and twentieth-century capitalism gradually came to accept a modicum of national and international regulation—to protect workers and consumers, to preserve price stability, to prevent monetary disasters, and so on—twenty-first-century global capitalism needs a regulatory framework that is less fragmented and fragmentary than what exists today. Global dirigisme is neither possible nor probably desirable. But a few important and sore points need to be addressed. I am thinking of the flaws, demonstrated by the Asian crisis of a few years ago, in the supervision of countries and banks by the IMF and its frequent indifference to the domestic effects of the deflationary policies it imposes, the disastrous effects of the volatility of private capital flows, the risks created by excessively rigid exchange rates, and the need to oblige foreign investors to take into account human rights and labor conditions, health standards, and environmental protection. I have neither the competence nor the space to redesign the institutional architecture, but the following guidelines may be essential. First, there ought to be one embryonic economic government that can oversee and try to guide the evolution of the world economy. Here, the model could be the European Union, whose supranational Commission functions as an economic executive and whose Council of Ministers sets the rules (for the global economy, a new economic and social council comparable to the Security Council would be needed). Harmonizing the activities of the World Trade Organization (WTO) with those of the International Labor Organization, the World Bank, and the IMF would be within the jurisdiction of this council, and a functional equivalent of the European Union's Commission would act as its executive agent. Divergences over economic philosophies and goals would persist, but these bodies could focus on setting common norms in the form of codes of good practices and on reducing the bad effects of capitalist competition—the rash of alliances and mergers that creates a need for a global antitrust mechanism. Second, the responsibility for assistance to development ought to be more centralized, the goals being an increase of development assistance and a reduction of the inequality between the rich and the poor countries' influence in world governance: this would entail a UN right to tax its members for economic development and to inspect, report on, and recommend changes in the development policies of the receiving countries. Third, a world environmental agency needs to be created that would be in charge of negotiating global protocols and be provided with the expertise necessary to supervise their enforcement and recommend to its assembly sanctions against delinquent states and enterprises. Fourth, UNESCO would have to be revamped; from the (valuable) concern for elite cultures and endangered local ones, the activities should partly switch to a global effort against fanaticism, parochialism, and intolerance, which would require major funds to influence and activate governments, churches, and school systems. An agency comparable, once again, to the EU Commission, would serve as this new UNESCO's executive.

The improvement of global governance requires not only more powers and resources for global institutions but also far greater democratization and representativity. Next to the new Economic and Social Council, there ought to be not only the UN General Assembly, to which this Council would report (along with the more specialized agencies, such as the [WTO, World Bank, and Environmental Agency), but also a consultative assembly composed of representatives of NGOs and of important multinational corporations (an official and public supplement to, if not a substitute for, the Davos conference). The General Assembly, which represents governments, needs to be complemented by an assembly of peoples' representatives that, in the beginning, might have only powers of general recommendation (rather than share the very specific powers of the General Assembly). But it would introduce unofficial voices in the global debates. As I have suggested before,[2] the control of the legality of the resolutions adopted by the Security Council, the General Assembly, and the new Economic and Social Council would increase the authority and legitimacy of these global bodies and be entrusted to the World Court.

IV. TOO LITTLE, TOO MUCH?

Short of being mobilized by a world catastrophe—a nuclear war that kills millions (but not us all), an economic recession next to which that of 1929 would appear insignificant, a meteorite colliding with the earth, a series of global epidemics that nobody would know how to stop, global warming turning into a boil (we now understand that Hollywoodian science fiction can anticipate real events)—the many tribes of the human race are unlikely to launch a world constitutional convention that would do away with the sturdy residues of the Westphalian order, abolish existing states and the creaky international institutions that serve them, and proclaim a world state. As, indeed, with global warming, changes are likely to be gradual and to respond to crises as they develop: piecemeal and not necessarily adequate. When one sees how difficult and controversial, after fifty years, remains the transformation of the European Union from a complex mechanism of interstate cooperation and pooling of state powers into what Jacques Delors likes to call, cryptically, a federation of nation-states, one has to realize that when it comes to global governance, the ideal is not in the realm of the possible, and the best may be the enemy of the good. In other words, I am the first to state that the changes I advocate are, at best, the passage from a puzzle to a mosaic.

The real problem lies not in the distance of my scheme from utopia but in the distance between it and current realities. The obstacles are too many to be examined in detail here, but the main ones need to be faced frankly. First, despite their loss of legal and operational sovereignty to new institutions that have been set up to reduce violence and to protect human rights, as well as to the global capitalist market, states remain the ultimate public decision makers, and this means, of course, that the traditional contests for power and states will continue—indeed, they may get even sharper as the states cling to what they still have and become more fearful of losing even more of their authority. The fact that power is as unevenly distributed as it is today while the number of states has multiplied and most of them have very little might makes an agreement on their respective weight in the institutions of global governance very dubious. Military and economic giants are unlikely to want to be outvoted or pushed around by hordes of pygmies. Moreover, the contradiction that, twice in the twentieth century, has undermined the attempt to submit all states to the same duties would persist: between the general and the abstract nature of these obligations and the concrete calculations of interests (such as those that make us more tolerant of states that sponsor or tolerate terrorism but are otherwise our friends or allies than of those states that treat us as our foes or of "friendly" nuclear proliferators, such as Israel, than of "rogue" ones, such as North Korea).

A second obstacle is this: despite the partial globalization of mass culture, the nationalisms of fragmentation we have witnessed in recent years, the politicization of religion such as that of a large part of Islam, the battles between enthusiasts of globalization as an engine of individual emancipation and collective modernization, and defenders of threatened cultures and practices—all this has made Rousseau's dictum about the absence of any unity of humankind (even, at times, against common ecological dangers) even more sadly true. In a world driven by economic and technological forces, where the political ideologies of the past two centuries have tended to exhaust themselves—through horrible excesses or humbling irrelevance—the split between globalizers whose hopes are with capitalism and parochialists who continue to distrust the inhumanity and the destructiveness of capitalism as an ideal type has made unity even more difficult.

There is another cleavage that would make it almost (or completely!) impossible to achieve some of the institutional reforms I have suggested and to push beyond the limits we have reached in trying to help human beings against state oppression, repression, and cruelty. It is the cleavage between liberal democratic regimes that respect human rights and the right of people to self-determination and authoritarian or totalitarian regimes that do not (the "decent" authoritarians of Rawls are a fiction of his ideal theory, for practical purposes). The progress toward a more humanitarian world that my scheme tries to promote, in which people, not only officials and experts, would be represented, would meet with fierce resistance from the many tyrants of this world (who have, for instance, no incentive to grant to other countries or to a global criminal court jurisdiction over those of their subjects who have committed crimes against humanity or genocide). States whose regimes need walls (even as their economies need hefty doses of openness) do not welcome the democratization of international institutions. An Assembly of Peoples' Representatives half based on free choices, half made up of disguised officials, would be a joke. Without the Kantian prerequisite—a world of liberal democracies—the institutions of world governance will remain battlegrounds, yet we need world governance in part because of the clash of regimes. In the realm of assistance for development, this same fundamental split is likely to make liberal regimes concentrate either on sanctions against evil regimes rather than aid for these regimes' subjects (who may never receive it anyway) or else on funds for their own progress.

The final obstacle that needs to be confronted happens to be the very superpower that sees itself as the upholder of world order and the champion of liberal democracy: the United States. Every scheme of world order needs, behind the international institutions it entails, actual states that provide them with resources and that act as the secular arms of the principles and procedures this order tries to preserve. This was the role of the great powers in the age of the Concert of Europe, that of the (unfortunately disagreeing) British and French under the League. It was the role of the United States and its main allies during the Cold War. But when unipolarity, not multipolarity, succeeded it, the dwindling enthusiasm of the United States for institutions that appeared, to a sizable section of the American establishment, either rather useless or actually constraining or even hostile gradually turned into a boastful unilateralism that is the very enemy of global governance: protocols and treaties abandoned or repudiated, discourses about the incompatibility between external judicial interventions and the U.S. Constitution or about the right of the United States to decide who is a threat to peace or when nuclear weapons should be used, resistance to those economic institutions that do not sing the gospel of the market, and so on. The underlying message is clear: the United States is the provider of global governance and the interpreter of last resort of what global governance requires. This is not exactly conducive to a consensual scheme. Other states do not want American governance of the world. Without a thorough rejection of this new doctrine and a return to a policy of leadership without dictation, the state of world governance can only get worse.[3]

NOTES

Chapter 5 was published in *Daedalus* (winter 2003).

1. John Rawls, *The Law of Peoples* (Cambridge, Mass.: Harvard University Press, 1999).

2. In *World Disorders* (Boulder, Colo.: Rowman & Littlefield, 1998), 185.

3. See Joseph Nye Jr., *The Paradox of American Power* (Oxford: Oxford University Press, 2002).

· 6 ·

A World Unjust and Belligerent

$\mathscr{P}$eace can be defined in two ways. The broad definition belongs to Giraudoux who describes it as "the interval between wars" (which he considers, as did Raymond Aron, to be the essence of international relations). A narrowly construed definition sees peace as referring specifically to peace treaties and their consequences for the former warring parties and the international realm. This is the definition that I will be using here, modified slightly to take into account those cases when, such as in 1945, the final ratification of treaties was prevented by the breaking up of the alliance that defeated Germany. These treaties were replaced with agreements that were both temporary and limited. But, as some have said, there is nothing more permanent than that which is temporary.

Georges Bidault once said that a good diplomatic agreement was one with which all parties were equally dissatisfied. This is an elegant way to acknowledge that the purpose of peace treaties was more to balance out injustice than to have justice prevail. (We can look here to the case of Poland, which lost its eastern border but was "compensated" with parts of Prussia and Germany's Silesia region.) In fact, many peace treaties that were imposed by the victors were seen as unfair (not only by the vanquished but also by some of the victors themselves, such as in the case of Italy after 1918). The Versailles Peace Treaty is a classic example. The accords of Yalta and Potsdam, which allowed Russia to impose its dominion over Eastern and Central Europe (I will not enter here into the debate over the margin of choices available to its allies), were seen as profoundly unfair by those behind what became the Iron Curtain. The peace treaty signed by Egypt and Israel in 1979 was seen as unfair not only by the Palestinians, who were left out, but also by a sizable portion of the Arab world. The status given to Austria, once it was finally determined in 1955, was unjust not because it was too harsh but because it cast in the role of victim a nation that had for the most part fully embraced Hitler.

Conversely, justice is often belligerent when it no longer resembles the traditional image of a scale but instead the image of a fighter with his sword. I am reminded here of wars (or guerrilla wars) against the oppression and the domination of the colonizers. Similarly, there have been those interventions in cases of human rights violations that are often more effective in establishing or reestablishing justice, as was the case with the wars stemming from the dissolution of Yugoslavia, than is the stubborn adhesion to the principle of nonintervention, as was the case with Rwanda. In addition, there are antiterrorist operations, the purpose of which is to bring aid to the victims of terror, insecurity, and fear. The expulsion of al-Qaeda and the Taliban from Afghanistan is a good example of belligerent justice.

Violence, therefore, is something just, or justifiable, when there is an emergency and when all other avenues have been exhausted. Armed interventions in ethnic conflicts aimed at ending massive human rights violations (as was the case in Yugoslavia) fall into this category. (In contrast, in the case of Rwanda, it was nonintervention that proved unjust.) The decision by Great Britain and France to go to war after the inglorious injustices of the "appeasement" might have also fallen into this category had the all-out war against Fascism and Nazism not taken aim at so many civilians and thus violated the long-standing principle of the just-war doctrine: the protection of noncombatants. As for peace, it has at times existed—I am thinking here of the fate of West Germany and Japan after World War II. This time there was no manifestation of the retaliatory violence that drove Hitler before and after his rise to power and that was similarly apparent in the *Organisation de l'Armée Secrète* at the time of the Evian Accords in 1962. This was not due only or even primarily to the military presence of the Western victors or the new threat posed by the Soviet Union.

Why then has peace been so often unjust, and why has justice been more often belligerent than peaceful? There are many reasons for this. First, there are many different types of peace. Peace was often imposed by the victor on either the vanquished or the unfortunate "little" countries trapped between the Great Powers. This was the case in Europe after Yalta, when one side was occupied by the Soviets and the other found itself under the imperfect influence of the Americans and the British. Thankfully, there has also been peace that stems from a compromise and creates little or less resentment. There is also grandiose peace that reshuffles the world order, such as the Westphalia Treaty or the peace following the Napoleonic Wars or World War I. Here, the adoption of new principles and the bartering over territory led to a patchwork of decisions, which governments or people considered unjust, and of attempts to repair past injustices, which are often inextricable. The former are usually perceived as unpalatable, and the latter are less celebrated than we could imagine. Finally, there are peace or armistices that serve only to put a temporary end to violence and leave all sides (or at least some of them) feeling dissatisfied (as is the case with the Israeli–Arab conflicts or the wars over Kashmir).

Second, there is a wide array of definitions of justice. The preliminary question is, Justice for whom? For the states involved in a conflict? For the individuals who are often victims of the compromises constructed by the states? Let us consider the Evian Accords in 1962. Both Algeria, which had obtained its independence, and France, which had freed itself from the Algerian quagmire, had good reasons to find these agreements acceptable. Could the same be said, though, of the *harkis* or of the members of the *Organisation de l'Armée Secrète*? Peace achieved through compromise has often entailed large transfers of populations, and thus individuals have suffered the consequences of the actions taken by states.

Moreover, there are different types of justice. Criminal justice, which deals with perpetrators of war crimes or crimes against humanity (even if they happen to be statesmen), is perceived as just by the victims (e.g., the victims of Milosevic) but is seen as partial and vindictive by those who had supported and even inspired those same criminals. The current ambivalence of the United States with regard to international criminal justice is quite typical: the Americans supported the creation of tribunals in the cases of Yugoslavia as well as Rwanda, where they had not wanted to intervene, but they have renounced the International Criminal Court because it could—theoretically —incriminate American nationals.

Distributive justice is the subject of even more fierce controversy because it can be viewed in many ways: equal opportunity, fairness (as defined by Rawls), or equality of results. In all these aspects, the opposition between states and individuals can at times be dramatically felt. In other words, this is the area where it might be most difficult to achieve an agreement between adversaries or rivals.

Although procedural justice is perceived as less contentious, it can nonetheless be very hard to achieve, particularly when the very type of procedure selected (recall the arguments over the shape of the table) can determine the outcome of a conflict.

The nature of international relations is another obstacle to the ideal of just peace. The universe in which these relations occur is by definition ruled by partiality. This is true in two ways: each actor tends to see things only from its own point of view (think back to de Gaulle with respect to Israel during the Six Day War), and there is no impartial judge empowered to decide what is just and impose its decision on the parties. In the Hobbesian universe, the Leviathan alone defines what is just, and it is therefore an arbitrary decision. No such global Leviathan exists today. Therefore, in a world where state and nonstate actors abound (from Doctors Without Borders to unscrupulous terrorists), each side tends to have its own idea of justice (which fuels wars if said actors are armed) and, of course, its own interests.

Finally, the traditional shortcomings of the "anarchical society," so well analyzed by Hedley Bull, are accentuated by contemporary international relations. Preoccupations with justice have intensified as the public, which plays a role in foreign policy, has gotten more and more democratized. This general public acts less like an inert object in the hands of diplomats or military professionals and more as a large group of concerned actors wanting to have their say. Between the end of the Napoleonic Wars and the end of the French-Prussian War, the habit of treating entire populations like cattle lost its legitimacy. Consequently, the negotiation of peace accords went from attempting to strike a balance between competing interests to attempting to achieve a weakening or a quieting of passions, which is much more difficult. Demands for self-determination have greatly sparked the political tinderboxes and have added fuel to the fires of wars, as was the case with internal demands and revolutions to obtain democracy.

As contemporary international relations have intensified, they have also worsened. This is due to the nature of modern warfare. With the increased sophistication of weapons, able to strike harder and farther, with armies becoming more and more civilian (as opposed to professional armies), wars that were once fairly limited now expose to view the most inflamed passions, such as patriotic or chauvinistic fervor, terror, and brainwashing, to name a few. Injustice has multiplied in a way commensurate with modern warfare. (On September 11, 2001, why were victims targeted in New York but not in Chicago or San Francisco?)

WHAT CAN BE DONE?

Political philosophy, which has always been more interested in the *polis*, or state, rather than the relations between the units, has focused its attention on the opposition between order and justice. In order to maintain the established order, grave injustices are often condoned, the resolution of which initially carries the risk of engendering disorder if not civil war. It bears remembering here the saying attributed to Goethe: better injustice than disorder. This is the near universal mantra shared by almost all right-leaning people such as Kissinger. In the realm of international relations, there is, however, a third participant: peace (or war, as the case may be). It is rare for regional or world order to be established without both injustice *and* violence. I am reminded here of the order imposed by the colonial empires. Although decolonization brought back a certain brand of justice, this was often achieved by the use of force (by the "decolonizers") and resulted in a perilous state of disorder. Many authors have viewed or continue to view empire (ancient or modern) as a form of government that puts justice below order and peace. But, in reality, such peace is usually a "peace of cemeteries," where maintaining order is a constant preoccupation and in the end there is neither stable order nor assured peace or justice.

What can be done then if one wishes (not as a naive idealist but as a realist, horrified by constant oppression, the human and material cost of modern warfare, and the surge in passions stoked by injustice) to get closer to a form of order that is both more just and more peaceful? The reader is well aware that such a vast subject cannot be addressed in just a few paragraphs. I will, therefore, limit myself to a few comments that are more consistent than might at first appear.

1. If it is at all possible to choose, it is almost always preferable to try to achieve justice through peace rather than war. Justice, like democracy, can rarely be established with foreign gun power. It was much better that apartheid was abolished by an agreement between blacks and whites than by way of a war between enemy races, which would have created a profound sense of injustice for the losing side.

2. Precisely because there is no all-powerful Olympian judge able to define "objectively" what constitutes justice, it behooves the leaders of nations to concern themselves with the feelings of injustice created by their decisions rather than focusing solely on objective justice. Objectively, the ragged edges of the Versailles Treaty were not scandalously unjust. But whereas a century ago the victors had refrained from humiliating the French, this time around the vindictiveness of the victors and the clause on the German responsibility left a sizable portion of the Germans feeling humiliated. Peace that feeds resentment is a bad peace. (However, peace that does not seek to bring to justice the perpetrators of horrific acts from the victors' own camp is neither wise nor just.)

3. States engaged in armed conflict often choose to bid farewell to arms (at least temporarily) rather than to continue their exhausting fighting. More often than not, outside mediators also tend to focus on achieving a cease-fire above all else. However, if the victory over violence is not followed by an effort to resolve the root causes of the conflicts and to reach an agreement that is acceptable (if not wholly satisfactory) to the warring factions, then peace will remain fragile

enough and the feelings of injustice strong enough for violence to start anew. For proof of this, we can look to the Middle East from 1947 to the present or to Kashmir. One should not mistake the temporary and deceptive order created by military reprieves for an order that is both peaceful and just, which should remain the primary objective.

4. In today's world, establishing or reestablishing justice (or eliminating injustice) often requires the use of force. Therefore, in order to legitimize this recourse, it is necessary to endow the United Nations with its own armed forces that would be able to act quickly on orders from the Security Council. This would be beneficial on two accounts. First, it would be more efficient and serve more as a deterrent than improvising a collective action in times of crisis. Second, it would prevent some actors who might be guided solely by their own self-interest from acting unilaterally.

5. From a Hobbesian perspective, if the international system becomes as dangerous for the survival of the habitants of Earth as civil wars, it is therefore necessary that states abandon their state of nature. Hobbes considered the state of nature to be less harmful for the states than the one individuals experienced before understanding the necessity to transfer their powers to a state able to protect them against the war of all against all and to ensure them with a modicum of justice. The logic of the Leviathan calls then for the creation of a world state, as was understood by Morgenthau during the advent of the nuclear age. This remains true, in my opinion, in the age of transnational terrorism. For various reasons (well understood by Kant), the world is not ready for this leap. This does not preclude us, however, from taking steps toward this goal by strengthening the power and legitimacy of international and supranational organizations. By the same token, it is of paramount importance to reduce the injustices caused by the global economy by making certain that the market is not ruled by the law of the jungle in areas ranging from trade to foreign investment and the environment. Here too, a just order will be achieved only if the cooperation between states and private actors leads to common rules and regulations.

6. Kant corrects Hobbes insofar as he is concerned less about the survival of individuals than about their sense of civic duty. For Kant, what constitutes the best antidote to war (whether civil war or war against outside forces) is not the transfer of the use of force to the state or a confederation of states but the internal transformation of the states: the transition to the rule of citizens in representative

democracies, which would prevent arbitrary rule and put a damper on the warring tendencies of the Leviathans both at home and abroad. This is why the slow process toward justice and peace must include free speech and the respect for human rights.

7. This brings us back to the true foundation of international relations: not states or transnational groups but individuals. Although democracy is often promoted as a guarantee for peace (with respect to relations between democracies), it can nonetheless be a cause of injustice and violence unless individuals endeavor to establish three conditions. The first has to do with viewing individuals in a manner that is closer to Kantian liberalism than to the often-weakened liberalism of the previous century. This latter liberalism tends to be concerned mainly with the rights of individuals: the primacy of individual rights over the common good and the primacy of freedom through independence over freedom through participation. Kant insists on the duties, the categorical imperatives present in the consciousness of the people, more than on freedoms. Second, despite an electoral process where the short term tends to prevail, it behooves the individuals who make up the democracy to find the necessary resources to put long-term interests ahead of short-term preoccupations. (This is possible only if there already exists a modicum of order, peace, and justice.) There are several forces that can enable or at least help citizens to rise above this tendency. Inside the states, a style of education is needed that is antiracist, antinationalist, and universalist (not, however, antipatriotic). Outside, international institutions need to focus on the common interest rather than the specific interest of groups or nations and need to favor the long-term view over the short-term view. Third, in the mind of citizens, reason and humanism must win over not only the secular religion of totalitarianism and the dark passions it ignites but also the religious fanaticism that calls stridently for the death of those who are ungodly, infidels, or "different." A tall order indeed.

In order to achieve justice and peace despite human nature, the nature of nations, and the nature of international relations, it is necessary to affect both institutions and values. As far as the latter are concerned, imagination, which allows one to understand the points of view and grievances of the Other, and its sister, compassion, are especially important. (I do not speak here of tolerance, as there are all manner of injustices and violence that are intolerable.) As for institutions, it is necessary gradually to circumvent and subvert the Westphalian order and the vast area of international law that stems from it. We need to both chisel away at sovereignty and create a series of obstacles to extreme sovereignty, which is one of the worst contributors to violence and injustice.

I recently had the opportunity and the somber pleasure of rereading *The Pest* by Camus. This, in my opinion, is not only the most beautiful novel of the twentieth century but also the most convincing guide for the twenty-first century. It does not promise that rats will disappear once and for all, but it does demonstrate to us why and how we must fight against them.[1]

NOTES

Chapter 6 was translated by the author from an essay written for Pierre Allan and Alexis Keller, eds., *What Is a Just Peace?* (New York: Oxford University Press, 2006).

1. I subscribe entirely to the conclusions of P. Hassner in "La revanche des passions," *Commentaire*, no. 110 (summer 2005): 312: "There is no other way than the rare, fragile and often conflictual alliance of moderation and passion," in a world where immoderate passions become "criminal and suicidal," and "moderation without passion is impotent."

·7·

The Debate about Intervention

$\mathcal{T}$he tragic series of disintegrating states racked by ethnic conflicts, sectarian quarrels, gang warfare, or huge human rights violations has, in the past decade, replaced the more traditional interstate "cold war" as the most salient aspect of the "diplomatic-strategic" arena of international relations. I have reviewed elsewhere the political and ethical issues raised by humanitarian interventions, especially those of a collective nature, and I have in particular examined the Yugoslav conflicts.[1] My purpose here is to reflect on the arguments for and against such interventions that have multiplied over the years. After a brief review of the opinions of theorists, I examine first the arguments that defend them and then turn to the criticisms of intervention before concluding in favor of the former despite the strength of the critics' points.

TRADITIONAL VIEWS OF INTERVENTION

It is often useful to return to the pronouncements of political philosophers about issues that recurrently plague statesmen and affect ordinary citizens. However, on our subject, the wisdom of the theorists tends to fall short. Realists, as analysts, look at interventions, unilateral or collective, as ordinary manifestations of power in an anarchic milieu; normatively, they don't go much beyond advocating prudence and moderation. Neorealism focuses on the determining role of the international system's structure; as most of the internal conflicts take place in states of limited importance or else in states of sufficient power to deter outside interventions, these conflicts are not deemed significant enough to affect the structure; as for collective interventions, they are seen as little more than fleeting coalitions of powers rather than as manifestations of any autonomous role of international institutions.[2] The policy advice that follows from this is for states to avoid interventions unless vital issues of state security and survival are at stake for them in an internal crisis elsewhere.

Liberal political philosophy has had to deal more forthrightly with foreign military interventions. It has been caught between the different implica-
tions of two related conceptions. One was its vision of a more harmonious
world in which representative regimes running states with powers sharply
limited by national and transnational civil society would have fewer reasons
to fight and compelling reasons to settle conflicts peacefully. Liberalism also
stated its conviction that such a world could come into existence only if nondemocratic regimes were displaced and replaced by democratic ones. The
vision entailed a defense of state sovereignty and a condemnation of outside
interventions, especially if they use force. The conviction suggested that
achieving the vision might require such interventions against obnoxious
regimes—both when they commit aggression against neighbors (hence the
theory of collective security) and when they massacre or oppress their people.

Immanuel Kant came down on the side of nonintervention "in the constitution and government of another state." The exception he mentions—the
case of a state "split into two parts" by dissension between two sides "which,
while constituting a separate state . . . lay claim to the whole"—turns out not
to be really an exception because "as long as this inner strife was not decided,
the interference of outside powers would be a trespass on the rights of an
independent people struggling only with its inner weakness . . . an actual
offense which would tend to render the autonomy of all states insecure."[3]

John Stuart Mill's position was more complex and elaborate but not as
profoundly different from Kant's as one might think. He justifies forcible
intervention in two cases. One is "the case in which one of the parties is of a
high and the other of a very low grade of social improvement,"[4] for the same
international customs and rules of international morality that exist between
civilized nations do not exist "between civilized nations and barbarians."
(Liberalism and imperialism were thus seen as perfectly compatible.) The
other case, among civilized states, is that of "a people struggling against a
foreign yoke, or against a native tyranny upheld by foreign arms."[5] Thus, outside intervention by force is admissible on behalf of self-determination—but
not for self-government: intervention to help a people set up free institutions
(rather than its own state) is rejected because it cannot be proven that "it
would be for the good of the people themselves." In contemporary terms, this
would mean Bosnia, Kosovo, and East Timor yes, Haiti, Somalia, and
Rwanda no.

Michael Walzer, a century later, adopted Mill's distinction and encased
it, so to speak, in his "legalist paradigm"—his conception of "an international
society of independent states" endowed with "the rights of territorial integrity
and political sovereignty."[6] In this society, "only aggression can justify war,"
but helping a nation secede and obtain, through self-determination, its own
independent state is legitimate; intervention in a civil war whose stake is the

control of the central government is not legitimate because each nation has a right to resolve the problem of who should govern it by itself without outside interference. However, Walzer added to the short list of justified military interventions humanitarian ones when they are "a response (with reasonable expectation of success) to acts that shock the moral conscience of mankind" because "government armies engaged in massacres are readily identified as criminal"[7] (his example is Pakistan in what was to become Bangladesh).

Most recently, John Rawls's *Law of Peoples* exemplifies another liberal tension—this time between the notion of a society of "peoples" bound by a series of principles that are those of modern interstate law (so that they are divided into two categories: decent peoples, democratic and "hierarchical," who respect those norms and "outlaw states" that don't) and the more contemporary international law that grants certain rights (and obligations) directly to individuals. Rawls resolves this tension by including in his list of principles to be observed by "peoples" the respect of human rights. This allows him to qualify his principle 4—"peoples are to observe a duty of nonintervention"—in the case of "outlaw states" that commit "grave violations of human rights." What is striking in Rawls's conception is that he moves away both from the rigid distinction between self-determination and self-government that Mill and Walzer advocated and from the tight embrace of the former. "No people has a right of self-determination, or a right to secession, at the expense of subjugating another people"; conversely, coercive interventions are allowed in "grave cases," when "domestic institutions violate human rights" or limit the rights of minorities living among them."[8] The question left open is how to bring outlaw states to honor the law of peoples in cases other than the "grave violations of human rights" that justify intervention. Rawls tells us that it is a question of foreign policy, political wisdom—and luck; he suggests economic and diplomatic pressures depending on "a political assessment of the likely consequences of various policies."[9] The shift from a license for intervention in defense of national self-determination to a justification for intervention in defense of human rights is part of the gradual, slow shift from a liberalism of nation-states endowed by international law with rights and duties to a liberalism of rights and duties for both states and individuals, the rights of the states—including the right to sovereignty—being increasingly subordinated to their respect and promotion of the rights of the individuals.

COLLECTIVE, FORCIBLE INTERVENTIONS

We turn now to the contemporary debate and to the arguments in favor of collective forcible interventions—or even unilateral ones in "egregious" cases (to use Rawls's adjective), when collective institutions are paralyzed or passive (we can think of India in Bangladesh or Tanzania against Idi Amin).

One argument is conspicuously absent or subdued: it is that of the need to help national self-determination when it is being resisted. Even in the case of East Timor, the clamor for an external military interference was based on the atrocities committed by Indonesian military and paramilitary forces after the UN-sponsored referendum on independence rather than on a duty to enforce the results of this referendum given Indonesia's noncompliance. In Kosovo, the Rambouillet document promised a referendum on the status of the territory after three years, but the agreement that put an end to the war in June 1999 referred only to an ill-defined autonomy. The focus throughout was on Serb atrocities, not on Kosovar demands for independence. (This had already been the case when the Security Council ordered Saddam Hussein to stop the massacres of Kurds and Shiites—there was no promise of self-determination for the Kurds.)

The Catholic doctrine of just war has been the traditional middle ground between Christian pacifism and theories justifying holy war to propagate a faith. It has developed in the context of interstate conflicts, but we find that today most of the justifications for interventions in domestic conflicts fall in the traditional categories of the *jus ad bellum*, which deals with just causes (self-defense and the vindication of rights), proportionality of values (the values destroyed should not exceed those that are being upheld), proper authority (who can legitimately decide the resort to force?), reasonable chance of success, and last resort (the exhaustion of all efforts to save peace). The causes deemed important enough to require intervention can be divided into two categories. The first one is the properly humanitarian one: the disinterested duty to put an end to or to reduce human suffering. This is the argument of Joelle Tanguy, speaking as an official of Doctors Without Borders. She makes a case for impartial aid agencies providing assistance to all the victims of humanitarian disasters and against linking it to "the kind of intervention carried out by political and military bodies," which condones the use of force. The latter will add to the suffering. "Both approaches are necessary, but in order to serve their purposes, we believe that they must be carried out independently."[10] In her view, politicizing humanitarian assistance makes it the hostage of political calculations and military priorities. Interference yes, force no. This is, obviously, the position of a nongovernmental organization.

The second category of arguments addresses the right of states to use force inside the borders of other states. Usually, the "just cause" that is invoked is the defense of human rights when there are massive violations of them—in cases of genocide or brutal ethnic cleansing or (as in Liberia or Sierra Leone) monstrous brutalities committed by rebel or rival gangs. This is both clear enough—and vague enough to leave room for argument. (Was the level of violence in Kosovo before March 1999 high enough to vindicate military action? Was the latter justified, rather, by the violation of past agreements Milosevic had signed and the anticipation of further ethnic cleansing?)

An elegant formulation comes from Kofi Annan: the UN charter is "a living document, whose . . . very letter and spirit are the affirmation of . . . fundamental human rights," whereas sovereignty is being "redefined by the forces of globalization and international cooperation."[11] Less diplomatically, David Luban argues that "there is nothing regrettable about violating the statist order in order to protect human rights; the justice and injustice of war should be assessed along the dimension of human rights protection, not state sovereignty protection, and the social ontology that places states above individuals is indefensible."[12]

To the argument made by realists, that the pursuit of such altruistic aims contradicts the very logic of international relations—a logic of selfishness—and that the promotion of such values is not in the nature of "the game," which aims at promoting state interests, the advocates of a new international law reply that these are false distinctions because the toleration of shocking or egregious atrocities is likely to lead either to chaos spreading through imitation or to regional destabilization through arms smuggling, massive flows of refugees, and self-interested interventions in support of feuding parties. (This does not, of course, address cases when such effects are not visible; paradoxically, East Timor was one such case. But here it could be argued that upholding the result of a UN-sponsored referendum was indeed both value and interest driven.)

The limitation, however vague, of causes of forcible intervention to particularly serious violations of rights is a way of dealing with the proportionality between values saved by force and values destroyed by it. Defenders of the war in Kosovo have replied to critics of the way in which it was waged—against civilian installations more than against Serb forces—by arguing that the damage was necessary to put an end to—and less horrendous than the continuation of—the ethnic cleansing of the Albanians.

On proper authority, the "interveners" have been, on the whole, champions of the United Nations. But on the one hand they have become aware of its limitations (about which more will be said), and on the other they have deemed the cause more important than the procedure of the Charter, the substance more important than the formalities. This is why many (but not all) did defend the bypassing of the Security Council in the case of Kosovo and the transformation of NATO from a military alliance (last used as a UN agent in Bosnia) into a regional organization, a "principal," substituting for a veto-ridden Security Council. Others would have preferred a resort to the

Council, followed by a resort to NATO or to a "coalition of the willing" if the Council had been paralyzed by a Russian and/or a Chinese veto.

It is because of both proportionality and the need for a reasonable chance of success that the defenders do not seem bothered by the contrast between action against Serbia (or in Haiti) and inaction against Russia over Chechnya. Reasonable chance of success is, of course, a very iffy notion. Those who went beyond a purely humanitarian delivery of food and medicines in Somalia thought they had a good chance of eliminating the warlord Aïdid; many believed that there was little chance of stopping the genocide in Rwanda after it began in the summer of 1994, despite later vehement arguments to the contrary. A reasonable chance of success requires a willingness to bear certain costs and to launch an effort sufficient to have such a chance. The United States had no such willingness in Somalia and in Rwanda, and despite British and Nigerian attempts, nobody was ready for a sufficient effort in Sierra Leone.

No less controversial is the last condition of *jus ad bellum*: that force be used only as a last resort. Not only can one think of cases where force was used too late to save many victims (Bosnia, Haiti) and would, if used early, probably have been less destructive of "enemy" lives than protracted sanctions that hit innocent civilians over many years, but opponents of military intervention will, it seems, never be satisfied that all hopes for a peaceful resolution had been extinguished before force was used or that the efforts presented by officials as honest attempts at reaching an agreement hadn't been designed to be rejected. Defenders of NATO's actions in Kosovo insist that even after Rambouillet, the Serbs refused any plan that would have allowed international forces into Kosovo. Critics point to provisions of the Rambouillet agreement (especially the right of NATO forces to move from Hungary to the disputed area) that, in their view, no self-respecting Serb government could have accepted. But if it couldn't accept this and yet had been willing to accept outside "peacekeepers," Serbia surely could have made it clear.

The key, for the defenders of forcible intervention for humanitarian goals, is the vision of an international order in which state sovereignty is not an absolute but a set of attributes that can be curtailed when essential human rights are being violated and in which the ban on aggression that has limited sovereignty since the Covenant of the League of Nations is completed by a ban on such internal atrocities as ethnic cleansing and systematic massacres of "enemies of the state." As in the Wilsonian view or in that of Hans Kelsen, war is either a crime or a sanction enforced by the international society, but what constitutes a crime is no longer limited to transgressions across borders.

CRITICISMS OF INTERVENTION

The opponents or critics of intervention have deployed a formidable arsenal of arguments. Many of them raise questions about the "justness" of defending human rights abroad. The most sweeping attacks are of two kinds. One is legalistic, the other is political. The legalistic stance proclaims the sanctity of the principle of national sovereignty as the cornerstone of the post-Westphalian world order and of its corollary, the principle of nonintervention. The latter is seen as protecting not only the state against outside interference and subversion but also its citizens, for whom the state is the precondition of order and the focus of social identity. It is this crucial role of the state, even in an age of economic and technological globalization, that the World Court has recognized when it gave an advisory opinion that refused to declare nuclear weapons illegal because of the right of states to defend themselves.

The political attack comes from the realists. They look at international relations from the viewpoint of the states and argue that a sound foreign policy is one that protects and promotes their essential interests. When they are in question, states need no human rights or humanitarian arguments to justify their interventions. When such interests are not involved, and even if one could argue, in legal terms, that there may be a right to intervene, say, against genocide, something, it must be added, these critics are not ready to concede, a distinction would still have to be made between such a right and an obligation to intervene. For military action to be an obligation, essential interests need to be at stake—as in the case of aggression. Risking lives "in the absence of any definable national interest"[13] can lead only to overcommitment, to serious damage to relations with other often far more important governments, and to an erosion of domestic support. There are too many dogs fighting in the world arena, and the United States has no dogs in most of those fights. Indeed, the truly vital interests—the protection of national security from foreign aggression, the preservation of America's world status and economic resources from challengers—are threatened by the external policies of rivals or rogues, not by their internal actions (which it may be impossible or far too risky to try to stop).

A specifically military variant of this position, well stated by General Colin Powell, stresses that the purpose of America's armed forces is to fight and defeat enemies. The "other new missions that are coming along"[14] are peripheral and must remain so. Otherwise, America's forces will be depleted by marginal operations and made unavailable and unfit for the real lurking dangers.

The neorealists, who look at international relations from the viewpoint of the system and of its stability, see internal wars as potentially destabilizing, at worst, when outsiders interfere and especially insofar as external intrusions can be interpreted as acts of disguised imperialism committed by a small coterie of Western powers, and, at best, as insignificant for structural change.

Thus, while the defenders of intervention are moved by a nightmare of human suffering spreading chaos if each state is left, so to speak, in possession of the people under its jurisdiction, the opponents are inspired by a nightmare of interstate chaos if the pillars of state sovereignty and nonintervention are torn down. In addition to realists, they include humanists such as Tzvetan Todorov, who see in interventions a display of the dangerous desire to do good, that is, to apply to others one's conception of the good and a lack of concern for the postintervention issues that will arise. Todorov contrasts the "right to interfere," which he rejects because it requires excessive means and often aims at dubious ends, and the duty of assistance to victims, which "cannot include military interaction."[15] They are also upset by the kinds of selectivity and inconsistency that crusades for good causes are bound to lead to. Responding to every "egregious" violation of human rights being physically and politically impossible, any criterion of choice other than the defense of essential national interests is likely to be morally shocking and politically embarrassing. Small states will be the targets but not the main powers; allies (such as the Turks) will be protected from "their" Kurds, but Iraq's Kurds will be favored. The Croats and Bosnians will be allowed to have their states, but the Serbs will be barred from extending their control over Serbs in Croatia and in Bosnia. Kosovo will be encouraged to secede de facto, but Katanga's attempt, in the early 1960s, was crushed. Ethnic atrocities in Europe will rouse to action states that will be far more indifferent to horrors in Sudan, Rwanda, or Sri Lanka.

Selectivity and inconsistency in choosing whom to attack are not the only inevitable effects of the moralistic approach; there will also be constant doubt and debate about what rights are to be protected. What constitutes a genocide (remember the State Department's reluctance to call genocide what happened in Rwanda)? Do random massacres and mutilations on a grand scale amount to genocide? Are deliberate policies aimed at starving opponents as "egregious" as massacres? What acts can be seen as barbaric? (Many in Europe believe that U.S. capital punishment is uncivilized.) Is there any consensus on what constitutes an attack on human dignity? Is political persecution always less obnoxious than atrocities and group persecutions because it attacks people for choices they have made or actions they have undertaken?

The conclusion is obvious: get out of this morass and return to the verities of realism. There is only one problem with this: the definition of the national interest. A mild form of realism would recognize that all powers must heed the *imperatives* of physical and economic security but also that many have sufficient resources to promote and protect *preferences*, especially about the kind of international milieu they would like to operate in; and among these preferences, the elimination of certain kinds of unacceptable behavior has every right to figure. Moving farther away from orthodox realism, one might argue that certain important values constitute interests both because, as moral persons, we have ethical interests about human behavior and because, as political persons, we have an interest in a certain kind of order that can no longer be limited to interstate relations, given the porousness of borders and the speed of communication and of communicable diseases, among which violence is one. Is risking lives to save others abroad less essential than risking them for the defense of unessential bases or redundant resources? Are inconsistencies and selectivity on a global scale any worse than those one finds in the application of domestic punishments, tax laws, or educational policies?

Another criticism of the cause for which intervention occurs is that it presupposes a clear distinction between oppressors and victims, whereas in reality the victims of terror may themselves have practiced terrorism and engaged in provocations. This charge has been leveled particularly against the Kosovars and their Liberation Army and (by the Russians) against the Chechens. In a world of few angels, it remains nevertheless necessary to distinguish between mere sinners and true devils. There is little doubt that Muslim Bosnians were more often the victims of Serbs and Croats than the instigators of terror against them or that Kosovars, since the revocation of their autonomy, had been grievously mistreated. War is often a contest between pure evil and part evil, as Koestler recognized about World War II. Indeed, this problem is not different from that of identifying an aggressor in interstate affairs.

Next comes the issue of the proper authority to wage a war of intervention. Here, the critics point out a dilemma. If—in true realist fashion—it is the United States that takes the lead (either unilaterally or as shaper of a coalition in the United Nations, NATO, or the Organization of American States [OAS]), it will risk both dissipating its resources and fomenting considerable resentment abroad, among foes, rivals, and even allies with little sympathy for the self-proclaimed "indispensable nation" and for the burdens borne by the "only superpower." If, in order to avoid all this, the United States turns the mess over to the United Nations, there is a grave risk of throwing away the required "chance of success," given the bureaucratic inefficiency of the organization (painfully evident in Bosnia) as well as its dependence on the political support of and guidance by a number of states with divergent concerns, different designs for the UN mission, and a tendency to dump on it more responsibilities than it can handle or to give it mandates that are unrealistic (such as the protection of free havens in Bosnia or the establishment of peace among armed factions in Cambodia, Angola, Somalia, and Sierra Leone).[16] Many of the critics conclude that the least objectionable formula would be entrusting the task to a regional organization. The problem, however, is that the Organization of African Unity, in the most troubled of continents, has shown itself both too divided and too devoid of resources to take the lead—hence its passivity vis-à-vis Sudan and its failure in Rwanda and the Congo. The OAS remains dominated by the United States, and the European Union has not reached the stage of strategic-diplomatic action so far. In the successful case of East Timor, where no interveners used force, it was a combination of U.S. diplomatic and economic pressures and of a "coalition of the willing" led by Australia that obliged Indonesia to retreat. Thus, there is indeed something Sisyphean about the problem of authorization.

Critics also question whether military interventions respect the principle of proportionality of values. They emphasize the very high costs the interveners often impose on the supposed beneficiaries. In the case of Kosovo, the immediate effect of the bombing operation was the massive expulsion of the Kosovars, whose protection was the objective of the war, and the American preference for the immunity of their combatants increased casualties among noncombatants, both Serbs and Kosovars. Conversely, in Bosnia, the limits put by the Security Council on the mandate of the UN Protection Force left the "safe havens" unprotected and Srebenica at the mercy of its genocidal conquerors. These were two opposite ways of violating the old rule, "do no harm."

Another set of criticisms concerns the principle of last resort. Waiting too long in the hope that diplomacy will work and is not just used by the "guilty" party as a delaying tactic can allow it to consolidate its forces and to begin to carry out its murderous designs. It can be argued persuasively that the United States should have intervened in Haiti when thugs opposed the arrival of American ships, which turned around and left, or in Kosovo just after Milosevic's violation of the deal he had made with Richard Holbrooke in October 1998. In Bosnia's case, it took more than three years to get to the "last resort." Critics point out that given the dangers of such delays and the human costs of military intervention, preventive action would be preferable. There was practically none undertaken in Yugoslavia in the spring of 1991. Both in Somalia and in Rwanda, the UN presence had been withdrawn before the tragedies that hit those countries, whereas in Macedonia, where observers have been stationed for many years, peace has been preserved. The case for prevention has, however, one major flaw. Unless the Security Council decides under chapter VII that a situation creates a threat to peace and security and orders a country to accept the stationing of an international force, the need for that country's consent can thwart the effort at prevention, as we saw in Kosovo, and not all countries are likely to obey UN "commands."

The most impressive critiques concern the "reasonable chance of success." In interstate wars, the definition of success is the defeat of one side's forces and the acceptance by the loser of the conditions set by the winner (for instance, the restoration of Kuwait's independence and integrity in the Gulf War and that of South Korea's sovereignty over its territory in the Korean War). In internal wars, defeating the violator of human rights is only the beginning of a long ordeal that often requires more from international society than it is willing to devote to areas that are not strategically or economically important. For what is at stake after military victory is, in these cases, the rebuilding or the building of a state, from the outside and by outsiders. The long experience of the United Nations in Cambodia has shown how difficult this is. Often the United Nations has not had the mandate and the means to disarm factions that can thus continue to make trouble, as in Angola, or else the mandate exists but the members lack the will to carry it out, as in Somalia. When the objective of the operation is the establishment of democracy in a place that hasn't practiced it and where most of the preconditions for it are missing, the outsider has a choice between, so to speak, reducing democracy to a mere free election and actively and gradually setting up the institutions and inculcating the values and the procedures that breed democratic government. The former may be too little, and the latter is likely to provoke charges of neocolonialism. What the United States, Britain, and France did in post-1945 Germany was not done by the United States in Haiti after the return of President Aristide. It is too soon to say whether a new stable Bosnia will emerge from the Dayton Accords. This is because success has been defined, both there and in Kosovo, as the establishment of a peaceful multiethnic society—that is, the organized coexistence of ethnic groups that have just gone through traumatic violence. There seems to be an unhappy choice between trying to reach what, in the short term, is an unreasonable objective (whose lack of realism, as in Kosovo, fuels endemic violence against the remaining Serbs) and a partition that may look, so to speak, surgically sound now but would be likely to create new territorial claims, reward the ethnic cleansers, and above all promote Balkanization. When, as in Kosovo, the hatreds are still incandescent, even the minimal objective—the elimination of ethnic violence—may require more of a military and of a policy presence than states are willing to contribute.

Thus, success after war requires the international fire brigade to spend a disproportionate amount of its resources on tasks that are unpleasant and difficult, in areas that, to quote J. K. Galbraith on Vietnam, ought to be allowed to return to the obscurity they so richly deserve. And success requires the outsiders to make extremely difficult choices: how far to go in enlisting the local political forces, whose objectives may be far different from those of the "liberators" or occupiers (as in Kosovo), versus how far to go in becoming the de facto rulers of a country, at the cost of fostering deep resentments and of perpetuating external tutelage. Another difficult choice is between encouraging a reconciliation of the previously warring factions or parties versus insisting on the punishment of those guilty of war crimes and crimes against humanity. Such punishment turns out, in fact, to be a necessary prelude to reconciliation, but in the short run it may have the opposite effect, and it may be beyond the capacity of the outside interveners to locate and detain the criminals.

A final charge needs to be mentioned. It is in the realm of the *jus in bello* and concerns the proportionality of the means used by the interveners to their ends. In interstate wars, often the military means have been excessive and violated the immunity of noncombatants. In internal conflicts, the means have tended to be both insufficient and inadequate. Yugoslavia in 1992–1994 is a clear case of insufficiency—Serbs and Croats pushed around and aside the hapless UN forces repeatedly. Somalia was another such case. Kosovo was a case of inadequacy: the "American way of war" ruled out ground forces far too long and resulted in high-altitude bombing that inflicted little punishment on the Serb forces that were driving the Kosovars out of the country.

The essence of the critique of intervention in internal conflicts is the argument that the present nature of international society dooms such enterprises or ambitions. By having to concentrate on cases that do not involve the domestic turbulence in major powers, they oblige states to devote to secondary or inessential areas resources and attention that they are reluctant to provide, thus almost guaranteeing fiascoes: peacekeepers with no mandate to use force if the parties resume fighting (Angola, Cambodia, and Croatia in the spring of 1995) and peacemakers who are far better at fighting than at the "social work" required after victory. States have to concentrate on essentials, for domestic as well as for geopolitical reasons, and international or regional organizations have neither sufficient autonomy (political and military) nor sufficient competence to be useful actors rather than parts of the problem.

TOWARD A GLOBAL SOCIETY?

If one recognizes that the traditionalist critique is often pitilessly correct, one is left with a fundamental choice.

One may conclude that, the world being as it is, military interventions in domestic crises represent "a bridge too far," that they should be undertaken only in exceptional circumstances: the atrocities committed amount to genocide, the effects of intervention will not be worse than those of inaction, there is a broad consensus among civilized nations, domestic support in those that will have to provide the bulk of the forces, and the willingness to stay the course for postwar rehabilitation and reconstruction. Paradoxically enough, Rwanda should have been such a case—but only the first condition was met. If one accepts this point of view, one does not thereby dismiss the importance of human rights, but one considers them as above all a domestic responsibility, and in the innumerable instances in which there are serious violations because of the nature of the regimes, outside prodding should be prudently limited to cases in which no vital interest would have to be sacrificed to the cause of human rights abroad and to methods of diplomatic and, exceptionally, economic pressure.[17]

However, if one believes that the toleration of, so to speak, fragmented chaos and bloodshed is dangerous even though the victims live in areas that realists tell us "don't matter" because they're poor and strategically insignificant—dangerous because murder and misery spread, refugees multiply, warlords and terror cross borders, and rich and powerful countries, unlike the wealthy in America, can't live as gated communities—then the realist prescriptions appear neither moral nor politically sophisticated. If one believes that a world of sovereign states and of international institutions tightly dependent on and controlled by them is both increasingly unrealistic politically, given the effects of globalization and the need for better international governance, and morally unacceptable when states fall into murderous chaos or regimes massively violate essential human rights, then one has to choose the path of reform of the international system so that it can begin to cope adequately with the protection of these rights.

This means, on the one hand, that the states that are concerned should prepare adequately for interventions when the violations and atrocities are sufficiently or very likely to be "egregious," adopt strategies that are capable of success yet that minimize civilian casualties and sufferings, and be ready to engage in protracted enterprises of state building or rebuilding. Given the hostility of the American military to what other nations have often considered perfectly valid peacekeeping tasks for its soldiers, the United States might consider forming a special police force separate from the army. Given the reluctance of American elites and of a large fraction of the American public to bear the main part of the burden, other states or groupings need to be enlisted. The recent decisions of the European Union to create an adequate common security policy that would allow for such interventions is encouraging.

On the other hand, international and regional organizations must be given the capabilities they lack in this domain. The United Nations needs "a UN-legion type force" in order to eliminate the problems of command and control that have plagued past efforts when national forces put at the disposal of the United Nations often received contradictory instructions from their governments and the United Nations. This "legion" could be either the kind of UN volunteer force that Brian Urquhart has repeatedly advocated or a force composed of contingents in readiness put at the disposal of the United Nations by national governments. It would be paid for on the UN budget. The United Nations should also revive the notion of trusteeships established for a limited duration (but for as long as necessary) in order to restore and consolidate failed or new and shaky states.

The reason why the second option is preferable is a doubly normative one. It is ethically normative because it is morally imperative to shift the balance from the states to the human beings and to curtail the sovereignty of the former whenever it is exerted at the expense of the latter. (In my view, the crucial determinant of the state's rights is not the consent of the citizens: there are too many instances of majority consent to measures of discrimination, racism, or xenophobia; it is the respect of human rights.) There is also a politically normative component: the states, even when they are as powerful as the United States, are increasingly incapable of solving their problems unilaterally, and the global economic system in a world of accelerated technological progress poses rising social and environmental problems that cannot be solved in the Westphalian legal framework or in the realist theoretical one. We are moving from an interstate "anarchical society" to a global society that ought to be at the service of human beings.

NOTES

Chapter 7 was published in Chester A. Crocker, Fen Osler Hampson, and Pamela Aall, eds., *Turbulent Peace: The Challenges of Managing International Conflict* (Washington, D.C.: U.S. Institute of Peace Press, 2001).

1. See Stanley Hoffmann, *World Disorders* (Lanham, Md.: Rowman & Littlefield, 1998), chap. 11, and *The Ethics and Politics of Humanitarian Intervention* (Notre Dame, Ind.: University of Notre Dame Press, 1996).

2. Compare Kenneth Waltz, "Structural Realism after the Cold War," *International Security* (summer 2000): 5–41.

3. C. J. Friedrich, ed., *The Philosophy of Kant* (New York: Modern Library, 1949), 434.

4. J. S. Mill, in Arnold Wolfers and Laurence W. Martin, *The Anglo-American Tradition in Foreign Affairs* (New Haven, Conn.: Yale University Press, 1956), 213.

5. Mill, in Wolfers and Martin, *The Anglo-American Tradition in Foreign Affairs*, 215.

6. Michael Walzer, *Just and Unjust Wars* (New York: Basic Books, 1977), 61.

7. Walzer, *Just and Unjust Wars*, 106.

8. John Rawls, *Law of Peoples* (Cambridge, Mass.: Harvard University Press, 1999), esp. 37 and 81.

9. Rawls, *Law of Peoples*, 93.

10. Berkeley Institute of Governmental Studies, *Public Affairs Report*, January 2000, 1.

11. Secretary-General's Report to the General Assembly, UN Press Release SG/SM7136, GA/9596, September 20, 1999.

12. David Luban, "Intervention and Civilization" (unpublished paper), 10.

13. Henry Kissinger, quoted by Ivo H. Daalder, "Knowing When to Say No: The Development of UN Policies for Peace-Keeping," 50.

14. Colin Powell, quoted by Daalder, "Knowing When to Say No," 41.

15. Tzvetan Todorov, *Hope and Memory* (Princeton, N.J.: Princeton University Press, 2003), 228.

16. Kissinger, quoted by Daalder, "Knowing When to Say No," 50, put it this way: "If international consensus is the prerequisite for the employment of American power, the result may be ineffective dithering. If . . . international machinery can commit US forces, the risk is American involvement in issues of no fundamental national interest."

17. Economic sanctions usually harm civilians, including those whose rights one tries to protect from abroad; the exceptional case is South Africa, where the representatives of the black majority approved of Western sanctions against apartheid.

· 8 ·

Intervention: Should It Go On,
Can It Go On?

$\mathcal{W}$hat I will address here is not "humanitarian" intervention, for reasons that shall be explained later, but outside interventions entailing a resort to force—or to forces—in the domestic affairs of a country in order to protect people from extreme violence.[1]

THE IMPORTANCE OF THE ISSUE

There have been many such examples in recent years: in Africa, in Asia, and in Central America. This corresponds to two series of factors. The first is an important evolution of the international system: the phenomenon of internal disintegration or malfunction of many states, resulting from a multiplicity of causes. Many states are devoid of national consciousness or effective integration: Somalia, Rwanda, Sudan, former Zaire, Sierra Leone, Angola, and Liberia. Other states are under attack from rebellious minorities: Indonesia as the occupier of East Timor, Sri Lanka, Ethiopia, Iraq, Turkey, and Russia. Several multiethnic states have disintegrated; Yugoslavia and the Soviet Union are the best examples. Transnational terrorism is a major contributing factor to that weakening of the units that constitute the foundations of the international system. Finally, there are many murderous states: Iraq, the Haiti of the military, Rwanda under Hutu rule, and the Khmer Rouge regime.

This is not a purely contemporary trend, but it has been masked for a long time by the bipolar context. It corresponds both to the release from forced communist cohesiveness imposed by and during the Cold War (on the late Soviet Union and on Tito's Yugoslavia) and to the unexpected dividends from decolonization, which left behind a large number of purely formal or pseudostates, many of which had been established by nationalists but were in fact not nations. The importance of this trend lies, of course, in the role of

79

the state and of state sovereignty as the cornerstone of international law and of the international system.

The second set of factors is subjective: the evolution of human consciousness. An international law rooted predominantly in the concept of state sovereignty is now challenged by an accelerating, if not yet universal, revolution against unfettered sovereignty. It began with the restrictions put on the state's right to go to war, especially after 1918 and 1945, and it continued with the emergence of human rights as an international concern. The information revolution has played a major role in this. This has amounted to a double innovation of enormous significance: the scope of international law now extends to a domain that has been the core of "domestic jurisdiction," and states are no longer the predominant subjects of the rights and duties conferred by international law; it now gives rights to and imposes obligations on individuals directly.

The effects of these developments are enormous. Just as there are different kinds of wars, there are different types of internal crises. They range from crises provoked by the absence of a genuine government (as in Somalia) to crises resulting from a struggle for the control of central power (as in Rwanda or the Congo) to crises provoked by the desire of minorities for self-determination and the creation of new states, as in East Timor, Yugoslavia, or Chechnya, and finally to crises created by the central government itself in its attempts at crushing secessionists or religious and political dissenters.

This complex scene forces a bewildering number of choices on outsiders. They can opt for nonintervention in the name of sovereignty and limit themselves to humanitarian aid for victims of internal strife (this has been the prevalent reaction to the civil war in Sudan). They can resort to traditional peacekeeping: the dispatch of observers or of lightly armed forces whose duty is to be politically neutral among the contending factions and to deal evenly with them, without using force (except if they come under attack). This has been the case in post-Dayton Bosnia and in Kosovo. There is also the option of what might be called mild coercion, diplomatic or economic: it worked against Indonesia in East Timor and was followed by the peacekeeping force led by Australia. Finally, there is strong coercion, that is, peacemaking, which targets one of the parties, as in Bosnia before Dayton, in Kosovo before Milosevic caved in, in Haiti, and so on.

SHOULD SOMETHING BE DONE AT ALL?

A neorealist view has been sharply critical of the interventionist trend. In this conception, what matters in world affairs has not changed: the relations between the great and potentially great powers (today, the United States, Russia, and China) and the fate of strategically and economically important areas (the Middle East, Korea, and Taiwan). Anything that threatens the security of the major actors is important. Thus, the destruction of terrorist cells and the punishment of states that support them is a priority. But many of the internal crises that rack states and pseudostates are in backwaters of no strategic significance and little importance for the internal and external security of the major players. If these crises occur in one of those players (China vs. Tibet, Russia vs. Chechnya), an external forcible intrusion is far too risky to be undertaken. This creates a conundrum of (in-)consistency: why intervene to protect Iraq's Kurds and not the victims of Russian repression in Chechnya? The neorealists also point to the dangers of intervention in secondary areas from the viewpoint of conserving one's forces and concentrating one's attention on the major flash points. Finally, they denounce the restraints imposed by such interventions if they are undertaken under international auspices or by coalitions of the willing, on a great power such as the United States: multilateralism for a "real" national security operation, yes if necessary; for a "trivial" cause, no.

This thesis is ultimately unconvincing. The legal argument on which critics of intervention often rely—the importance of respecting internal sovereignty—has been badly frayed both by frequent violations during the years of the Cold War (remember U.S. subversive intervention in Guatemala or Santo Domingo, for instance) and, more recently, under the rubric of "self-defense" by war against the Taliban. The old distinction between "possession" and "milieu" goals also argues against an excessive priority to strategic and economic possession goals: a major power needs a milieu that will support world order (or its conception of it), and the benign neglect of domestic upheaval abroad risks producing epidemics of regional disorders, with massive flights of refugees, interstate tensions among neighbors (as around Congo), and risks of escalatory intervention by states or by mercenaries. In addition, when is a "backwater" trivial, when is it not? After all, Zbigniew Brzezinski, President Carter's national security adviser, once predicted that Ogaden was of vital importance for victory in the Cold War because of Soviet involvement. In addition, the rising costs of chaos, left unattended, provide fine opportunities for tyranny. At this point, the problem of moral duty cannot be avoided. Economic assistance has been advocated for a combination of ethical (i.e., non-selfish) and self-interested arguments. Intervention to protect victims of tyranny or repression can be defended for exactly the same mix of reasons: all states have an interest in order, and order without a modicum of (international and global) justice can lead only to disaster (surely this is also one of the lessons of September 11, 2001).

WHAT IS TO BE DONE?

This is the toughest issue. A criterion of "humanitarianism" is both elusive and unsatisfactory. The kind of humanitarianism offered by an organization such as Doctors Without Borders both advocates a "duty of interference" in case of humanitarian disasters yet distrusts the self-interested states that may want to intervene; they trust disinterested agencies like themselves, for the relief of human suffering. They particularly dislike state military interference because it tends to create more victims—which is indeed frequently the case. However, "pure" humanitarian action is often insufficient: if the causes of the humanitarian crisis are not addressed, such action risks being no more than a temporary band-aid: important, to be sure, but limited in time and scope. Moreover, even pure humanitarians cannot avoid taking political decisions at every turn. For instance, in cases of ethnic cleansing, does humanitarianism dictate a refusal to contribute to it by trying to encourage its potential victims to stay in their homes and hereditary provinces, or does it mean accepting such cleansing and relocating its victims in order to save their lives? Another example: what to do when the humanitarian aid provided to refugees in camps is confiscated by armed guards and when the camps become places for the forcible recruitment by such guards, eager to enlist more fighters for guerrilla actions? This was a dilemma faced by and divisive of humanitarian organizations both in Sudan and in Rwanda. Indeed, pure humanitarianism can even be counterproductive: in Bosnia, these organizations were often at the mercy of the Serbs; their lack of means of self-defense often led to the pilfering of aid by the Serbs and thus to a prolongation of the war. One doesn't need to be a realist or a neorealist to understand that wars, internal and interstate, are about politics, whereas humanitarianism, insofar as it wants to be nonpolitical, is insufficient at best and counterproductive at worst. The evolution of Bernard Kouchner, the founder of Doctors Without Borders—from a doctor's view to the choice for political action as a cabinet minister and international civil servant—is instructive.

Of course, this does not mean that intervening with armed force is easy. Let us begin with traditional peacekeeping. It presupposes, by definition, an agreement of the fighting parties to call in the peacekeepers. If one party resists, delays, or violates such an agreement, the peacekeeping mission is in a quandary (in East Timor, it took strong pressure on Indonesia to get it to accept one, and during that time many people died). Moreover, the duty of such forces to remain neutral and to use weapons only for self-defense places them at the mercy of the "bad guys": the most frightening example was what happened at Srebenica; the observers—sent with Serb consent—to Kosovo at the end of 1998 were powerless to stop Milosevic's attempt at subjugating the

Kosovars. Often, these peacekeepers are at the mercy of events too big and murderous for their size and their means: the withdrawal of UN peacekeepers from Rwanda before the massacres began, the fate of General Allaire's mission and pleas, are a tragic reminder of this frequent impotence. Attempts to mix peacekeeping and peacemaking, entrusted to forces established only for the former task, have turned out disastrous, as in Somalia, when the change of mission—from protecting the people to feeding the people to disarming those who were disrupting the mission—led to the collapse of the attempt and, as in Bosnia, where, in 1992–1995, peacekeeping, favored by Britain and France, became an obstacle to coercive peacemaking, which would have put the peacekeepers in peril (in Somalia, peacemaking "sank" peacekeeping; in Bosnia, peacekeeping prevented peacemaking).

Let us move from "peace after war" and its problems to "war for peace" in internal crises and its obstacles (i.e., to the difficulties of military intervention for peacemaking). A first issue is a double question of when. On the one hand, what is the right threshold for intervention? Too low, it sacrifices completely the legitimate claims of sovereignty in order to protect human rights. Too high, it limits intervention to the most extreme cases of human rights violations, which means, in practice, that by then it is already much too late and that genuine (although perhaps not genocidal) atrocities may end up being tolerated. On the other hand, at what moment in an internal crisis is it right to intervene? The argument of "last resort," derived from (interstate) just-war theory, is doubly troublesome: opponents of military force will rarely concede that all possibilities of peace have been exhausted, and proponents of intervention will tend to argue that an early one will save lives (think of Rwanda), whereas a late one will allow for abominations (like the expulsion of Kosovo's Albanians) to occur.

A second issue is that of authority to intervene: who, not when. Here also there are two questions: on the one hand, who has the right to intervene or to authorize external intervention? The Charter gives this authority to the UN Security Council. But here we face a paradox. Under international law (which includes the Charter), the use of force is justified only for self-defense against armed attack or for collective security in conformity with the Charter; all other uses of force violate the principle of domestic jurisdiction. As a consequence, interventions because of human rights violations have to be presented to the Security Council as violations of global or regional security. An intervention provoked by a massacre committed in an island far from any neighbor would be challenged by many states as incompatible with the Charter. Let us assume that the "threat to regional or global security" case can be made. What happens if serious violations of human rights are committed by both sides, as is presently the case of Israel's repression of Palestinian resistance and of Palestinian terrorism? What happens if the Security Council is paralyzed? In Kosovo, the United States and its allies anticipated paralysis and acted under their own (or rather NATO's) authority—a deviation that was, so to speak, semilegitimized by the Security Council's failure to protest but also a potentially dangerous precedent. What about regional organizations if the Security Council is paralyzed? Unfortunately, as we saw in Rwanda, they are often not up to the task and as divided as the United Nations or (as in the Middle East) missing. Coalitions of the willing, even when they act in good faith, take time and preparation to be able to exercise authority. On the other hand, the question of external authorization is not the only one. Intervention also needs domestic support, which is often lukewarm (as in Kosovo: would it have lasted if Milosevic had not given up?) or missing (as in the United States after the killing of American soldiers in Somalia). This issue may become particularly troublesome in the United States, needed for many interventions that require advanced weapons or sophisticated technology. It may well be in a country where a sizable part of the public and of the politicians are or have become highly susceptible to the neorealist arguments and suspicious of international organizations not controlled by the United States—that there will be support only for interventions à la Afghanistan (i.e., against attacks perpetrated on U.S. civilians by foreign states and terrorists) but not for the interventions that try to protect peoples from their regimes or from civil wars.

A third issue is the necessity for effective intervention. Multilateral action is never easy. Often, the partners are divided, and the results risk being catastrophic: as in Bosnia, until the spring of 1995, or in Somalia, when the United States and the United Nations had rival strategies. Even when, as in Kosovo, there is a firmer unity, each member may have its preferred strategy and targets. This is not only caused by divergent preferences among allies; it is also because the strategy most likely to succeed is not always obvious. In Kosovo, the ends—preventing or stopping ethnic cleansing—may not have been reachable with the means available (and with the timing selected), and it was the concern with minimizing U.S. losses that both limited and dictated the targets.

The fourth issue concerns not effectiveness but ethics: the necessity for intervention to be just. The categories that have been (illegible) have been those of traditional just-war theory. They are not fully adequate either for internal conflict or to the international relations of the twentieth and twenty-first centuries. I have already questioned the "last resort" criterion. Proportionality of means to ends is a notoriously elastic concept: it all depends on the importance the actors attribute to the ends. Reasonable chance of success is a highly iffy and subjective condition (in Kosovo—as later in Afghanistan—observers within a few weeks went from deep pessimism to eating their hats). As for noncombatant immunity, however careful the targeting, "collateral damage" (a hideous euphemism) has turned out inevitable and sometimes horrendous.

From the points of view of both effectiveness and ethics, there is the difficult problem of unintended consequences. In Kosovo, the foreign intervention contributed to the speedy ethnic cleansing of the Albanians; later, the coalition's victory made possible the ethnic cleansing of the Serbs (as in Croatia in 1995).

After the headaches of action come those of the aftermath of war. If the crisis ends by agreement, there are likely to be vast unresolved issues. Is there really a future for a multiethnic Bosnia or Kosovo? What will the final status of Kosovo be—independence? partition? autonomy within a new Yugoslavia? Will peacekeeping survive the postwar tensions? The record in places like Angola or Cambodia has been mixed. Next come the long-term issues of reconstruction. What will be the fate of the refugees? Many are still in camps (Rwanda) or incapable of returning (East Timor, exiled Serbs from Kosovo). Who will pay for economic reconstruction? Can outsiders really engage in "nation building," especially when there had never been a genuine nation? In Haiti and in much of Africa, the "rescuers" have tacitly abandoned that goal. When they have not, as in Kosovo, there is the risk of crossing the border between helping the local factions set up a new state and establishing a kind of protectorate, thus creating tensions with one's protégés. Lastly, there is the familiar dilemma of criminal justice. One option has been purely judicial: international criminal justice for war crimes, crimes against humanity, and genocide, as well as domestic justice. It has been a slow and rocky road, both in the case of Yugoslavia and in that of Rwanda; the question of bringing the accused and the suspect to trial has not been resolved. The other side of the dilemma is that of "reconciliation" rather than trials. Truth commissions have the merit of dampening polarization and facilitating a return to a kind of normalcy, but they upset human rights defenders, and it is far from clear that there can be "closure" and firm reconciliation without a modicum of criminal justice.

"I CAN'T GO ON, I MUST GO ON . . ."

This long and sketchy list of difficulties is not aimed at a negative conclusion about the wisdom of interventions. It is meant to goad their champions into a realistic assessment of the magnitude of their task. In my view, some interventions may be unwise, but the principle itself is not; ultimately, what is involved is a choice of values and goals. In my view, there should be no retreat. We owe it to the victims of internal crises and crimes. We saw what happened when opportunities were missed, as in Yugoslavia in 1991, and when Rwanda turned into a bloodbath with the flight of the United Nations and the inaction of the great powers. The coddling of Indonesia, especially by the United States, and the abdication of the "world community" confronted by Tibet and Chechnya (and also, until September 2001, by Taliban atrocities) are enough to induce nausea. In addition, it is in the direction of a far more energetic priority for human rights that lie the signs of a new kind of world order in which states would be at the service of their inhabitants rather than the other way around, in which statecraft would be guided by an enlarged definition of what is in the national interest by a greater commitment to multilateral cooperation and action, and in which nongovernmental organizations (NGOs) and "world public opinion" (i.e., the opinions of foreign publics) would play a greater role. In this new world order, the norms restricting sovereignty would clearly extend to serious violations of human rights (including those that terrorism, public and private, entails). Norms and institutions that extend to individuals directly would constitute revolutionary progress in international law (which is why America's hostility to the International Criminal Court is absurd).

The problem will be managing the coexistence and interpenetration of two very different types of international relations. The traditional competition of states for resources, prestige, and power, motivated by ambitions and fear, licensed by the paucity and weakness of supranational institutions, will continue. But there will also be a global politics, with more actors—individuals and groups both constructive and destructive in addition to states and public international agencies—with greater centralization, although no world government yet, more of a role both for public international organizations and for an incipient (if flawed) global civil society, and above all more of a concern for individuals, both the victims and the guilty. *Raison d'état* and *raison des individus* will compete and partly blend.

The new global politics will also have to deal with conflicts among its own concerns—for instance, between stopping "internal aggression against people" (if necessary by force) and defending the environment against the ravages of war, between priority to economic development and priority to human rights and democracy, between capitalist growth and social justice, between self-determination and the need to limit fragmentation and parochial nationalisms, and between sanctions on criminal leaders and punishing their populations. Such tensions—and the major one behind the world of Machiavelli and that of the idealists—will not be easy to resolve. The agenda of the new global polity will require action on multiple fronts: an effective network of international criminal justice, with sanctions if the criminals are not delivered; far greater coordination among the NGOs and between them and public international organizations; measures making it possible for the latter to act preventively and quickly, which means having forces in readiness; reviving a nonpostcolonial form of trusteeship for the restoration of collapsed states; encouraging adequate forms of democracy in a highly heterogeneous world; and so on. These are just examples.

Obviously, the responsibility of the "lone superpower," the United States, is enormous. The present mix of "sovereignism," neorealism, and unilateralism, enhanced by American power and by the new challenge of terrorism (even though no part of that mix is well adapted to it), is both dangerous and paradoxical. Let us hope that it does not prevail. The questions for American statecraft are, Leading for what? And with whom? The reality, in world affairs, is the colossal erosion of the differences between what is domestic and what is global. It occurs both through globalization and through violence. Insofar as intervention is concerned, to borrow and adapt a title from Samuel Beckett, some say it can't go on but it must go on, if we want the progressive components of the new global politics to prevail both over the traditional "state of war" and over the destructive aspects (such as global terrorism) of the emergent world society.

NOTES

Chapter 8 was published in Dean K. Chatterjee and Don E. Scheid, eds., *Ethics and Foreign Intervention* (Cambridge: Cambridge University Press, 2003).

1. This chapter tries to be a reasonably comprehensive survey of issues and viewpoints about intervention. It does not try to discuss them in depth—fortunately, there is a vast literature of high quality that does so. For my own previous writing on the subject, see *World Disorders* (Lanham, Md.: Rowman & Littlefield, 1998), chaps. 10 and 11, and *The Ethics and Politics of Humanitarian Intervention* (Notre Dame, Ind.: University of Notre Dame Press, 1996).

·9·

Intervention, Sovereignty, and Human Rights

I.

$\mathscr{T}$he problems raised by the armed intervention of states in the internal affairs of other states have been discussed in numerous books and articles over the past sixteen years. There are many distinctions that we find in them:

> Between traditional unilateral interventions in the "state of war" for a world without any central power and the collective interventions undertaken by or in the name of the international "community"
>
> Between the legal norms that are supposed to regulate the interventions and the practices that attempt to substitute less restrictive provisions to these norms
>
> Between different conceptions of an ideal international order, for instance, modern versions of the theory of just war applied to interventions and modern versions of what might be called the theory of holy war: obviously much more permissive.

It is not my purpose here to review all those distinctions and quarrels. My intention is more limited: what are the imperatives, the risks, and the obstacles that open, block, or close the road to collective interventions aimed at protecting human rights in countries where these rights are in danger? These rights may be endangered for many reasons: moderate or tyrannical regimes (Saddam Hussein's Iraq or Mugabe's Rhodesia); ethnic and religious conflicts that tear a country apart, often because the government supports one ethnic group or one religion against others (Rwanda, Sudan); disintegration of countries where peace and security had for a long time been maintained by coercion (Tito's Yugoslavia); abuses committed by a colonizing power (Indonesia in East Timor); a return to anarchy after the fall of a dictator (Somalia, Zaire); confrontations between a majority and a minority that belong to different ethnic groups or religions (Sri Lanka, Chechnya, Kosovo, Tibet);

endemic and bloody civil war between classes or ideological factions (Columbia, several countries of Central America during the Cold War).

A thorough study should not deal exclusively with the role of states in a world in which internal conflicts have often stolen priority away from interstate wars, partly because such interstate wars are often extraordinarily devastating and dangerous but partly because a very large proportion of states has no solid institutions or are not based on true nations. Nongovernmental organizations play an important role in internal conflicts, and the choices they have to make are often difficult and controversial, insofar as they are in reality political and not merely humanitarian choices. Here, however, I will deal only with states.

II.

Let us begin by looking at a radical thesis that corresponds in fact to what classical international law and the Charter of the United Nations actually say. It is the thesis that is hostile to collective interventions in the domestic affairs of states. The best defender of this point of view, at present, is Tzvetan Todorov. The arguments against the interventions are many. They deal with the inevitable arbitrariness of choices: few states are ready to take the risk in intervening by force in the domestic conflicts of great powers, and, as a result, such force will be used almost always at the expense of the small ones only. This is of course not false, but force is only one of the means of pressure that can be used, and there are many cases in which other means are not devoid of some effectiveness. There is also the argument of the interveners' likely ignorance or even partiality. This warning is useful, but the dangers are not insurmountable. Finally, let us add the argument related to the previous one of the conflict or at least tension between the role of the interveners even and especially if they are wrapped in the coat of a legitimate international or regional organization and the sovereignty of the state in which intervention takes place or the aspirations to independence of the minority that one seeks to protect. The profession of tutor or of trustee is difficult and delicate but is not merely a choice between flagrant ineffectiveness and an authoritarianism that quickly becomes unpopular. Todorov sees in military intervention a manifestation of the nefarious "temptation of doing good," and this is indeed sometimes the case. I am thinking here of the "coalition" covered by the Americans in Iraq. But it seems to me that in most cases collective military intervention (or, as in Haiti a few years ago, the intervention of the United States undertaken with international legitimation) has rather corresponded to attempts at putting an end to evil and has even sometimes been abandoned too soon. The main charge one can bring against the thesis of nonintervention is that it gives up any attempt at trying to close a door to evil, with results that are often much worse than those of an ill-prepared intervention. We have seen this in Rwanda, and we are seeing it in Darfur.

Let us then admit that there are good reasons for sometimes resorting to collective or legitimized military intervention, and let us try to indicate what are the main types of cases and the problems that they raise.

III.

Let us begin, alas, by what is most frequent: serious violations of human rights committed either by the governments or by the inhabitants of countries that are deeply torn or reduced to the state of nature.

The problem that continues to trouble lawyers, political scientists, and politicians is that of the level of violations at which military intervention can be justified by international organizations or by a regional organization, such as NATO in Kosovo, in a case where the United Nations is, or is almost certain to be, paralyzed. There is no agreement on this point. What appears very serious to some (the suppression of the freedoms of speech and information, of political pluralism) appears to others to be less awful than the perversion of justice, the arbitrariness of condemnations and punishments, or the persecution of innocents. Despite the increase in the number of states that call themselves democratic, the violations of the rights that are listed in the Universal Declaration and in the two treaties on political and civil rights and on economic and social ones are so frequent and widespread that the "methods" used in the 1990s (i.e., a case-by-case empirical approach) is probably the only possible one. As a faithful disciple of Judith Shklar (and therefore of Montesquieu), I will only say that everything that lies in the domain of terror, violations of the physical and mental integrity of individuals, seems to me intolerable. As for the somewhat macabre problem that has preoccupied many people during the Kosovo affair—how many hundreds of deaths one has to be able to count before one seeks to intervene—I certainly cannot resolve it.

It seems to me, however, that when the cause for an armed intervention, to use the vocabulary of just-war theory, presents itself as a just cause, two other problems are raised at once. The first one is a military problem: there have to exist in a state of availability and preparation forces capable of acting quickly. The proposal made a few years ago by the pillar of the United Nations, Sir Brian Urquhart, which aimed at providing the United Nations with military forces furnished by the states and capable of intervening rapidly,

remains wise and essential and deserves to be extended to regional organizations such as the African Union. Only if such forces exist permanently can
the other serious problem that one has to confront be capable of being if not
resolved, at least attenuated: that of the proportionality between the values
protected or saved by the intervention and the inevitable human and material
costs of it.

IV.

The second category of cases is that of genocide. Just as much as in the case
of violations of human rights, the problem of identifying a genocide is controversial and can lead to interminable arguments. Was the massacre of the
Armenians in 1915 a genocide? Is what is happening in Darfur a genocide?
Does Russia in Chechnya seek to exterminate an ethnic group or "only" to
impose its domination? What about the Bosnian Muslims, caught between
the Croats and the Serbians in Bosnia, that is, those people who were the
tragic victims massacred in Srebenica? A definition that would be in rigorous
conformity with the terms of the International Convention on Genocide
might perhaps be applicable only in the most sinister case of a failure of the
international "community," the case of Rwanda (i.e., of the massacre of the
Tutsis by the Hutus). It seems to me, however, that any massacre that spares
only the "collaborators" and the exiles deserves to be termed a genocide.

What has been said about international and regional forces ready to be
used is even more important here. We are in a domain where one of the criteria of the theory of just war is deeply flawed: the idea that the resort to force
must be postponed until the failure of all attempts at peaceful settlement.
This idea is very wise in the case of relations among states (although even
there one can think about situations where it does not apply), but when a
genocide is foretold or predictable, this idea could have disastrous consequences. Once massacres have started, one would need much larger forces to
put an end to them, and it might then be too late. The genocide convention
of 1948 clearly defines genocide but says little about enforcement. It needs to
be supplemented by a text that makes clear that the states as well as the
United Nations have not simply a right but a duty to intervene against a
genocide and also to do whatever may be necessary to prevent it. Needless to
say, states that may fear that such a text may be used against them or that
remain jealous about protecting their freedom of choice—that is, of inaction—are likely to oppose it.

V.

The last type of case that has caused so much ink and blood to be spilled since 2001 is that of the overthrow of an evil regime. Michael Walzer, in his classic book on just and unjust wars, treated it very negatively.

The overthrow of the Taliban regime in Afghanistan in 2001 was presented to and recognized by the UN Security Council as a case of legitimate defense exerted by the United States against a regime that had supported Osama bin Laden's terrorists, who had caused the attacks on American soil on September 11. The elimination of the Iraqi regime eighteen months later did not in any way belong in this category. Those who supported the intervention in Iraq as they had that of NATO in Kosovo or defended the former after having criticized the latter did not sufficiently take into account the following differences. In the first place, let us remember that American intervention in Iraq was presented to the public and to the United Nations as a sanction against violations of disarmament measures to which Saddam Hussein had committed himself after the end of the Gulf War. He was accused of having weapons of mass destruction and of having provided support to terrorism; he was not accused of violations of human rights. In the second place, military interventions aimed at such violations have been endorsed by the United Nations only when those crimes were obvious and ongoing (Bosnia, Timor—in those cases the interventions took place with the consent of Serbia and Indonesia, obtained by pressure). The equivalent in the case of Saddam Hussein would have been the massacres of Kurds and Shi'ites at the end of the Gulf War in 1991, but none of the states capable of intervening wanted to get into that hornets' nest. In the third place, when, in the case of Kosovo, NATO was substituted for the Security Council, there had been no resolution submitted to the United Nations, and the Security Council refused to condemn NATO. In the case of Iraq, in February–March 2003, the American resolution, which had as its goal legitimizing military action, had to be withdrawn because it did not have sufficient support in the Security Council, and quite apart from the geographical obstacles, NATO would not have supported the United States with the necessary unanimity.

None of this means that the problem of changing an execrable regime does not arise. But it is a much more delicate problem than encroachment on national sovereignty in cases of human rights violations not accompanied by regime change. It is precisely because changing a regime through a coup d'état led from the outside (Iran, 1953) or through invasion (Czechoslovakia, 1968; Dominican Republic, 1965) openly violates state sovereignty that one can oppose only partially the liquidation of Pol Pot's regime by the Vietnamese or that of Idi Amin's regime by Tanzania and that one should beware of any unilateral intervention that has not been legitimized by an international organization or by a well-established regional organization if the United Nations is paralyzed.

There exists a conception—the version of just war that wishes to go beyond the traditional approach. It is ready to discard state sovereignty when states have unjust governments, and it is ready to support resorts to force beyond cases of legitimate defense or serious violations of human rights or cases of collective security against aggression. This conception unquestionably risks encouraging calls for holy war against such or such category of infidels or against states deemed unjust by nature. In a case where no international or regional organization would be ready to legitimize a collective action for the establishment of a democratic regime, it would be necessary to create an association of states that are totally democratic that could provide such legitimacy if it is proven that the violations of human rights within the targeted state and the threat that this regime constitutes for regional or world security are such that regime change is a matter of public utility. But it is clear that such an association could replace the United Nations or regional organizations only when the latter are paralyzed and would have to be constituted not of purely formal but of genuine democracies: in other words, democracy could not be defined merely by a constitutional text or by the holding of often debatable elections.

VI.

The problems that exist in Kosovo and even more in Iraq show that the installation by force of regimes assumed to be willing to protect human rights and to promote democracy face difficulties that should not be underestimated. In Kosovo, the multiethnic ideal is being undermined by hatreds that will only diminish with time in the best of cases. In Iraq, ethnic and religious tensions that were repressed for many years are making the birth of a democracy extremely difficult, especially as the Sunni insurrection, material difficulties, rivalries among clans and personalities, and the presence of an occupying force that is popular only in Kurdistan and is caught between the temptation of controlling too much and the aspiration to get out are not ready to disappear.

Thus, two conclusions come to the minds of observers. The first one is that the example of Germany and Japan after 1945 is very difficult to replicate. Democracy requires a group of institutions and customs that take root only slowly and, if they have been created from abroad, materialize only gradually and in part. The second conclusion is that if *jus ad bellum* and *jus in bello* apply to intervention, it is essential that a *jus post bellum* be added. Intervening powers in the cases discussed here need to take much more seriously than they have not nation building (one cannot build a nation from the outside) but state building, the erection of institutions, and the development of practices and procedures that will allow a just and livable state to take its place in a world that remains too often unjust and murderous.

VII.

The suggestions presented here point to the need for a new conception of state sovereignty: conditional and limited sovereignty. Some of the limits have been indicated here. In the vast domain of internal sovereignty, the violations of human rights enumerated in this chapter provide other states, acting with the legitimacy conferred by the United Nations or by regional organizations or, in the case of regime change, by an association of democracies with a right or (in the case of genocide) a duty to intervene. Another major set of restrictions are those that curtail the external aspects of sovereignty with respect to the use of force. These limitations began after World War I, and they deal with the problem that has been central for liberalism, the problem of war. The restrictions on internal sovereignty in the matter of human rights came into play much later—when it became obvious that the liberal dream of representative democracies becoming the norm was not realistic and that the violations of such rights could reach intolerable dimensions. As a result, what collective security against aggression is to the unjustifiable state use of force in the realm of external sovereignty, the emergence of a duty of states, when they receive a collective seal of legitimacy, to protect victims of genocide or of massive violations of human rights in other states or to rescue them, is to the unjustifiable abuse of such rights in the realm of internal sovereignty.

These restrictions suggest a new conception of sovereignty. It is conditional. We are moving—slowly and controversially—from a kind of Weberian notion of sovereignty as the exercise of the state's monopoly of legitimate violence to a new conception. State sovereignty remains justified, abroad, as providing the state with the means not only to promote and protect its interests and those of its citizens on the world scene but also to protect the rights of the citizens of other states from serious violations. At home, sovereignty is justified as the guarantee of democratic self-government and the protection of the citizens from forcible or subversive intrusions. One could call this conception sovereignty as a mission instead of sovereignty as pure power. This points, in turn, to a conception of international society not as a group of states or (as in Rawls) of peoples but as a complex network of states representing the collective interests of their people (including security and survival), of individuals endowed with rights (both political and economic and social), and of groupings of individuals forming a global civil society (and also, alas, often an incivil society).

There are, of course, many "sovereigntists" who resist such a new conception—either because of the nature of their regimes (as in China or Russia) or because of profound distrust of outside interferences after decades or centuries of external domination or because of a self-righteous conviction of national superiority (as expressed in the United States recently). We are in a transitional phase of world affairs—no longer conceivable only as the affairs of sovereign states and certainly not approaching anything like a world government. The fate, in 2005, of far-reaching proposals for UN reform shows how much resistance states can still muster against the mutation of sovereignty. But an age of instant communications, global threats of violence and chaos, global diseases and disasters, and failing states and colossal inequalities leaves us only with a choice between the anarchy bred by the traditional conception of sovereignty and the new one I have sketched out here.

NOTE

Chapter 9 is the translation of an essay called "Intervention et droits de l'homme." The French version is the introduction to Gilles Andréani et Pierre Hassner, ed., *Justifier la guerre? De l'humanitaire au contre-terrorisme* (Paris: Presses de Sciences politiques [Collection références], 2005).

·10·

The United States and Collective Security

I.

𝒯he U.S. relation to the notion and to the practice of collective security has been complex and ambivalent. Americans can legitimately claim to have invented the concept—not once but twice: in the Covenant of the League of Nations and in the Charter of the United Nations. When it had to be put into practice, the record is mixed, and today, at the beginning of the twenty-first century, Washington seems to be—in a familiar swing of the pendulum—reverting to a policy that puts the self-assertion of American predominance and the practice of unilateralism ahead of multilateralism.

What Woodrow Wilson had in mind at the end of World War I was nothing less than a return of the international law of war to a conception close to the old Christian just-war theory. In the nineteenth century, with the triumph of the principle of state sovereignty, the resort to war, whose legitimacy had been the central issue in the traditional *jus ad bellum*, was accepted as both a fact of interstate life and a corollary of sovereignty. International law was there only to regulate the means used in war and to protect the rights of neutrals. Wilsonian collective security was a resurrection of the requirement of just cause, the core of the *jus ad bellum*. Wars of aggression were henceforth to be seen as crimes and banned. What would remain legitimate were wars of individual self-defense and of collective support to victims of aggression.

It was a bold leap toward a new age in which sovereignty would be sharply limited by international law and organization and the essential manifestation of sovereignty—the use of force among states—would be curbed. War would from now on be either a crime or a collective sanction. But this revolution raised a host of legal and political issues. Legally, article 10 of the Covenant, which aimed at protecting the territorial integrity and political independence of states, remained vague about the way in which this protec-

97

tion ought to be ensured. Would it be a collective military move against the aggressor? Would the interpretation of the duty to protect be left to each state? Would economic sanctions suffice? Should one count on "the court of public opinion" rather than on force (as Wilson would have wished)?

Moreover, the Covenant seemed to lean strongly in favor of the postwar status quo—which left defeated powers, such as Germany, and disappointed winners, such as Italy and Japan, deeply dissatisfied. To be sure, the Covenant contained a provision for peaceful change, but it required a consensus of the Council's members, which was most unlikely. This put a huge strain on the absolute (but a bit fuzzy) ban on the unilateral use of force in article 10 and allowed the revisionist and the revolutionary states (such as the new Soviet Union) to denounce the League as an instrument for the "haves" and the beneficiaries of the status quo.

Politically, as defenders of the "Westphalian system" of state sovereignty pointed out, the weakness of the notion of collective security was its incompatibility with the logic of interstate relations. States have allies and enemies. They naturally tend to fight enemies even if the latter had not violated anyone's political and territorial integrity and to protect allies even if these states had done so. International politics is about concrete stakes and alignments; collective security requires states to put an abstract principle above all these. International politics is about the right of states to stay out of frays that they don't consider threatening to their interests (hence the status of neutrality). The new order required "all" to come to the help of "one" if the "one" was a victim of aggression. Given the clash between the logic of collective security and that of foreign policy, it was to be feared that article 10 would often be ignored, or else there would be endless disputes on what constituted legitimate self-defense or violations of territory and political integrity.

The biggest political blow to collective security was, of course, the defection of the United States, that is, the Senate's refusal to ratify the Covenant and the peace treaties. This left the leadership of the League in the hands of two powers neither of which fully endorsed Wilson's concept. Great Britain was still closer to old notions of the balance of power and was currently more suspicious of French preponderance on the continent than of German revanchism; its diplomats tended to interpret article 10 in the loosest and least mandatory way possible. France was interested in using the League as an instrument of collective defense against a resurgent Germany—that is, more as an alliance than as a universal collective security system. And we all know what soon happened to the League.

Collective security was reinvented at San Francisco in the Charter of the United Nations. Eager to prevent a recurrence of the 1930s—of Japanese, Italian, and German aggressions—the drafters of the Charter not only restated the principles of Wilsonianism (and of a modernized *jus ad bellum*) but also made it clear that the Security Council was the sole legitimate authority in calling for the application of the mandatory provisions of chapter VII, with the power to plan and conduct collective security operations. What the Charter, having thus exorcised the 1930s, had not predicted was the Cold War—a split of the world into two camps, each one led by a power with a right of veto in the Council. This guaranteed Council impotence, except in the rare cases where the two superpowers would be on the same side against an aggressor. If one of them was the aggressor, collective security would, in fact, mean either simply words of condemnation emanating from or mere sanctions recommended by the General Assembly or else a world war. Once again, the world was divided into rival alliances (and the Western one often tried to present itself in collective security language, as in Korea in 1950). The Uniting for Peace resolution of 1950, which aimed at transferring the cloak of legitimacy from the Security Council to the General Assembly, was something of a fluke—in any case, the General Assembly could not issue commands. A tacit agreement developed against any resort to chapter VII in violent conflicts external to the Cold War; they were treated as cases of settlement of disputes under chapter VI, not as occasions for collective security. When the Soviet Union turned aggressor—as in Eastern Europe in 1956 and 1968 or in Afghanistan—the United States either did nothing (except verbally) or resorted to covert action. When the United States—rather frequently—breached the political independence of Central American states, the only collective sanction ever applied to Washington was the condemnation of the mining of Nicaraguan waters by the World Court—which led the United States to reject its compulsory jurisdiction.

II.

After the end of the Cold War, two problems arose. In the case of interstate conflicts, many hopes were expressed for a new golden age of the Charter, in conformity with its drafters' hopes—this was the idea of a new world order, made possible by American–Soviet cooperation. Such cooperation was seen as allowing the Security Council, at last, to perform the role that chapter VII had envisaged for it. Indeed, the Gulf War was the one shining moment for collective security against an aggressor: Saddam Hussein. It was a success insofar as the Security Council endorsed the use of force for the restoration of Kuwait's independence and as the "coalition of the willing" forced Iraq to withdraw. However, partly because the provisions of chapter VII aimed at providing the Security Council with a military potential had never been carried out, collective security here was more a U.S.-led operation under UN pavilion than a UN mission—and the coalition tended to fall apart after victory. The lack of support provided to the United States after the war by its allies (other than the United Kingdom) for either the use of force or continuing economic sanctions against a leader who seemed determined to frustrate UN inspections has shown the persistence of traditional state calculations based on national interests rather than on the duty of collective security. It has also promoted dissatisfaction with collective action and multilateralism in the United States—a dissatisfaction already fostered in the 1980s by the lack of support the United States had experienced in actions against state terrorism. For American critics of collective security's failures and shortcomings, the only acceptable alternatives against threats to peace and acts of aggression are either military alliances dominated by the United States (such as NATO) or unilateral American action. With a return to estrangement between Washington and Moscow, China's own pursuit of traditional diplomacy and the administration of George W. Bush's distrust of the United Nations, the chances for an effective practice of collective security through the Charter seem once again very meager. American sympathy for preventive war in cases that do not meet the Charter's conditions for collective security limits further the possibilities for it, say, in the case of nuclear proliferation by Iran or North Korea.

A second issue has, in the past ten years, almost eclipsed that of collective security for interstate peace. It is the issue of extending the "new" law that curbs the use of force by states to internal conflicts and that legitimizes collective interventions that may entail the use of force against a state that massively violates human rights at the expense of political opponents or ethnic groups inside its borders. The Security Council has repeatedly resorted to chapter VII in such cases whenever it decided that the internal use of force by a government constituted a threat to regional or international security.

This time, the purpose is no longer the preservation of the interstate status quo from attempts at changing it by force—indeed, the new humanitarian interventions may well transform that status quo by encouraging the creation of new states, based on the principle of self-determination, as in Yugoslavia (or East Timor). Since there is no agreement, informal or codified, on what constitutes a violation of human rights sufficient to trigger a legitimate outside intervention, the extension of the ban on unacceptable uses of state violence is even more open ended than the Charter notions of breaches of peace and acts of aggression. Since many states are strong opponents of interventions in domestic affairs, there are still major controversies about this extension. It proceeds through case law, not through well-established principles of international law. Moreover, the role of the Security

Council as the necessary legitimizer of collective security operations raises, in cases of humanitarian intervention, the same question that had proven so disruptive in cases of interstate conflicts: what happens when the Security Council is paralyzed by vetoes? In the case of Kosovo, we saw, in effect, a repetition of what had happened during the Cold War. Just as NATO, a military alliance, was established as an instrument for collective defense capable of protecting its members should the Soviets commit aggression and the Security Council be incapacitated by a veto from Moscow, NATO in 1999 was used as a "coalition of the willing" against Serb atrocities in Kosovo because its members anticipated Russian and Chinese opposition in the Security Council.

Thus, almost ninety years after Wilson, the conundrum of collective security remains the same. While the causes of legitimate multilateral resorts to force have enlarged—from cases of external aggression to cases of extreme internal brutalities—and while the secretary-general of the United Nations has defended this extension despite the criticisms of states intent on protecting their internal sovereignty, the possibility of enforcing collective security through the United Nations in all these instances where the cause is legally or morally "right" remains limited because states' concern for doing what is right remains often far smaller than their desire to promote and protect their interests. Whenever this happens, the states that want right to triumph have to choose between inaction, a "coalition of the willing" outside the United Nations (but with a debatable legitimacy), and unilateral action (easily—and often correctly—attacked as imperialistic, specifically when what constitutes aggression for the United States is not recognized as such by an important part of the UN membership). Among the reasons why the champions of the latter have gained influence in the United States are, on the one hand, the perils (and probability) of Security Council paralysis and, on the other, the multiple inefficiencies of the United Nations as an enforcer of collective security even when the Council is not paralyzed—as we have seen in Bosnia in the early 1990s and also in Somalia and in Rwanda.

We must contemplate a near future in which resistance to interstate aggression will largely depend on American willingness to act alone or to mobilize allies and in which collective resistance to intrastate aggression (to give a name to the internal crimes against human rights) may well not materialize if American leaders decide not to intervene by force in internal conflicts in areas where no vital American interests (other than the fates of the innocents) are at stake, where victory is often a murky concept, where "exit strategies" are hard to plan and to execute, and where countries other than the United States lack the means or the will to send fighting forces. This it not a pretty picture, but reality has to be faced even by idealists (like this author) who would, in the long run, like to see collective security prevail both in its original and in its expanded versions. It is only if one faces reality that one can devise strategies to change it. Denial and complacency are the twin enemies of progressive change.

· 11 ·

The United States and International
Organizations: The Clinton Years

I.

$\mathcal{A}$ ll states, in the pursuit of their interests, either try to enlist the support of the international organizations of which they are members or attempt to prevent these organizations from serving as obstacles on the road to their goals. Membership in several organizations with overlapping scope or purposes allows them to maneuver so as to take advantage of those agencies that are likely to be most favorable to them. There is therefore nothing new or shocking in finding that the United States is often very adept at playing this game—which might be called the search for the most advantageous (or least disadvantageous) use of multilateralism. In this chapter, the brand of multilateralism I examine is that which international and regional institutions embody; the range of these institutions goes from organizations with formal charters, complex rules, and numerous components to informal bodies with limited powers, scope, or membership, such as the G8: multilateralism is also a defining characteristic of international law, that is, of treaties and customs that assign rights and obligations to states, often depend on international or regional agencies for their enforcement, but do not necessarily set up collective agencies for their purposes. A study of the United States versus both international law and international organizations is beyond the scope of this chapter.

States, in theory, always have a choice between resorting to multilateral action in defense or pursuit of their interests and unilateral action, when it promises to be more effective and less cumbersome. In reality, this freedom of choice is often limited. All states are legally obligated to act multilaterally when international law or the charter of an international organization prescribes such a course, and many states act accordingly, either out of a concern for world order, a sense of ethical duty, a worry about their reputation, or a calculation of costs. But unilateral action remains the corollary of sovereignty, and in many areas of foreign policy there are no obligations to act in concert with others. Even among the members of the European Union, there exists no legal restriction on their right to recognize states and governments as they see fit. Even when obligations exist (such as the ban on the use of force by article 2, paragraph 4, of the UN Charter), states, large and small, sometimes violate them blatantly, as Iraq did when it invaded Kuwait.

For a hegemonic power such as the United States, there is a perpetual tug-of-war between the desire to push its vision of world order through the intricate mechanisms of regional and international organizations so as to have it shared by others and to be seen and accepted as the leader of the flock and the itch to act unilaterally whenever these mechanisms are deemed to be hindrances or inefficient. Much depends on the outcome of this calculation because American statesmen have not only to try to figure out, case by case, whether a resort to multilateral action would enhance or constrain or serve or reduce America's power but also to deal with the fact that most international and many regional bodies need American leadership or cooperation in order to succeed. They must therefore include in their calculation the short- and long-term effects of weakening, through unilateral action, agencies that may well be, on the whole, important levers for American influence. This is a special concern that few other countries share (although Britain and France know the same tug-of-war with respect to the European Union).

II.

In the Clinton years, the United States behaved in a multiplicity of ways toward the UN system and regional organizations. There was a fundamental inconsistency between the faith in multilateralism proclaimed by the members of the president's foreign policy team in the early months of the new administration and a course that turned out to be anything but straight. In the beginning, the word from Washington (particularly from National Security Adviser Anthony Lake) was about the need for the United States, despite its status as the only superpower, to cooperate with the rest of world society in order to resolve common problems. As Ivo Daalder has shown,[1] the Clinton administration began with a review of U.S. peacekeeping policy inspired by Lake's "pragmatic neo-Wilsonianism" and Secretary of State Madeleine Albright's "assertive multilateralism"—assertive because of the evident need for U.S. leadership both to steer the United Nations toward common goals and to prevent multilateralism from harming U.S. interests, hence a promise to strengthen the UN capacity to manage peace operations. But the policy review, begun in early 1993, resulted in a directive—PDD 25—in May 1994 only, and while it reaffirmed American support for UN operations, it qualified this support heavily. There would have to be "realistic criteria" for ending the operation, it would be undertaken only if inaction's consequences were clearly unacceptable and if the risks to U.S. troops were acceptable, U.S. forces would remain under U.S. command, and no support was given to the idea of a standing UN army or of earmarking U.S. forces for UN operations. Indeed, where earlier versions had mentioned the need for "rapid expansion" of UN peacekeeping, it was now presented as a limited task, "more selective and more effective" than before. What had happened between February 1993 and May 1994 was the fiasco in Somalia.

This does not mean that "assertive multilateralism" withered away. In the case of Bosnia (1992–1995), American diplomacy was anything but assertive at first because of a protracted disagreement with the European effort at reaching a peaceful settlement, which reflected Britain's and France's reluctance to switch from peacekeeping (although there was no peace to keep) to peacemaking (which would have required the use of force). But by 1995, Washington did become assertive—using the so-called Contact Group rather than the Security Council yet succeeding thereby in putting some force behind the previously empty warnings the Security Council had addressed to Milosevic. In East Timor in 1999, the United States provided the diplomatic pressure that was necessary to get Indonesia to consent to the peacekeeping force led by Australia. Clinton's leadership of the Organization of American States and of the Security Council resulted, again after many delays, in the return of President Aristide in Haiti, with an international as well as a regional mandate for the restoration of democracy. Nowhere was assertive multilateralism more successfully displayed than in the establishment of the World Trade Organization (WTO). In these cases, U.S. leadership served as the catalyst of a consensus that was more than a simple recognition by others of America's superior might.

However, next to this practice of "superpower multilateralism," we find two series of cases that can hardly be described as examples of a multilateralist disposition. First, there are instances of what one might call the unilateralism of dictation: these are exercises of American power *in* international bodies, but they go beyond leadership. What distinguishes them from the previously listed cases is not the pursuit of American objectives—this was evidently also the case in Bosnia in 1995 or with respect to free trade—but the way in which the United States used its dominant position in order to obtain outcomes about which it would be hard to prove that a general consensus existed. Preponderance facilitates leadership but does not necessarily amount to dictation. Dictation there was, in the International Monetary Fund (IMF).

As Joseph Stiglitz and Benjamin Cohen have shown,[2] it was the United States that pushed the IMF into making imprudent loans and into pressing for financial liberalization resulting in the Asian crisis of 1997–1998. And when that crisis hit a number of countries' currencies and financial institutions, it was the United States that insisted on the imposition by the IMF of familiar, intrusive, and highly unpopular austerity measures.

In several African conflicts, the United States decisively limited the effectiveness of Security Council attempts to cope with disintegrating countries. It was U.S. opposition to a timely intervention in Rwanda—an opposition based on the constricted principles of PDD 25—that led to the Security Council's decision to withdraw its peacekeeping mission. It was U.S. reluctance to commit forces to UN-sponsored peacekeeping operations that obliged the Security Council to keep them limited and largely ineffectual in Sierra Leone and in the Democratic Republic of the Congo. The way in which the United States blocked the appointment as head of the IMF of the candidate of the German government, despite previous understandings, and even more the way in which Albright demanded and obtained the nonrenewal of Boutros Boutros-Ghali's mandate as secretary-general of the United Nations are other, rather egregious examples of "bossism." Both Boutros-Ghali and his successor had to accept American demands for administrative reform of the United Nations, and so did the IMF in 1998–1999.

There has been another, even more spectacular kind of unilateralism: that which, in effect, dismisses international institutions whenever this seems more convenient for the United States. Here, the list is long. One might begin, if only in order to give a qualified verdict, with the U.S. decision to bypass the Security Council and to rely exclusively on NATO in order to intervene in Kosovo in March 1999. On the one hand, action by NATO was an exercise in multilateralism, for even though U.S. predominance in NATO is a political, technological, and military reality, there was no American *diktat* in this instance: the NATO allies had been preparing a collective operation against Milosevic for some time, and the only unilateral American move was Richard Holbrooke's surprise agreement with the Serbian leader in October 1998—which Milosevic quickly violated.[3] Rambouillet, for all its peculiar flaws, was a collective exercise by the United States and its key allies. But, on the other hand, resorting to NATO rather than to the Security Council was more than just choosing a smoother path instead of the rocky road of an agency in which the Russians and Chinese had a right of veto. The Charter of the United Nations gives to the Security Council only the authority to launch military operations and to empower regional bodies to do so. We all know that the Security Council would have been paralyzed, that such paralysis was unacceptable, and that it was less humiliating for the Council, for

Secretary-General Annan, and for the Russians and Chinese to be pushed aside than to be deliberately ignored after a veto. Nevertheless, the precedent that has been set by not following the procedures of the Charter in a case in which there existed an international alternative is dangerous insofar as it could be used in cases where there is neither a NATO nor a regional organization capable of filling the void—and where the United States might want to act alone without having first proven that the United Nations could not act.

Far more clear-cut are a whole series of unilateral American decisions with respect to the United Nations. There is, of course, the continuing failure to pay America's dues. There was the decision to pull out of Somalia after the casualties of October 1993. There was, once the genocide in Rwanda began, Washington's refusal to support UN and African countries' attempts at preventing it from worsening and to provide logistical aid to efforts by Rwanda's neighbors to organize an intervention. Washington, in its policies toward "rogue states," has gone pretty far in using force (against Iraq) on a slender legal basis—including just at the moment when the Security Council was examining the Butler report—and in using extraterritorial measures and secondary boycotts against states designated by the Helms-Burton and D'Amato-Kennedy bills. The use of force against the Sudan and Afghanistan, aimed at targets assumed to be terrorist bases of Osama bin Laden, certainly stretched the notion of self-defense.

One must also mention the refusal by the United States to join 121 other countries that, at a conference in Geneva in 1996, had agreed to ban antipersonnel land mines and the nonratification of the comprehensive test ban treaty, rejected by the Senate.

In several other important areas, unilateralism has been particularly pugnacious. One example is the failure of the United States to sign the treaty setting up the International Criminal Court (ICC), even though it was Washington that, in 1997, had asked the General Assembly of the United Nations to establish such a tribunal. The final vote on its statute was 120 to 7, the only allies of the United States being Iraq, Libya, Qatar, Yemen, China, and Israel. Many of the concerns expressed by the United States and France in the course of the negotiations were addressed in the statute, but the United States, unlike France, remained unsatisfied: opposed to a prosecutor capable of initiating investigations and to an excessively vague reference to the "crime of aggression." Even the clear principle of "complementarity" under which the court can assume jurisdiction only if national courts fail to investigate or (if necessary) to prosecute, the fact that the prosecutor needs the approval of two panels of judges, and the accountability of the judges to the governments that accept the ICC's jurisdiction did not appease the critics of the court (see the discussion later in this chapter).

The other triumphs of unilateralism in the UN system concern the environment and are more fully described by Robert Paarlberg. The Kyoto agreement of 1997, concluded by the administration despite a unanimous resolution of the Senate two years earlier against any binding treaty that did not apply to the developing countries, has never been ratified. And the 1992 convention on biodiversity never received the necessary support of two-thirds of the members of the Senate. Finally, despite the creation of the WTO, which was supposed to limit America's resort to unilateral reprisals based on section 301 of the Trade Act of 1974 and on the "super 301" provision of that of 1988, the American trade representative has kept the capacity to resort to such measures.

In the case of non-UN organizations, several U.S. exercises of unilateral power have been in evidence. In Latin America, we are told by Robert Pastor that "the American predisposition to addressing" the problems of illegitimate traffics "has often been unilateral and insensitive to the sovereign needs of its neighbors," and the same tendency has determined recent policy moves aimed at helping the embattled and far-from-democratic regime in Colombia in its fight against guerrilla groups suspected to rely for funds on the drug traffic. In NATO, the decision of the Clinton administration in 1996 to move from its "partnership for peace" policy, open to Eastern European countries and to states of the former Soviet Union, to the admission of three former Soviet satellites into the alliance was taken with practically no consultation of Washington's partners and indeed with minimal participation by the Pentagon and a divided National Security Council and State Department. This is a story in which the initial unilateralism in decision making led to dictation in enforcement.[4]

III.

Thus, despite the original intentions and statements of the key members of the Clinton administration, behaving as a responsible "multilateralist" power that seeks the support of international organizations has not been the norm. What are the reasons for these inconsistencies and these lapses from multilateralism? One is the difficulty the Clinton administration had in defining a coherent and workable strategy for the post–Cold War world (except insofar as the world economy is concerned: there, the United States has been the champion of globalization—with, however, a very mixed record on environmental issues). The administration focused on relations with Russia and

China and on a number of trouble spots of great strategic importance for the United States (North Korea, Iraq, and the Arab–Israeli conflict). But it did not provide convincing guidelines about when to intervene in domestic breakdowns, even though the disintegration of states has become a far more ominous feature of world politics than interstate conflicts. When does a murderous civil war or a murderous regime constitute a threat to America's national interest? (In the case of Bosnia, before the spring of 1995, the president oscillated from treating it as a kind of atavistic tragedy that required a quarantine to proclaiming that vital American interests were at stake.) In shaping the world economy, the United States has frequently resorted to what I have called bossism—not merely using international agencies as instruments of U.S. policy but as if they were agencies of the U.S. government. In coping with a world in which Washington had to keep its eyes on ex- or potential superpowers, on an epidemic of internal disasters, and on traditional conflicts between neighbors, *ad hocism* has prevailed. For instance, all "rogue states" have not been treated in the same way (compare the policy toward Cuba or Iraq with the approach to North Korea). In the cases of internal breakdowns, the most bloody, Rwanda, has been the most blatant example of U.S. failure to act. One might argue that the common characteristic of those interventions accompanied by force that did occur is that they were triggered by a combination of massive violations of human rights and American "realistic" interests—stopping a flow of refugees from Haiti and preserving overall security in the Balkans. But in the case of the Balkans, the hesitations were as noticeable as the subsequent interventions.

The second and third reasons for America's behavior are provided by the peculiarities of the American political system. First, within the executive, it can be said that the Pentagon, on issues that involve the use of force and the composition of forces, has behaved increasingly as a sovereign agency, animated by a deep distrust of limitations imposed by foreigners and an equally deep dislike of casualties and high risks. In the list of unilateral acts provided earlier in this chapter, many resulted from Pentagon vetoes. The elaboration of PDD 25 reflected not only the Somalian experience but also the "reluctant military," whose views were expressed in September 1993 by General Colin Powell: the mission of the U.S. armed forces is "to fight and win the nation's wars" (a "warrior culture" that clearly subordinates humanitarian interventions to the need for preserving the ability to fight the "big wars"—and that, not so incidentally, distinguishes the U.S. Army from the armies of many of its allies, less reluctant to embrace "social work" activities, in some cases—the Scandinavians, for instance—for traditional reasons of self-image and in other cases—Britain and France—because of the legacy of an imperial past). General Powell opposed successfully the idea of a rapid reaction force that he saw as a commitment to send Americans "to an unknown war, in an unknown land, for an unknown cause, under an unknown commander, for an unknown duration."⁵ The guidelines that led to the final text of PDD 25 reflected the Pentagon's requirement that intervention not have unacceptable effects on military readiness and its reluctance to place U.S. forces under UN operational control unreservedly. It was the Pentagon's concern for its forces in Korea that led it to oppose the ban on land mines. It also weighed heavily against the comprehensive test ban treaty and the ICC—in the latter case, the Pentagon feared that the treaty did not go far enough in protecting the military from charges that the operations they conducted violated the laws of war. For reasons that have more to do with his past than with his philosophy, Clinton has been eager not to overrule the defense establishment (cf. the move toward a limited antiballistic defense system, at the expense of the ABM treaty, which the president left for his successor to decide). For very different reasons, a George W. Bush administration might be even more "Pentagonistic," as statements by him and by his adviser Condolezza Rice and as the influence of General Powell on him suggest.

Second (this is the third reason), since 1994 the United States has provided the world with a stark display of the weakness of a presidential system with a sharp separation of powers. The old (and often much exaggerated) bipartisan tradition in foreign affairs has vanished, along with deference to the experts on foreign policy in the key committees of the House and the Senate; many of these leaders have actually disappeared from Congress. Indeed, Congress has, at times, been dominated by a coalition of neoisolationists, anti-internationalists, and Clinton haters—hence not only the failure of the administration to get Senate approval for many of its appointments but also the administration's defeat in the case of the test ban treaty, the rejection by Congress of the "fast track" for trade deals, the repeated attempts by Congress to dictate reforms to the United Nations, and the difficulty the administration has had in prolonging the presence of U.S. forces in Kosovo. The case of the ICC is particularly interesting; at this occasion, the Pentagon's horror at the idea of American soldiers being charged with crimes by foreign states and Republican contempt for such states' hypothetical pretenses of judging American war behavior converged. The most egregious example of congressional foreign policy was Senator Helms's appearance before and his speech at the Security Council of the United Nations—lecturing the United Nations about its flaws and treating it as, at best, an occasional instrument of U.S. foreign policy—and pretending to speak in the name of the American people.

IV.

The deeper reasons for what might be called a drift away from Wilsonianism or from the internationalism that was the spirit of America's foreign policy after World War II deserve some analysis. One factor, hard to evaluate with precision, is undoubtedly the hubris of being the only superpower, the "indispensable nation," in a world in which the main rivals are still (China) or currently (Russia) weak and in need of American goods or money. In this world, the United States alone can project technologically superior forces all over the globe. In the days of the Cold War, the existence of Soviet power, especially in Europe, obliged the United States—even before it lost its nuclear monopoly—to behave—even in its relations with dependent allies—in a way that distinguished it from the brutal methods of Soviet domination (with rather frequent glitches in Central America). The one American disaster of that period—Vietnam—fueled the Pentagon's distaste for open-ended interventions, the high costs of ground warfare, and casualties.

A second factor is a gradual disillusionment with political internationalism. In the realm of trade, a United States that had repudiated protectionism and understood that worldwide free trade was a royal road both to prosperity at home and to economic growth abroad obviously had a vital interest in institutions such as the IMF and the World Bank—which it dominates—or the WTO—which can be most helpful in dismantling barriers to U.S. goods and services. But in the strategic-diplomatic arena, a cost-benefit analysis gives less favorable results. Acting with others sometimes means being stopped by them (as when Mr. Christopher suggested to Britain and France in 1993–1994 a "lift and strike" policy in Bosnia) or pressured by them in undesired ways (as when Mr. Blair advocated forcefully a ground war in Kosovo). It is not by coincidence that the United States has kept the General Assembly—and also its European allies—at arm's length and often used its veto in the Security Council in order to protect Israel from the wrath of Arab and other Third World countries and to keep control of the peace process (even after it had been temporarily lost by Washington in Oslo). Being the "lone eagle" does not make one more popular, and even though American hegemony has been sufficiently "benevolent" or "benign" to prevent efforts at balancing American power from taking off, many non-American statesmen have been annoyed by America's championing of what they see as Western liberal values (cf. the debate about "Asian values") or peculiarly American conceptions of democracy. The fact that most countries seek the advantages of economic globalization does not prevent them from resenting the "Americanization" of their cultures and daily lives and the way in which political globalization—the agendas of nongovernmental organizations and of international institutions—also wears, more often than not, an American face. All this means that the United States, for all its indispensability, often finds the marshaling of support and consensus arduous.

One may add to this difficulty in translating power directly into results American disillusionment with the United Nations. It has, at times, been a scapegoat (as in Somalia); but often, its bureaucratic heaviness and inefficiency and its inexperience in running military operations or civilian activities of "nation building" have frustrated Americans raised on "can-doism," impatient with delays, overlapping jurisdictions, and poor preparation. It wasn't only Congress that has kept pressing for reform.

A final factor, itself resulting from what precedes, has been a backlash against internationalism and multilateralism. Within the Democratic Party, the voices for it have become less audible—in the Clinton years, Lake dropped out, Holbrooke was imperious and proconsular than multilateralist, and Albright, in whom the old faith was still burning, was often more shrill than adept. Al Gore's campaign was startlingly unfocused on foreign affairs. Among Republicans, unilateralism gained ever more ground, both in the form of "bossism"—when we have leaders who lead, others follow—and in the form of a rejection of external constraints. The latter is also characteristic of such backlashes against the traditional mainstream as the two antiglobalization movements of the right and the left, Pat Buchanan's nativism and Ralph Nader's populism, respectively.

Indeed, there are many ways of championing a multilateralism à la carte, that is, of justifying a policy of picking and choosing from the menu offered by international organizations only those items that enhance America's power and of rejecting as indigestible all those that might constrain it. The most candid and nationalistic is the stance of those whom the French, who have their share of them on the left and on the right, call *souverainistes*—the self-righteous protectors of national sovereignty against foreign encroachments. These are the "realists" who explain that world order is based on might, that the network of international law and organizations is a frail scaffolding that holds only as long as there is a structure of power behind it. They also argue that "under our Constitution, any Congress may, by law, amend an earlier act of Congress, including treaties, thus freeing the US unilaterally of any obligation." They "proclaim unequivocally the superior status of our Constitution over the claims of international law." In their view, for instance, the prosecutor of the ICC usurps "a powerful and necessary element of executive power, the power of law enforcement"; his real "potential targets" are America's "top civilian and military leaders." International bodies, such as the ICC, are politically unaccountable and therefore dangerous.[6] The counterargument, about the United States giving up its ability to shape international institutions by withdrawing from them (as in the case of the biodiversity protocol), does not impress those "realists," who are convinced that our absence would doom such agencies.[7]

Another defense of unilateralism is more sophisticated. Where the previous one assumes that the only thing that matters is what is good for the United States, the rest of the world be damned, this one posits that what is good for the United States *is* good for the world. If there is such a thing as internationalist unilateralism, here it is: a kind of deformation of Wilsonianism, a curious mélange of international messianism and national self-righteousness (to which Wilson himself was often prone). It explains that the United States plays "a prophetic and reformist role" because its "sense of mission has led it to conceive and support the establishment of international institutions." And the United States also plays a "custodial role as guardian and actor of last resort" for world order.[8] The reformist role may require that the United States withdraw or withhold funds from, so to speak, incorrect institutions (the International Labor Organization, UNESCO, and so on)—often for purely unselfish reasons. The custodial role may clash with "the formally prescribed procedures of multilateral institutions" when the way these work is "unlikely to produce the decisions that are called for" (as defined, presumably, by the United States) and to reach "the ultimate goals" at stake—hence American opposition to the ICC, "viewed as likely to obstruct the custodial role the US could expect to be called upon to perform militarily" and also to the land mines treaty seen by some in the executive as depriving the United States of weapons "indispensable to the performance of certain international security functions that would remain a US responsibility for several decades."

Thus, whether in realist uniform or in Wilsonian disguise, the case for unilateralism has progressed in a country where battle fatigue with external entanglements, proud awareness of America's power (hard and soft), and a desire to show the way to others produce neither consistency nor coherence in foreign policy. Between an American government sure of America's power but unsure about the best uses of it and international organizations that are increasingly important as sources of legitimacy and stabilizing forces but often mismanaged and devoid of adequate means, there can be no easy fit. The public seems more "internationalist" than much of the U.S. political class or elite, but its willingness to incur high costs or losses is in doubt, and its interest in the world outside is limited.[9]

114   *Chapter 11*

NOTES

Chapter 11 was published in Robert J. Lieber, ed., *Eagle Rules? Foreign Policy and American Primacy in the Twenty-First Century* (Upper Saddle River, N.J.: Prentice Hall, 2002).

1. Ivo Daalder, "Knowing When to Say No: The Development of US Policy for Peace-Keeping," in *UN Peacekeeping, American Policy, and the Uncivil Wars of the 1990s*, ed. William Durch (Basingstoke: Macmillan, 1996).

2. See Joseph Stiglitz, "What I Saw at the Devaluation," *New Republic*, April 17–24, 2000, 56–61, and Benjamin J. Cohen, "Containing Backlash," in Lieber, *Eagle Rules?*, chap. 14.

3. See Pierre Martin and Mark R. Brawley, eds., *Alliance Politics, Kosovo, and NATO's War: Allied Force or Forced Allies?* (New York: Palgrave, 2000).

4. See James Goldgeier, *Not Whether but When: The US Decision to Enlarge NATO* (Washington, D.C.: Brookings Institution Press, 1999).

5. Daalder, "Knowing When to Say No," 41, 42, 43.

6. These quotations come from John Bolton in, *Toward an International Criminal Court?* (New York: Council on Foreign Relations, Alton Frye, project director, 1999), 42–43.

7. For a sharp critique of this point of view, see Peter J. Spiro, "The New Sovereigntists," *Foreign Affairs* (November–December 2000): 9–15.

8. See W. Michael Reisman, "The United States and International Institutions," *Survival* (winter 1999–2000): 62–80, at 63, 66–71, and 75.

9. This chapter owes a great deal to Justin Vaïsse's still-unpublished study of the United States and international law.

·12·

American Exceptionalism—The New Version: "The National Security Strategy of the United States of America," September 2002

I.

*E*ach nation tends to see itself as unique. Two—France and the United States—consider themselves as exceptional because—or so they claim—of the universality of their values. One only, the United States, has tried to develop foreign policies that reflect such exceptionalism. Whereas France and most of the European powers have tended or been forced to practice balance-of-power politics for their protection and for the creation of minimal order in the international jungle, the United States has had much leeway to be original. The main component of its exceptionalism has been, for more than a century after its independence, its geographically privileged position: far enough away from Europe and Asia to be able to be safe and uninvolved yet capable of expanding into contiguous territories easily and without much of a contest. A second component was its institutions: it grew into being the greatest representative democracy, with greater participation of the public and of the legislative branch in foreign affairs than anywhere else. Finally, American principles turned geography and institutions into guidelines for behavior: a distaste for the rule of force that characterized European diplomacy and colonialism and the repudiation of aristocracy and its wiles, enshrined in a sacred text, the Constitution, which served and still serves as the glue that amalgamates all the ingredients of the melting pot (France, with its vast number of constitutions, could only use its language and culture as the glue of Frenchness).[1]

The sense of special mission imparted by these components left ample room for contradictions and complexities. The lofty feeling of democratic

115

superiority and universal relevance was perfectly compatible, in practice, with a pursuit of national interest and advantage that was just as fierce as elsewhere—indeed, geographical position and political faith facilitated and licensed quite ordinary crass behavior, as continental expansion was going to show; the usual behavior of states never became the policymakers' ideal, with a few exceptions, such as Hamilton, but this was not the only domain in which the ideal and the real were allowed to diverge. The complexity was provided by the two very different forms that American exceptionalism took and that I called elsewhere the Wilsonian syndrome. One form, of increasing less relevance as U.S. might grew, was isolationism. As Wilson said when World War I began, the United States was "too proud to fight"; it was a beacon of light, a model perhaps for others, but it wasn't going to get involved in others' fights—hence the founding fathers' imperative of "no entangling alliances." The other face was more crusading and militant: making the world safe for democracy, which entailed working with others yet did not supersede distrust of European-style alliances, marinated in secret diplomacy and cynical deals. Rather, it meant a willingness to build global institutions, good both for the promotion of U.S. interests and for the expansion of America's mission and ideals yet designed in such a way that the risks of unwelcome entanglements would be minimized (remember that article 10 of the League of Nations Covenant, which Wilson's intransigence refused to water down, left it to each state to protect the political independence and territorial integrity of another state from aggression). One thing that was common to the two versions of exceptionalism: the desire to protect (in both cases) and to project (in the second) what made the United States, in American eyes, unique: its values and institutions.

Indeed, Wilson had not given up isolationism for power politics: he joined the war as an associate, not an ally. The League, even with imprecise commitments, was too much for the public, and the design, especially in its preference for open diplomacy, anticolonialism, and self-determination, was unwelcome among Wilson's traditional foreign associates and often unrealistic. The result was a return to isolationism in the age of the totalitarian tyrants.

II.

After Franklin D. Roosevelt's death, U.S. foreign policy had to be reconstructed. Roosevelt's vision of the "four policemen" who would rule the world (through the UN Security Council), designed to be more effective than the League, was quickly crippled by the Cold War. The shapers of the new strategy of containment were all intensely aware of and responsive to the formidable new power of the United States—the rest of the West and much of Asia were down and the only challenger: Stalin's Soviet Union could be dealt with in only one of two ways: preemption, at a time when the United States had a monopoly of nuclear power—but the Soviets had the means of invading Western Europe—or containment, which became the doctrine and entailed military alliances with the countries that had to be saved from Soviet domination. This was the realist moment, whose chief theorist, Hans Morgenthau, excommunicated Wilsonian idealism and moralism. But the policymakers tried to mitigate the realists' celebration of power with various kinds of appeals to idealism that Wilson could have applauded. The struggle against communism was not presented as a power contest but as a crusade of the good (the democracies) against evil. The creation of a vast new network of international and regional organizations, Truman's four-point program for development, were dimensions of the power struggle but also presentable as idealistic measures for peace and welfare. The realism of the dark side of the struggle (such as subversion) was sugarcoated by a genuine idealism (think of American cultural diplomacy in Western Europe, animated by the Central Intelligence Agency). A synthesis of traditional power politics, in the prudent forms advocated by George Kennan, and of American idealistic and multilateralist exceptionalism seemed to be accomplished.

After more than forty years, the outcome was of course complex. On the one hand, the synthesis won great victories: the collapse of the Soviet Union (in a way close to "Mr. X'"s prediction in 1947), the rebirth of Western Europe and Japan as protégés of Washington, the subtle management of the Sino–Soviet split, the acrobatic success of having Israel as well as several Arab states as clients, and the waning of colonialism. But on the debit side, decolonization produced failed states with often miserable populations and violent ethnic conflicts; a permanent U.S. military presence was needed in Western Europe and Japan both because of a potential of continuing external threats and because the United States was needed to preserve harmony in Western Europe and the Far East. The end of the Soviet Union deprived the U.S. network of often disparate alliances of its glue and created new headaches. Above all, there was the scar of Vietnam: a bitter lesson in the impotence of force in some situations, a demonstration of the limits of doctrines as well as of America's appeal, and a discovery of the fragility of America's domestic front—points that present-day policymakers should not forget.

III.

After the Cold War, the United States talked about a new world order, but what it faced was a bewildering and disorderly new world. The end of the

Soviet Empire meant anything but a peaceful scene. The Arab–Israeli conflict continued, and the Gulf War was for the military both good (because of the rise in military credits) and perplexing (were the stringent conditions of the Powell doctrine a tough road map for future conflicts or a warning against most limited uses of force?). Once more, the unexpected struck: ethnic conflicts (some of horrendous scope) that raised each time the question of whether, where, and on which side to intervene and that provoked a debate between realists resistant to foreign policy as "social work" and the idealists of humanitarian interference. In these new circumstances, allies began to diverge. American diplomacy found itself pressured both by a public eager to return to domestic affairs (as Clinton understood in 1992) and by the military eager to avoid any new Vietnam (hence Powell's decision to end the Gulf War far indeed from Baghdad and his reluctance toward humanitarian expeditions).

The first indication of a new attempt by American strategic thinkers to define a doctrine for so complicated and elusive a world was provided by what has been called "Dick Cheney's masterwork,"[2] the Defense Planning Guidance draft of 1992, which was toned down before it was published, given the outcry it had produced. It was doubly important. In 1947, the containment rationale was written by a diplomat (one who wanted to deter, not to wage, war and was particularly suspicious of a militarization of America's alliances as well as of any resort to nuclear weapons). Forty-five years later, the tract that was the first draft of the Bush doctrine of 2002 was produced by a group of civilian and military officials of the Defense Department. Moreover, it launched a new form of exceptionalism and carried the American enthusiasm for power way beyond that of the late 1940s. There had been nothing exceptional then about what I previously called the U.S. discovery of the need for and utility of power—a rebuke and corrective to the two alternative forms of American exceptionalism until then. But there is something wondrous about its new incarnation, for it is an exceptionalism based almost exclusively on military domination. The 1992 draft went not so much beyond the Powell doctrine (when using force, do it overwhelmingly enough to win and only if the chances of success are good) as in a different direction. The document introduces explicitly the idea of the possible necessity of unilateral action, of the preemptive use of fore, and of a U.S. nuclear arsenal strong enough to deter the development of nuclear programs elsewhere. It was clearly aimed at reducing the challenges Russia and China might want to launch someday as well as the constraints imposed by America's allies. This still left one with one puzzle and one serious tension. The document proposes a strategy capable of deterring all challengers and of carrying out interventions anywhere, but it provided little guidance about where the more dangerous challenges and the more necessary interventions might occur (it soon became clear that Powell had no intention to intervene in Yugoslavia, prompting Madeleine Albright, then Clinton's UN representative, to ask him what he was keeping his force for). The tension was between this implicit ideal of a liberation of U.S. force from restraints and the agreements, based on reciprocity, reached with so many governments in the previous forty-plus years. It was not just a turn to a doctrine of the national interest pure and simple, now that the Cold War no longer required alliances and an idealistic stance, but something radically new that led away from the Wilsonian syndrome: it called on the United States neither (obviously!) to cultivate its own garden nor to pursue a world mission by leading others toward directions acceptable to them through multilateral organizations defining and legitimizing the common goals. Exceptionalism now meant being, remaining, and acting as the only superpower, and its substance was capabilities, not ideals and missions.

Let us look more closely at this new exceptionalism. When George W. Bush came to power, the doctrine that seemed to be in favor was a return to realism: a concentration on those conflicts that could impair the global or important regional balances of power, a retreat from involvement in conflicts devoid of such significance (as in Africa) or hopeless (such as the Palestinian issue). However, this is not what prevailed. Already before September 11, 2001, we find a remarkable mix of "sovereignism" (an avatar of the old isolationism's suspiciousness) and distrust of the opinion of others. The rejection of the Kyoto Protocol, the withdrawal from the ABM treaty, and the scuttling of the land mines treaty and of the comprehensive test ban treaty—most of these marks of defiance of the United Nations had appeared before George W. Bush came to power, when Congress was already in Republican hands. The extraordinary vendetta conducted (largely but not exclusively by John Bolton) against the International Criminal Court (ICC) brought out not only the Bush administration's paranoia about how a malevolent United Nations and ICC could indict innocent American soldiers and officers but also how punitive the United States could become against states (allies or not) unwilling to meet U.S. demands. As Michael Ignatieff has quipped, here exceptionalism meant exemptionism.

What are the new exceptionalists' main arguments? One—rather bizarre—insists on the idea that the U.S. Constitution is the law of the land, excluding any kind of superior law—such as international law—and any transfer, pooling, or delegation of sovereignty (a British judge commented that even Mrs. Thatcher had subscribed to such transfers to the European Union; so had General de Gaulle). Then there is the theme of benevolent imperialism, developed in particular by Robert Kagan, who has called the United States "a Behemoth with a conscience." In an article in which valid criticisms of the new "Kantian" Europe (i.e., toothless and preoccupied by "challenges" such as immigration and ethnic conflicts, whereas mighty America focuses on threats) are mixed with a great deal of condescending hubris, he explains that the new sense of "civilian" mission of the Europeans is made possible by the military power and presence of the United States and expresses only their own weakness.[3] A third argument, presented by Michael Reisman, states that the United States, being by its might responsible for world order, is justified in rejecting those parts of international law that would make order more difficult[4] (thus, he gives to the United States the right to decide what parts contribute to world order and what parts do not—a strange position for a professor of law). Finally, there is the argument of brute force. The United States has it in abundance, others do not; hence allies, when they do not bend to the will of the United States, are both nuisances and unnecessary. International law and organizations are constructs that can be discarded whenever they stand in the path of American power. This case has been made by John Bolton and Donald Rumsfeld; in their view, U.S. might is at the service of a very narrowly defined national interest (which excludes humanitarian flings). It is clear that those arguments all agree on downgrading restraints and on preserving American preponderance, even though opinions on the nature of America's mission range from a responsibility for world order to pure self-interest.

Who are the proponents of these ideas? They are, on the whole, variants of familiar types, of the stock figures of American exceptionalism. What is new is that they are extreme in their conviction that the United States is the only country that matters. There are the sheriffs who see the world through the epic of *High Noon* with the eyes of Carl Schmitt—a world in which politics is seen as a struggle for power between foes and friends. In this sense, they are the heirs of the Cold War (for whose ending they credit Reagan). They are suspicious of diplomacy (in the Cold War days, they distrusted arms control and found Kissinger, with his policy of détente, too soft). Now that the United States is the sole superpower, they deem allies less necessary and insist on a very selfish notion of the national interest (as Condoleezza Rice has said, the role of the U.S. Army is not to conduct children into the kindergarten of troubled countries). A second group is that of the imperialists with a good conscience because the United States offers others the public good of order and pays the price of preserving it. They share with the previous group a desire for "moral clarity," for a world in black and white, divided between the good (represented by the United States) and the bad (whereas Reinhold Niebuhr, once so influential, saw a world of multiple moral ambiguities).

Both these groups were well represented in the Reagan administration and had populated the Committee on the Present Danger of the late 1970s.

The sheriffs were disappointed by the turn of Reagan from his evil empire days to his embrace of Gorbachev, which softened the Soviet Empire's fall. The imperialists—men like Charles Krauthammer or William Kristol—had been frustrated by the (in their eyes truncated) ending of the Gulf War in 1991. These two groups react to the new challenges and troubles as displaced, partly triumphant but also partly scared, ex–cold warriors who behave a bit like Kafka's beast in the burrow: they see threats everywhere. A third group is less important, except insofar as it shares the Manichaean vision: those for whom the world is a contest between America's traditional conservative and religious values and all those who attack them, be they modern secular and dissolute liberals or Islamic fundamentalists. These are the American fundamentalists.

To these clans, one has to add a group that could be called "friends of Israel," who believe in the identity of interests between the Jewish state and the United States: both are democracies, both are surrounded by foes, and both need to rely on force to survive. Israel is seen as the one sturdy ally in a crucial area in which Israel's enemies are either also America's enemies or else very dubious and flawed allies and clients of Washington. These men and women look at foreign policy through the lenses of a dominant concern: is it good or bad for Israel? They are a potent force in American politics. Never in very good odor at the State Department—since 1947—they became well ensconced in the civilian offices of the Pentagon, around such men as Paul Wolfowitz, Richard Perle, and Douglas Feith.

IV.

A discerning reader might object that many of my new exceptionalists are no more than realists drunk with America's new might as the only superpower. This is true, but whereas the lesson of past realists (Niebuhr, Morgenthau, Kennan, and even Kissinger) had been the kind of discerning prudence and moderation that Thucydides had praised, the new voices are exceptional in their paean to American might (many of the more traditional realists, in academia and in government, are worried by the excesses of the present ones, so much closer to Alcibiades than to Pericles).

Moreover, things changed after September 11. Before that traumatic day, the new exceptionalism was a doctrine in search of a cause (or defining its cause as America's own national interest). After September 11, it found its cause, just as the post–World War II United States had found its in the Cold War. It was the war on global terrorism—on the terrorists and on those states that protected them. This was going to be the rationale of the Bush presidency, the great simplifier, the chief new foreign policy doctrine. It had the advantage of providing a lever for domestic mobilization (and diversion from controversial domestic issues), given the shocking discovery of palpable vulnerability. It flattered the exceptionalists of all tendencies by emphasizing the indispensable role of the United States, and it appealed especially to the more idealistic ones by stressing that the defense against terror, America's cause, was also the world's cause: self-interest and morality, power and values, and the sheriff and the missionary were back together.

But there were signal difficulties. Already during the Cold War, many issues could not be squeezed into the corset of the Soviet–American conflict. Could all important issues now be fitted into the new straitjacket, and could those that could be treated by primarily military means (two questions raised by Hubert Védrine)? The phenomenon of terrorism is extraordinarily heterogeneous. If terrorism means deliberate attacks on the innocent, one would have to amalgamate the gangs of "private" terrorists and state terrorism (carpet bombings, totalitarian terror, and so on) as well as the multiplicity of reasons for the resort to terror: the will to self-determination (as in the case of the Palestinians or the Chechens), a fight over territory (as in Kashmir), a form of domestic action against a repressive regime (in Sudan and in the Algeria of the 1990s), a religious holy war (al-Qaeda), and so on. Obviously, one size doesn't fit all, and concentrating on the acts of terror at the expenses of the causes could well contribute to the global destabilization sought by the terrorists.

Another difficulty is the choice of a method to combat them. Should it be through a coalition of states, or—given their own diversity of regimes and situations—should it be primarily America's war? Both alternatives seemed unpromising. Should the United States focus on the threats to American lives and installations? This would have clashed with the new verbal universalism of the doctrine. Being the sole superpower does not help resolve such issues.

Moreover, there is the danger of a slippery slope, of a constant extension of the new "war." From September 11 on, the Bush administration widened the war against transnational terrorists into a war against the regimes that gave them shelter (but hasn't al-Qaeda found hiding places in a very large number of states, the United States included?). A much more controversial extension has been that from terrorism to states with weapons of mass destruction (and hostility to the United States, unlike, say, Israel, Pakistan, or India). This makes world order even more shaky; it incites others to use the new American doctrine for their own very special ends: the Indians against Pakistan, the Russians against Chechen rebels and occasionally Georgia, and the Sharon government against not only Palestinian terrorists but also the Palestinian Authority and Arafat. This blurs the distinctions that a more discerning United States should be able to observe. The war on terrorism becomes a vast tent under which all kinds of settlements of accounts can fit—including our own quarrel with the bizarre "axis of evil." Within a year of Bush's characterization of three very different states, he has been obliged to diversify American responses in order to limit the dangers to peace and the risk of American "imperial overstretch." At present, Iran is left largely to the United Nations and to a European triumvirate, North Korea is being treated with diplomacy, and only Iraq is under the American gun.

Bush, during the campaign of 2000, had spoken about the need for modesty in foreign affairs. How far from this we are now is shown both by the doctrinaires of the new exceptionalism and by the final avatar of the 1992 defense draft: the new "National Security Strategy of the United States of America," dated September 2002. It is something of a hodgepodge, speaking about primacy *and* balance of power, using also traditional Wilsonian language ("we will actively work to bring the hope of democracy, development, free markets, and free trade to every corner of the world"). It talks about organizing coalitions but also about not hesitating to act alone for self-defense. Still, in the main, it codifies all the new aspects of exceptionalism: the doctrine of preemption so as to destroy threats before they reach U.S. borders (while warning others not to use preemption as a pretext for aggression), the emphasis on the deadly threat of rogue states that try to acquire threatening weapons of mass destruction and "reject basic human values and hate the U.S. and everything for which it stands," the promise to maintain the capability needed to defeat any attempt by any state to impose its will on the United States and its allies and to dissuade potential adversaries from building up their forces to equal or surpass the power of the United States, and last but clearly not least, the determination to protect U.S. nationals from the ICC.

The promise of preemption, which the UN Charter rules out (as a form of aggression) except when an aggression is obviously imminent, is a formula for chaos if it becomes a frequent claim by others and if disputes break out about how urgent the need for anticipatory self-defense really is. The document never refers to the United Nations as a body whose endorsement would be needed—clearly, it would be the United States that would judge both on the legitimacy of its own preventive acts of force and on that of others: the exceptionalists are protected by their good conscience (which does antedate Bush: it was Albright who described the United States as the indispensable nation who sees farther than the lesser breeds). The whole new doctrine is pervaded by the view that we see not only farther but also better what is good and bad and that others are not to be allowed to act like us.

This imperial conception risks plunging the United States in a morass of double standards. For this administration, Palestinian terror is bad, but Sharon's attacks on Palestinian civilians are, at worst, imprudent; proliferators are bad if they are anti-American tyrants and thus candidates for American preemption but not otherwise (it is fortunate we did not practice this doctrine on the Soviet Union in the 1940s or China in the 1960s). As Pierre Hassner has noted, the United States pressured Serbia into sending Milosevic to the Hague tribunal but refuses to accept the jurisdiction of the ICC for itself.[5] The reduction of international politics to the fight against enemies of the United States raises in acute form the problem of unsavory allies: after all, many terrorists hate us not because of our democratic values and system but because of what we are and what we *do* (or what they think we do) and because of our policies that support antidemocratic regimes. To be sure, we vaguely promise democracy for all, but short of universal intervention, we cannot reach that goal—and even with universal intervention, we would have trouble maintaining democracy in countries that have no experience of it. Indeed, if our goal is really not just rhetorical but also genuine, reaching for it would destroy many of our alliances and, by revolutionizing and depacifying world affairs, actually risk wounding the process of economic globalization for which the United States also stands.

In sum, the Bush doctrine means more than the emancipation of a colossus from constraints that are based on an ideal—and on the practical benefits—of reciprocity (constraints that the United States, for all its superiority, had restored and enshrined in networks of international and regional organizations after 1945). It amounts to a doctrine of global domination, inspired by the fact of U.S. might, founded on the assumption that America's values are universally cherished except by nasty tyrants and evil terrorists.

The design may be grandiose, but there is something breathtakingly unrealistic about this unilateralist power and grand exceptionalism coated in all too familiar moralism—what Hassner has called "Wilsonianism in boots."[6] There are two main obstacles. One is the world itself, and the other one is the U.S. public. The world is not reducible to two cleavages—between terrorists and antiterrorists, between democratic and nondemocratic regimes (as U.S. alliances and occasional unilateral interventions, as in Central America, have shown). We have helped terrorists abroad when we deemed them useful (such as even the Taliban against the Soviets); some of our allies (from Guatemala to Pakistan) have practiced state terrorism on a grand scale. Charles Maier reminds us that empires have always had troubles with those excluded from their benefits (inside and outside their borders).[7] Just as Cold War "globalists" never paid enough attention to the regional and local causes of conflicts, our exceptionalists today pay far too little attention to such problems as development or the environment, whose relative neglect (in the latter case) or dogmatic treatment (in the former) feed hostility to the United States. Going way beyond the banalities of the National Security Strategy document, they have, under the rubric of "regime change," promised an energetic effort at replacing tyrannical regimes with democracies; this, if attempted, would not only topple friendly tyrants but also manifest a blind hubris: we don't have the skill or knowledge to manipulate the domestic politics of a large number of other countries, to tell others who their leaders should or should not be, and to "improve" the world by projecting on them a model of democracy that has worked—not without upheavals—in the rich and multicultural United States but that has little immediate relevance in much of the present world. "Regime change" in Germany and Japan required a prolonged occupation and came out of a total war. These are not the circumstances of today. What we would see as a selfless or benevolent policy of democratization would be received as a policy of satellitization and clientelism. Even Palestinian reformers did not respond kindly to George W. Bush's call for a displacement or replacement of Arafat, whose waning power was bolstered by Bush's excommunication.

Here is where the other flaw lies: the misfit between this democratic imperialism (a fine contradiction in terms from the start) and the American polity. A strategy of frequent preemptive use of force and of domestic restrictions on public liberties necessitated by the global wars against evil is unlikely to get public support for very long, especially if the claims for prosperity and well-being are pushed behind the necessity of winning these wars (and today's would-be imperialists cannot simply rely on exploiting the resources of others). Sooner rather than later, the public would suffer from battle fatigue, especially if its officials continue to explain simultaneously that the United States is the most powerful nation in history and that it is the most threatened. A world order based on American might but whose imperial master has little enthusiasm for peacekeeping operations and little patience with nation building would be doomed. A world order, to have a chance of stability and especially if it is threatened by pervasive terrorism, would require among its states a code of cooperation, rules of behavior and engagement (as during the Cold War), and restraints in order not to appear even more threatening than the enemies they hope to defeat by a mix of violence and incantations. But, alas, all the new exceptionalism offers is a mix of force and faith—a huge force that is often not usable or counterproductive and a grandiose faith in the appeal of an American model that is a cause of resentment as well as of admiration (and envy, closer to the former than to the latter). Taming a tempestuous world, overcoming its uncertainties, by military power and a variety of bribes would be insufficiently effective abroad and increasingly unacceptable at home.

V.

Iraq was seen by the new exceptionalists as the best place to test the new doctrine: it had a horrid regime, a record of aggressions and of violations of UN demands, and—we were told—a patient and relentless quest for weapons of mass destruction. What better case could be found? If the United States should succeed, even alone (or with only Tony Blair), in destroying Saddam and his arsenal, what a wonderful lever for transforming the whole Middle East, for furthering modernization in the Muslim world, for assuring the victory in that world of the moderates over the rabid, and for a settlement of the Israeli–Palestinian issue on terms more favorable to Israel than those that Barak had appeared to offer Arafat or those that Clinton had offered at Taba? What Mark Danner has called "a vision of great sweep and imagination: comprehensive, prophetic, evangelical—. . . wholly foreign to the modesty of 'containment'" (which was the "ideology of a status quo power") signals a determination "to remake the world" and to deal with the "evil of terror" by "making new the entire region from which it springs."[8] It may be this vision that inspired the new exceptionalists to focus on Iraq, whereas an attack on North Korea does not have the same potential for transforming a whole unstable and dangerous area. Nor does it have oil, certainly a potent factor in the drive to oust Saddam at a time when the Saudi alliance is in trouble. But what if the risks exceed the expected gains?

That Saddam Hussein was an evil man and a threat to his neighbors and to U.S. interests is undeniable. But was it a threat that called for and justified preventive action? What were the risks of acting now? Were there alternatives worth trying?

Iraq's alleged arsenal of weapons of mass destruction and quest for nuclear arms were worrisome but not unique. Saddam was not suicidal and was much more likely to resort to these if attacked, by us, against either U.S. forces or Israel. We hesitate to "preempt" against North Korea because it could incinerate Seoul. Indeed, we hesitate to impose on it sanctions comparable to those we apply to Iraq because North Korea could respond by accelerating its nuclear program. Iraq, "as far as nuclear weapons are concerned, is much less of a threat now than it was in 1991."[9] If Saddam had still had weapons of mass destruction, our attempt to eliminate him and his weapons might well have provoked the disaster we were saying we wanted to prevent. We contained the Soviet Union, its huge army, and its enormous weapons for almost fifty years.

Indeed, the risks of such an attempt were very high. The case against it was both political and moral. The burden of proof lay on those who told us that we'd win easily, that his regime would crumble, and that democracy would then prevail in a liberated nation. Even if official optimism was based on more than wishful thinking (remember Vietnam!), the aftermath of victory was likely to be awesome—and so it proved to be—war was fought on false pretenses: the intelligence services' misinformation about weapons of terror, and the government's assertions about links between Saddam and al-Qaeda. The opposition to Saddam's regime, in Iraq and among the exiles who returned, both Shiite and Kurdish, remained divided. The Sunnis, who had supported and been favored by Saddam, have remained hostile and provided the bulk of the insurrection of 2004 and 2005. Despite two sets of elections, Iraq is still devoid of experience in democratic rule and traditions. A U.S. administration with deep doubts about nation building and very little help from other nations has been stuck with running a vast Muslim country racked by internal ethnic and religious divisions and aspirations for revenge. This has fostered more anti-Americanism and terrorism in the Muslim world. Indeed, the unilateralism of the administration risked, if the United States acted alone, shaking many of our carefully built alliances—in Europe and in the Middle East. If we wanted them to last and to help, our interest required that we concentrate on the Israeli–Palestinian issue and on the "war" on terrorism *before* we turned on Iraq (indeed, for some of the hawks in the administration, one of the attractions of an early war on Iraq was that it would postpone and render even more difficult an evenhanded solution of the Palestinian problem).

Our unilateralists tell us that a superpower does not need to have its hands tied by international agreements and the United Nations. What they forget is that, as in the war on terrorism, we cannot achieve any of our goals alone and that it was the United States—the dominant power after 1945—that had the wisdom of understanding this. An order founded on force and American beliefs alone does not create legitimacy or guarantee effectiveness, and it instigates anti-Americanism.

It is said that critics of a U.S. attack on Iraq fail to understand "the moral clarity" the president wants to impose on world politics. It is argued that Hussein's regime gives us a moral foundation for action. In Bryan Hehir's words, which have inspired the paragraphs that follow, "The invocation of moral reasoning for any contemplated policy decisions is to be welcomed as long as the complexity of moral issues is given adequate attention. Moral reasoning can indeed support military action, at times obligate such action. It also, equally importantly, can restrain or deny legitimacy to the use of force. To invoke the moral factor is to submit to the full range of its discipline."

The proposed strategy had three characteristics pertinent to its moral character. It was proposed as a preemptive strike, an intervention, and a unilateral action. Each characteristic raises serious moral questions. Preemption is morally conceivable but only within the most stringent limits. The case against it lies in the need to legitimate the use of force only in the most extreme conditions. Self-defense is the most obvious case, but the arguments proposing that a presumptive attack on Iraq met the self-defense standard were thin. Eroding the restraints against preemption—especially in the policy of the world's most powerful state—is a dubious moral move. Deterrence is more complex today, as the president has argued. But maintaining deterrence rather than preemption as an international standard is of the highest moral and legal importance.

There is a solid case for expanding moral legitimation of military action in cases of humanitarian intervention (Somalia, Rwanda, Kosovo), but the abiding value of the principle of nonintervention must be recognized and protected. Its basic role is to preserve order among sovereign states that acknowledge no higher political authority. Action against Iraq is clearly not a case—after many years of Hussein's tyranny—of humanitarian intervention. It was not comparable to the overthrow of the Taliban: Saddam's links with al-Qaeda are unconvincing. It was classic Great Power intervention, the principal case that nonintervention was meant to restrain. Like deterrence, nonintervention is designed to produce a conservative pattern of world politics, giving primacy to order and restraint. Preemptive military intervention, save in the most extreme cases, erodes basic principles of international order.

Finally, a unilateral intervention, undertaken without authorization and with little or no allied support, intensified the moral and legal problem. Authorization for the use of force, embodied in the UN Charter, is an extension of the moral principle that force should not be invoked quickly or easily. Unilateralism, however much lauded as the prerogative of a Great Power by supporters of a preemptive strike, in fact omits other meanings of Great Power responsibility. Great Powers set precedents in world politics; hence, each choice they make must be measured by the consequences of the precedent they set. Eroding deterrence, nonintervention, and authorization in one stroke is at least morally reckless.

There was an alternative to America's acting as the self-appointed policeman and promoter of "regime change" (a daunting task in areas unfamiliar with democracy and something of a potential boomerang for a country like the United States, many of whose allies are highly dubious regimes whose support Washington needs). It was a collective, UN-supported policy of containment, entailing a strong border-monitoring system and the return of weapons inspectors to Iraq. Indeed, instead of acting alone and justifying military action by the risk of future Iraqi aggression, the United States ought to have pleaded for collective enforcement of past UN resolutions and the fulfillment by Iraq of obligations it had accepted after the Gulf War (i.e., the dismantling of weapons of mass destruction), to be followed by a lifting of sanctions. The United States, in other words, should have presented itself not as the lone sheriff but as the trustee of the society of states. The greatest chance of success in the task of eliminating Iraq's arsenal lay not in attacking Saddam but in creating a coalition on behalf of the objectives most states had subscribed to—*not* in acting alone, entangled in difficulties with allies and encumbered by the Israeli–Palestinian issue. The administration, obviously divided, seemed to have begun to understand this by going to the Security Council in September 2002, but it still insisted on preserving the possibility of unilateral action either if the United Nations didn't meet American demands or if the Iraqis made the inspections impossible.

The zealots who celebrate America's might and its benevolent imperialism forget that world order requires more than force, that a modern "empire" needs a consensus of states, and that it undermines its leadership by acting as a bully or a spoiler. As for eliminating evil regimes and leaders, especially when their successors might turn out to be no better, it is a form of arrogance the wiser conservatives and liberals in our past (and today) have always warned us against.[10]

VI.

Empire—or the dream of empire—has invariably gone to the heads of the imperialists. The dream of Wilsonian missionaries, deeply suspicious of any force other than that of world public opinion, still inspires many international agencies and nongovernmental organizations. The dream of a benevolent empire sustained by an illusion of the world's gratitude but resting in fact only on the opinion of its own establishment and on a determination to avoid clear obligations shows how wide the gap has become between America's ever more flattering self-image and the image of the United States abroad, even in countries so pro-American for so long as Germany and Britain. Given the fact of America's preponderance in many forms of power, hard and soft (to use Joseph Nye's useful distinction[11]), the United States is bound to remain the most important state actor in the world. But there is a major difference between a leader and an empire: "The choice is between authoritarian, if not tyrannical rule tempered by anarchic resistance, and hegemony tempered by law, by concert and by consent."[12] The Bush administration remains a puzzle, with grandiose ideas floating over many improvisations. It has a State Department that still believes that imperial power can be maintained only if accompanied by a measure of reciprocity, even if it is partially illusory or contrived, in its obligations and dealings with others. It has, in the Pentagon and the White House, the new exceptionalists whose vision is one of an American worldwide "mission civilisatrice" with Roman Empire or Prussian methods. And it has a president who talks mainly like the latter but often acts more cautiously. Maybe, as Andrew J. Balevich has written, "no one is really in charge; ours is an Empire without an Emperor,"[13] given the domestic restraints on the presidency. Such an empire functioning not by direct rule over others but in a world of states of all kinds faces a Sisyphean task. It is not reassuring, either for Americans with little desire to be the twenty-first-century Romans or Britons or for the foreign tribes. It is time to remember Vietnam. Nevertheless, there is no reason to believe that the lessons of Iraq will be more potent than those of Vietnam. Even if the recent form of exceptionalism—unilateral and militaristic—recedes, traditional views of American uniqueness in power and in vision and in attractiveness and in "can-do-ism" are still well represented all over the political class. It is time to reread Thucydides.[14]

NOTES

Chapter 12 was published in Michael Ignatieff, ed., *American Exceptionalism and Human Rights* (Princeton, N.J.: Princeton University Press, 2005).

1. See Stanley Hoffmann, *Gulliver's Troubles* (New York: McGraw-Hill, 1968), pt. 2.
2. See David Armstrong, "Dick Cheney's Song of America," *Harper's Magazine* (October 2002): 78–83.
3. See Robert Kagan, "Power and Weakness," *Policy Review* 113. Kagan also mocks France's "punching far above his weight class" (*Washington Post*, November 3, 2002, B07). What would, in 1940–1945, de Gaulle have obtained for France if he hadn't "punched above its weight class"? Can the United States today, with all its power, really dominate the world?
4. See W. Michael Reisman, "The United States and International Institutions," *Survival* (winter 1999–2000): 62–80, at 63, 66–71, and 75.
5. See Pierre Hassner, *The United States: The Empire of Force or the Force of Empire*, Chaillot Papers No. 54 (Paris: European Union Institute for Security Studies, 2002), 41 ff.
6. Hassner, *The United States*, 43.
7. Charles Maier, "An American Empire?," *Harvard Magazine* (November–December 2002): 20–31.
8. Mark Danner, "The Struggles of Democracy and Empire," *New York Times*, op-ed, October 9, 2002, A31.
9. Norman Dombey, "What Has He Got?," *London Review of Books* 24, no. 20, October 17, 2002.
10. For another critical evaluation of the Iraq policy of the administration, see John Lewis Gaddis, "A Grand Strategy," *Foreign Policy* (November–December 2002): 50–57.

11. See Joseph S. Nye Jr., *The Paradox of American Power: Why the World's Only Superpower Can't Go It Alone* (Oxford: Oxford University Press, 2002).

12. Pierre Hassner, "Definitions, Doctrines, Divergences," *The National Interest* 69 (fall 2002): 34.

13. Andrew J. Balevich, "New Rome, New Jerusalem," *Wilson Quarterly* (summer 2002): 56.

14. For more on Iraq, see my *Gulliver Unbound* (Boulder, Colo.: Rowman & Littlefield, 2004).

• *13* •

"Why Don't They Like Us?"

I.

$\mathscr{I}$t wasn't its innocence that the United States lost on September 11, 2001. It was its naïveté. American officials and citizens have tended to believe that, in the eyes of others, the United States looked very much like the boastful clichés that were propagated first during the Cold War (especially under Reagan) and later during the Clinton administration. We had been seen, we thought, as the champions of freedom against fascism and communism; as the advocates of decolonization, economic development, and social progress; and as the technical innovators whose mastery of technology, science, and advanced education was going to unify the world. Some officials and academics explained that U.S. hegemony was the best thing for a troubled world and would, unlike past hegemonies, last not only because there were no challengers strong enough to steal the crown but above all because we were benign rulers who threatened no one. In recent months, the debate in the United States had not pitted the satisfied celebrants of the single superpower against those who warned about what C. Wright Mills once called the national celebration, against the perils of self-righteousness and the pitfalls of self-satisfaction. It had been a debate between those who thought that even a mighty superpower needed to rely on "soft power"—the power of attraction and persuasion—in order to enlist other actors for the task of managing world order and those who thought, like the blunt and shrill John Bolton, that we should essentially count on our might and give up our illusions about international norms and multilateral entanglements: if we led, others would follow. It is this debate that has dominated the discussion, in and out of the government, even after September 11. It is fundamentally a dispute about the best way of being the hegemon—a prudent way versus a rash one.

What, however, we have averted our eyes from is looking at the hegemon's clay feet, at what might both neutralize our vaunted soft power and

133

undermine our hard power. Like the swarming insects that come to light under a fallen tree, all those who doubt about, dislike, or distrust the hegemon have suddenly been exposed, much to our horror and disbelief. Having become a major actor in world affairs at a time when the dominant European powers were weakened by their "thirty years' war" (1914–1945) and when we faced a rival that seemed to stand for everything we had been fighting against—tyranny, terror, ideological brainwashing—we thought that we would benefit from standing for both liberty and stability (as we still do in much of eastern Europe). We were not sufficiently marinated in history to know that, through the ages, nobody—or almost nobody—has ever loved a hegemon. Those who had to gain by serving the hegemon's purposes and receiving his favors in exchange often sneered at him as a way of preserving their self-esteem. These were bargains of mutual accommodation in which affection or sympathy has little part. Past hegemons tended to be quite realistic in this respect, from the days of Rome to the age of Great Britain. They wanted to be obeyed or, as in the case of France, admired. They rarely wanted to be loved. This, however, was what the Americans expected. They were bound to be disappointed; gratitude is not an emotion one associates with the behavior of states. Indeed, those who owe their tranquillity or their prosperity to a greater power are often the least grateful because they massage their self-esteem by counting the reasons for feeling superior to their benefactor. As a combination of *High Noon* sheriff and proselytizing missionary, the United States has tended, unlike the United Kingdom, to expect gratitude and affection.

This is an old story. What makes the present one so original is a double set of factors. First, there is the collapse of the so-called Westphalian world, the world of sovereign states, the universe of Hans Morgenthau's and Henry Kissinger's realism. The unpopularity of the hegemonic power has been heightened to incandescence by two aspects of this collapse. One is the irruption of the publics, or the masses, in international affairs. Foreign policy is no longer, as Raymond Aron had written in *Peace and War*, the closed domain of the soldier and the diplomat. Domestic publics—their interest groups, religious organizations, and ideological chapels—either dictate or constrain the imperatives and preferences that the governments fight for. This puts the hegemon in a difficult position: he has to work with governments that often represent very little and cannot engage in fishing expeditions of public support abroad without alienating leaders whose cooperation he needs. The United States paid heavily for not having had enough contacts with the opposition to the shah of Iran in the 1970s. It discovers today that there is an abyss between our official allies in Pakistan, Saudi Arabia, Egypt, or Indonesia and the publics of these countries. Diplomacy in a world where the masses, so to speak, stayed indoors was a much easier game.

The collapse of the barrier between domestic and foreign affairs in the state system is now accompanied by a disease that attacks the state system itself. Many of the "states" that are members of the United Nations are pseudostates, with shaky or shabby institutions, no basic consensus either on values or on procedures among their heterogeneous components, and no sense of national identity. The hegemon, in addition to having to suffer the hostility of either the regimes of certain countries (Cuba, Iraq, North Korea) or that of the publics in "friendly" countries, can easily become the target of some of the factions that fight each other in disintegrating countries or the pawn in their quarrels, which range over such increasingly borderless issues as drug traffic, arms trade, money laundering, and crime. Nineteenth-century great powers imposed their order, their institutions, on huge parts of the world. The current hegemon is threatened by the disorder and the institutional vacuum in many of these parts.

Today's hegemon suffers from the volatility and turbulence of a global system in which ethnic or religious or ideological sympathies have become transnational and in which groups or individuals uncontrolled by states can act on their own. This explains only in part why the hegemon is easily unpopular, disliked by all those who thrive on shaking the powers that would contain them or on resisting the vision of a political, economic, and social order that the hegemon would like to impose. What makes the hegemon especially vulnerable—not so paradoxically—is the fact that the "American Empire" offers a historically unique combination of assets and liabilities. One has to go back to the Roman Empire to find a comparable set of resources. The United States *is* the only superpower. Britain, France, and Spain had to operate in multipolar systems. The United States is at the top of the holders of military power, economic and technological power, and cultural and scientific influence. While each of the arenas of world affairs—strategy, trade, investments, environmental issues, human rights, and so on—has a certain autonomy, the capacity of the United States to link them all, to provide a framework of institutions and of rules for the games played in each arena, and to block alternative frameworks and rules is unique.

But if America's means are huge, the limits of its power are also vast. Abroad, the United States, unlike Rome, cannot simply impose its will by force or through satellites. The world we live in is not "uni-multipolar," as Samuel P. Huntington has suggested. It is "uni-multipolar" insofar as the hegemon has to take such states or groupings as Russia, China, the European Union, and India into account. But it is also multistate insofar as small "rogue" states can defy the hegemon (remember Vietnam), and it is anarchic in the sense that chaos can easily result from the huge new role of nonstate actors. At home, the reluctance of Americans to take on the Herculean tasks of policing, "nation building," democratizing autocracies, and providing environmental protection and economic growth for billions of human beings provides both resentments among those who believe that all these tasks require America's resources and attention and the hostility of those who discover that one can count on American presence and leadership only when America's material interests are gravely threatened. (It is not surprising that the "defense of the national interest" approach of realism was developed for a multipolar world. In an empire, as well as in a bipolar system, almost anything can be described as a vital interest since even peripheric disorders can unravel the superpower[s]'s eminence.) Also at home, the infinite complexities of the American foreign policy decision-making process result, alternatively or simultaneously, in disappointments abroad when these twists and turns thwart policies on which others counted (Kyoto Protocol, International Criminal Court, and so on) and in persuading enemies that the United States is basically incapable of pursuing long-term policies consistently (e.g., in the Balkans).

II.

None of that means, of course, that the United States has no friends in the world. The Europeans, both western and eastern, have not forgotten the liberating role played by Americans in the war against Hitler and in the Cold War. Israel remembers the way in which President Truman sided with the founders of the Zionist state and all the help received since then. The democratization of postwar Germany and Japan has been a huge success. The Marshall Plan and "Point Four" were revolutionary initiatives. The decisions to resist aggression in Korea and in Kuwait were farsighted and so on.

But Americans have a tendency to overlook the dark sides of their course (except on the protesting left, which is thus constantly accused of being un-American or of hating America), perhaps because of a conception of international affairs in terms of crusades between good and evil, which entails formidable pressures for unanimity. It is not surprising that the decade that followed the Gulf War was marked both by nostalgia for the clear days of the Cold War and by a lot of floundering and hesitating in a world without an overwhelming foe. When we look at anti-Americanism today—without, at first, judging its fairness and validity—we need to begin by distinguishing between those who attack the United States for what it does or fails to do and those who attack it for what it is (some, like the Islamic fundamentalists and terrorists, do both).

The main criticisms of American behavior have mostly been around for a long time. Perhaps the main one is the contrast between the ideology of universal liberalism propagated by the American government and establishment and policies that have all too often consisted of supporting and sometimes of installing singularly authoritarian and repressive regimes. (One reason why these policies often elicited more reproaches than Soviet control over satellites was that, as time went by, Stalinism became more and more cynical and the gap between words and deeds far less wide than in the United States. One no longer expected much from Moscow.) There is no need here to recount what was appalling—in Guatemala, Panama, El Salvador, and Chile; in San Domingo in 1965; in the Greece of the colonels; in Pakistan; in the Philippines of Marcos; in Indonesia after 1965; in the shah's Iran; in Saudi Arabia; in Zaire, and, of course, in South Vietnam. All this has fed various forms of anti-Americanism and has been reinforced by the inconsistency of American behavior: the enemies of these regimes were shocked by American support for them, and those whom we supported were turned into enemies (or at least bitterly disappointed) when our cost-benefit analysis changed and we dropped those who had relied on us (the shah, Mobutu, and Thieu at the end; the Haitian military when we restored Aristide; and so on). These twists and turns of Machiavellianism occurring behind a Wilsonian facade have alienated many clients as well as potential friends.

A second grievance concerns America's frequent unilateralism and the difficult relation between the United States and the United Nations. For many of the smaller countries—and some not so small (India)—the United Nations is, for all its flaws, the only universal provider of legitimacy and both the essential agency of cooperation and the protector of its members' sovereignty. The tendency of the U.S. Congress in recent years and of the administration in 2001 to act as if the United States could export its legislation abroad; impose sanctions or even bombings (of Iraq), for a variety of reasons, all by itself; veto treaties it doesn't like even when American objections had been met; and conduct military operations outside the United Nations, as in Kosovo, has been very badly received by a great number of critics abroad—even when, as in the case of Kosovo, the cause itself was not seen as unjust. The way in which U.S. diplomacy has "insulted" the UN system, sometimes by ignoring it and sometimes by rudely imposing its views and policies on it, has also been costly in terms of foreign support.

Third, the sorry record of the United States in the area of international development has been a source of dissatisfaction abroad both because the U.S. interest in and financial contributions for narrowing the gap between the rich and the poor have declined since the end of the Cold War and because international institutions such as the International Monetary Fund and the World Bank, dominated by the United States, have often dictated (as before and during the Asian economic crisis of the mid-1990s) financial policies that turned out disastrous either when they were too lax or when they were too restrictive. The fact that the greatest amount of foreign aid has gone to Israel and to an Egypt at peace with Israel but incapable or unwilling to use U.S. assistance to raise the conditions of living in a country with a growing population and growing inequalities has not helped either.

The last grievance about U.S. behavior is, of course, about American support of Israel. Much of the world—not only the Arab or the Islamic world—considers U.S. policy there as biased, and despite occasional American attempts at evenhandedness, notices that the Palestinians remain under occupation, that the Israeli settlements continue to expand, and that the Arab terrorism that Arafat could not completely control is condemned more harshly than the killings of Palestinians by the Israeli army or by licensed assassination squads. This is not the place to go into this long, sad, and intractable conflict, but objectively one can't help but note that in the Israeli–U.S. relationship the smaller and dependent power has been more successful in circumscribing the superpower's freedom of maneuver than the United States has been at getting Israel to enforce the old UN resolutions adopted after the 1967 war. And subjectively, many in the Arab world (and outside) have attributed this to the power of the "Jewish lobby" in the United States. They have noted that President George W. Bush, after having proposed a "road map" for a settlement (one that left, like the Oslo agreement of 1993, all the tough issues for the end of the road), accepted Prime Minister Sharon's view of the settlements on the West Bank as "facts on the ground." While the (unilaterally decided) evacuation of Gaza by Israel and the reinsertion of the European Union into the diplomatic game (for the monitoring of the newly Palestinian Gaza) have been signs of progress, there is little doubt that Sharon intends to pursue a unilateral separation between Israel and the Palestinians that will, if carried out, leave them, on the West Bank, both walled in and reduced to a shrunken and disjointed piece of land.

We have thus reached anti-Americanism caused not by specific policies but by dislike of America's values, institutions, and society—and of their enormous impact abroad. Indeed, for many of those who share this dislike, America represents the vanguard, definer, and promoter of globalization. Here we have to be careful. The Islamic fundamentalists of al-Qaeda, whose hatred of the United States is unsurpassed, make excellent use of the communication and information technologies that are so essential to the spread of globalization (as Ayatollah Khomeini had already done almost thirty years ago). But attitudes are sharply divided. There are those whose most eloquent spokesman is Osama bin Laden, for whom America and the globalization it promotes relentlessly through free trade and the institutions it controls represents evil (because it symbolizes the domination of the Christian Jewish infidels for some or the triumph of pure secularism for others): a society of materialism, laxness, corruption in all its forms (including sexual), fierce selfishness, and so on (we know the charges well, if only because they are an exacerbated form of right-wing anti-Americanism in nineteenth- and twentieth-century Europe). But there are also those who, while accepting the inevitability of globalization and eager to benefit from it and while preferring a society of individual initiative to the rigid hierarchy of feudal and traditional societies, are incensed by the contrast between America's promises and the realities of American life—by the lack of sufficient social protection, by the vast pockets of poverty amidst plenty, by racial discrimination, by the role of money in politics, and by the domination of elites whose role in business, in government, or the media is denied or minimized by the official ideology of equal opportunity—charges we again know well because they are an exacerbated version of the left-wing anti-Americanism still powerful in western Europe.

The attacks on America that focus on what it is (or is seen to be) draw a picture of the United States that could be called the underdog's vision. On the one hand, the United States is condemned for being an evil force because its dynamics and dynamism make it naturally and endlessly imperialistic, imposing its form of society on others, its culture (often seen as debased) on respectable older cultures, its flawed version of democracy on other regimes, and its unbalanced conception of human rights on more communitarian and more socially concerned approaches. It is also seen as a brutal society, both at home, where the poor and the jobless are treated as if it was all their fault, and abroad, where the United States often acts as a bully ready to use all means, including overwhelming force, against those who resist it: hence Hiroshima, the horrors of Vietnam, the rage against Iraq, and the war on Afghanistan.

On the other hand, the underdogs draw hope from their conviction that the giant has clay feet. They look at American society as one that cannot tolerate high casualties and prolonged sacrifices and discomforts, whose impatience with protracted and undecisive conflicts should encourage others to be patient and relentless in their challenges and assaults. They look at American foreign policy as one that is often incapable of overcoming these and of sticking to a course that is fraught with high risks—as against Saddam Hussein at the end of the Gulf War, as in the flight from Lebanon after the terrorist attacks of 1982, as in Somalia in 1993, and as in the attempts to strike back at bin Laden in the Clinton years. Thus, America stands condemned not because its enemies necessarily hate our freedoms but because they resent what they see as its Darwinian aspects and often because they despise what they see as the softness at its core. Those who, on our side, note and celebrate America's power of attraction, its openness to immigrants and refugees, and the uniqueness of a society based on common principles rather than on ethnicity or on an old culture are not wrong. But many of those who, for instance, come to study here and fall in love with the gifts of American education return home, where the attraction often fades, and those who stay sometimes feel that the price they have to pay in order to assimilate and to be accepted is too high.

<h2 style="text-align:center">III.</h2>

This long catalog of grievances and complaints obviously needs to be picked apart. They vary in intensity; different cultures, countries, and parties emphasize different parts of it, and they are often wildly excessive and unfair. But we are not dealing here with purely rational arguments; we are dealing with emotional responses to a condition: responses to the omnipresence of the hegemon, to the sense many people outside the United States have that the United States dominates their lives both when America acts as a force of change that destroys old habits, institutions, and protections, filling the void with the gale of the market, and when Washington buttresses and preserves regimes seen by their subjects as oppressive, corrupt, and incapable of helping the underprivileged and of providing an adequate future to the young who experience the bitter dashing of the hopes they had put in getting educated.

What we find around the world is an anti-Americanism that rests on both amalgamation and scapegoating. Complaints that are often contradictory (America has neglected us or dropped us when we no longer needed to be courted, but America's attentions are corrupting, and America doesn't care about how they are distributed) end as a gestalt of resentment that strikes Americans as absurd: we are damned, for instance, both when we fail to intervene to protect Muslims in the Balkans and when we use force to do so. And the extraordinary wealth of roles America plays in the world, underlined by American boasting and, especially recently, by American unilateralism, ensures that many wrongs caused by local regimes and societies will be blamed on the United States—it is no coincidence that many terrorists of September 11 came from America's protégés, Saudi Arabia and Egypt. Thus, we end up being seen as responsible for anything bad our "protectorates" do—and for much our allies do, as when Arabs incensed by racism and joblessness *in France* take up bin Laden's cause or talk about *American* violence against the Palestinians. Bin Laden's extraordinary appeal and prestige in the Muslim world do not mean that his metaphysical nihilism (to use Michael

Ignatieff's term) is fully endorsed by all those who chant his name. It is partly based on the fact that he symbolizes the success of this bloody Robin Hood in inflicting pain and humiliation on the only superpower.

He doesn't represent only revenge for what he called "eighty years of humiliation and disgrace" imposed on "the Islamic nation." He also represents something that had marked the twentieth century from World War I to the fall of the Soviet Union: the need for people who, rightly or not, feel collectively humiliated and individually in distress and despair to attach themselves to a savior, to entrust their fates to him, and to avert their eyes from the most unsavory of his deeds. (American leaders ought to be careful not to use the kind of insulting and derogatory language toward him and his followers that would only offend not just his brand of fanatics but many other Arabs or Muslims as well.) This need to replace one's own feeble and disoriented brain with the brain of a charismatic and single-minded leader was at the core of fascism and of communism. With the fall of the most essential form of the latter, Soviet communism, many young people in the Muslim world who might have once turned to it—and many who would have been deterred from it by Islam—were ripe for Islamic fundamentalism and terrorism—or not only the young and the less educated (although they are always the foot soldiers of political or religious totalitarianism).

What we find in such movements is always the same psychological reductionism: the search for simple explanations (and what is simpler than the machinations of the Jews and the evils of America?) and a highly selective approach to history. (The fundamentalists of Islam are convinced that the United States and the United Kingdom are persistent enemies of the Arabs. They remember the promises made by the British to the Arabs in World War I and the imposition of British or French imperialism after 1918 rather than the support the United States gave to anticolonialists in French North Africa in the late 1940s and in the 1950s. They remember British opposition to and American reluctance toward intervention in Bosnia before Srebenica but forget about NATO's actions to save Bosnian Muslims in 1995, to help Albanians in Kosovo in 1999, and to preserve and improve Albanians' rights in Macedonia in 2001.) Such reductionism is of course fostered and developed by indoctrination either through the controlled media and the schools of a totalitarian regime or through the religious schools, the conspiracy rumors, and the propaganda of fundamentalism.

IV.

There is very little Americans can do about the most extreme and violent forms of anti-American hatred—except fight them in ways that do not strengthen their appeal. But they can try to limit this appeal by dealing with those grievances that have justification, even though this would entail a drastic reorientation of U.S. policy not only in the Palestinian–Israeli conflict but also in helping to establish, in the developing world, the kind of social safety net that even celebrators of the market and of globalization such as Thomas Friedman deem indispensable (rather than counting simplistically on trickle-down expectations that are based more on faith than on experience). It would mean prodding one's allies and protégés toward a gradual democratization of their regimes, not condoning violations of essential rights that can only, in the long run, breed more terrorists and anti-Americans. It would mean a return to internationalist policies and, in our approach to international agencies, paying far greater attention to the representatives of the developing world—making fairness prevail over arrogance. It would also mean paying greater attention, wherever the regimes are undemocratic, to the needs and frustrations of the people than to their governments' demands.

We are in the midst of a clash between foreign perceptions and misperceptions of the United States and of an American self-image derived more from what Reinhold Niebuhr would have called pride than from reality. If we want to affect those external perceptions (which will be very difficult in extreme cases), we need to readjust our self-image. This means getting more curious again about the outside world, which our media, after the Cold War, have tended to downgrade, and it means listening to views we may find outrageous, both for the kernel of truth that may be present in them and for the stark realities that may account for these views' excesses, the realities of fear, poverty, hunger, disease, social hopelessness, and injustice that are as important as the strategic realities we have tended to concentrate on.

A terrorism aimed at the innocent and using old and new means of mass destruction is of course intolerable. Safety precautions and the difficult task of eradicating it are not enough. If we want to limit its appeal, we need to keep our eyes and ears open to conditions abroad and confront our self-image with our actions. There is nothing un-American about this. We should not meet the Manichaeanism of our foes with a Manichaeanism of self-righteousness. Indeed, self-criticism and self-examination have been the not-so-secret weapon of America's historical success. It is those who demand that we close ranks not only against murderers but also against shocking opinions and emotions, against dissenters at home and critics abroad, who do a disservice to America.

NOTE

Chapter 13 was published in *The American Prospect*, November 19, 2001.

· *14* ·

After 9/11/2001: The Pitfalls of War

I.

$\mathcal{A}$s soon as the shock of the terror attacks on New York and Washington was felt, commentators began stating that September 11, 2001, marked the beginning of a new era in world affairs. It is a misleading interpretation of a stunning and horrible event. What was new was the demonstration that a small number of well-organized conspirators could cause thousands of victims in the "only superpower" and thus show that the United States was not any safer from attack than far less mighty nations. But the change of scale and the location of the targets do not represent a transformation of international relations. The terrorists brutally drew our attention to a phenomenon that had long been partly hidden from sight by the Cold War and by decoloniza-tion, two sagas that were quite traditional: an epic contest between two great powers and the troubled birth of a large number of (more or less shaky) new states. While these struggles went on, something drastically new was emerg-ing: a global society in which states were no longer the only—or even the essential—players. Insofar as they keep the appearance and trappings of sov-ereignty, the states are still, on the surface, the shapers of their foreign poli-cies. But unlike in the dominant model of world affairs taught to future academics, statesmen, and businessmen, states' goals are only partly "geopo-litical": territory, resources, security from rivals, prestige, and so on. Increas-ingly, states have had to take into account the demands and wishes of their people—jobs, welfare, ethnic or religious sympathies and hatreds, protection from internal or external wars, and so on. Governments that neglect such preferences and pressures do so at considerable peril. Nothing is purely domestic or purely international anymore.

Even more important has been the recent emergence of a global civil society, made of individuals and groups that operate across borders and whose decisions and acts sharply reduce the freedom of maneuver of governments:

multinational corporations, nongovernmental organizations, investors able to move their money at lightning speed from one stock market to another (and thus to shake up domestic currencies), but also terrorists. The distinction between state and civil society is of course artificial. Many of the components of the latter have among their goals the adoption by governments of measures aimed at satisfying their grievances, and few are the "private" actors who do not need and obtain financial or political support from the governments. But global civil society has suffered both from neglect by students of world affairs and from being even more unmanageable than a world of states with only fragmentary collective governance. The shock of monetary crises in the 1990s was fortunately not strong enough to destroy the world economy. The shock of September 11 has been so great because it resulted from an attack not by anonymous speculators on national currencies but by a small group of barely armed individuals on the national security and sense of confidence of the world's greatest power. Suddenly, rogue states lost their status as the greatest potential threat. A world of millions of private actors means a world of unlimited vulnerability.

This is, paradoxically, especially frightening for the country that has done most to destroy borders and walls and to shape a world market to promote freedom of communications, information, and movement: the United States. Americans have known, since the Vietnam War, that awesome firepower does not guarantee victory against a determined small nation. Unevenness in will compensated for inequality in economic and military might. The fact that American power was partly unusable (i.e., nuclear weapons) and partly ineffective when used was disturbing enough when the foe was a tiny state. It is even more disturbing to think that a few thousand terrorists may have the same effect: Gulliver no longer tied by Lilliputians but assaulted by clever gnats. The weapons of economic and military warfare (including for mass destruction) are now available not merely to states but to the peoples of the world as well.

II.

How do we cope? The Bush administration has shown a great deal of schizophrenia. On the one hand, it has declared war on terrorists and regimes that support them, thus evoking images of massive campaigns fueled by the huge American arsenal. And it has proclaimed that whoever does not support us will be considered to be against us. But on the other hand, this grand display of threats has been tempered by increasingly numerous references to the duration, complexity, and uncertainty of this war, to the nonmilitary requirements of it, to the fact that we expect certain states to support us for some tasks and other states for different ones. This schizophrenia reflects both division within the administration and the difficulties of the task.

The first question that comes to anyone's mind has still not been answered. Whom are we fighting? If it is the enterprise of Osama bin Laden, formidable as it may be, we risk finding that dismantling its network is likely to be a slow and frustrating task in this world without walls and that even successes in this struggle will not put an end to many other murderous forms of terrorism. To proclaim a war on terrorism in general, even if one means only "private" terrorist cells and forces, is ambitious indeed. For we need to distinguish among types of terrorists. Some have limited missions—those who see themselves as "freedom fighters" using the weapons of the weak, as in Sri Lanka or Northern Ireland, in Corsica or Chechnya, in Palestine, or in Sri Lanka or in the Basque province. It is hard to imagine the United States doing other countries' police or army work for them. It is the groups that have declared war on America or on the whole of the Judeo-Christian world that ought to be our targets.

There are many who ask also for war against states that serve as hosts and helpers of terrorists. Here again distinctions are essential. Are all the states in which terrorists operate their willing accomplices? In this case, the category includes states incapable of exerting control because they are too weak (Lebanon) or because they are insufficiently vigilant (the United States and many of its democratic allies). Should it be only the states that sheltered or aided bin Laden? This has, indeed, sent us into an Afghan quagmire of considerable proportions, causing a huge new exodus and creating revulsion among many Pakistanis. Should it be all those whom we have declared to be terrorist states, even if the links to bin Laden are hypothetical or dubious? This list includes states that have now promised to help us (Syria, Sudan) and enemies (Iraq) or semi-enemies (Iran) whose "punishment" could all too easily boomerang in terms of international support. Ridding the world of all rogues and terrorists is a dream that would be seen abroad as a demonstration of rabid imperialism. Modesty in goals is imperative.

The second question is that of the means of this war. The current emphasis on diversity of tactics is wise. Terrorism should be fought as a crime against the innocent, just as organized crime is at home. The patient collection of information, the silent penetration of cells, and the dismantling of the networks' communications (i.e., the instruments of police and counterintelligence) are likely to be more effective than military operations. These risk provoking both political damage, by weakening further regimes that would let us operate from their soil, and what is so annoyingly called collateral damage, that is, killing innocent victims, among whom the terrorists have learned to live. Indeed, the scope of our military means makes surprise attacks difficult. By the time our planes and forces arrive, the training camps will be empty. This was particularly the case in Afghanistan, as all past attackers have found out.

As Reverend J. Bryan Hehir has argued,[1] attacks that do not take every precaution against killing the innocent or destroying the infrastructure of the society in which the civilian population lives would be both immoral and supremely counterproductive. This brings one to the third question. How can we fight terrorism without undermining our position in a world where the support of other governments and peoples is essential? One reason for prudence in punishing governments that help terrorism is that, at best, it is their societies we will punish (and we'll fill the reservoir of their hostility) and, at worst, we'll be faced, after the collapse of those currently in power, with the formidable task of finding new leaders who will not appear as our puppets. Our choice of local allies during the Cold War days has often been sufficiently catastrophic to make one dubious about the kind of nation building or rebuilding we could undertake in areas we don't fully understand. After all, the Taliban was one of our (or the Central Intelligence Agency's) creatures not so long ago.

To command the often besieged governments of other countries to be with us, or else, makes sense only if they are in a position to be with us without committing suicide or reinforcing their internal enemies. Such a command may be less good at getting hostile or critical governments to side with us out of fear of American power than at getting friendly but frightened governments looking for a fence to sit on out of fear of their domestic foes.

III.

A last question is that of American unilateralism. Commentators may have announced its demise too soon. In a situation infinitely more complex than the one we faced when one pretty unpopular leader (Saddam Hussein) invaded and annexed a small Arab state, was the coalition that Secretary of State Powell was skillfully building being seen by all his colleagues in the government as a partnership in which our allies will not only provide various forms of support but also take part in the major decisions? As often before in NATO, we looked at our allies as junior partners of our firm, asked to supplement our forces and to pay for the common good.

There are two reasons to worry about this. One is that we have a large enough number of critics in the world to need and seek a seal of international legitimacy (especially at a time when Russia, as in 1990, is cooperative and

China discreetly nonhostile). This could have been provided by the UN Security Council. If ours is the cause of humanity, if terrorism against civilians is something that threatens everyone, if security from terror attacks is a universal public good, we should behave not as a country that seeks revenge for what it has endured and has the power to twist arms all around but as a country that seeks a broad mandate and accepts the norms and constraints of international law. The involvement of the United Nations would have had legal and practical advantages. Legally, the International Criminal Court (resisted so frivolously by American "sovereigntists") should be allowed to extend its jurisdiction to crimes against humanity committed by terrorists. Practically, a UN agency or office against terrorism could facilitate—especially among states that are not particularly friendly with one another yet have their own reasons to combat terrorism—exchanges of intelligence and modes of cooperation.

Another reason to resist the itch of unilateralism and of what I have elsewhere called bossism[2]—the use of international and regional institutions to impose our views—is that in order to succeed, the struggle against terrorists and the states that support them needs to begin with an adequate understanding of our adversaries' grievances, if only so as to allow us to shape a discriminating policy and to avoid acting in a self-destructive way. Reading newspapers and listening to public officials and commentators after September 11 was a disconcerting experience. While the media in friendly countries have, mostly without animosity, discussed why the United States is the target of so much hostility (not only in the Islamic world), in the United States the question has been dismissed, or the answer has been self-serving, simplistic, and summary (it's the virtues of democracy, of capitalism, or of an open society, which makes others envious).

It would be far better to realize that this hostility has many layers. Some of the terrorists and their supporters are religious fanatics who see in the United States, the West, and Israel a formidable machine for cultural subversion, political domination, and economic subjection. The kind of Islamic revanche that bin Laden sketches out in his statements is both so cosmic and so peculiar an interpretation of the Koran that there is very little one can do to rebut it but a great deal one can do to limit its appeal. This kind of an ethics of conviction feeds—like so many other forms of totalitarianism—on experiences of despair and humiliation. But there are more limited bills of indictment. Sometimes, the targets are corrupt or brutal regimes propped up by American economic and military assistance and presence. Sometimes there is solidarity with the Palestinians' demand for an end of occupation and, at last, genuine self-determination. Sometimes it is a sense of having been used and discarded (acute among many Pakistanis after the end of the war against the Soviet Union in Afghanistan) or a protest against the misery of refugees or continuing mass poverty in much of the developing world. It is easier to cope with arguments about American actions or omissions than with those that reject American values and institutions, and it is dangerous to confuse those different categories. We have tended, since the end of the Cold War, toward a form of self-congratulation that is grating for others: we are the "indispensable nation"; the carriers of a globalization that will bring peace, democracy, prosperity, and so on; the champions of an economic system that will eventually lift and spruce up all the boats; and the catalysts of world order. We have not been sufficiently sensitive to other peoples' fears for their cultures and to others' sense of shock at the inequities that come with capitalism and globalization.

None of this can justify the horrors of September 11. But we need to know why others sometimes feel threatened by us. We have been celebrating the solidity of our status as the dominant nation after the collapse of Soviet power and of the Soviet threat. There are, in terms of power, no rivals in sight, and benign American hegemony, we often say, provides a modicum of order without threatening anyone (indeed, our power of attraction, what Joseph Nye calls soft power, is unique). And yet one can both attract and repel. In conventional terms of power, we may be unbeatable, but we now know that those who feel threatened by us or annoyed by our self-righteous predominance can do us great harm. We need not only to protect ourselves better at home (instead of waiting for a decisive victory abroad) but also to understand why even nonterrorists sometimes feel smothered by America's cultural, economic, political, and military omnipresence.

Who will wage "America's new war"? The (mainly civilian) professionals of violence, or those who realize the limits of our power? A prudent policy would concentrate on the bin Laden networks of underground plotters and the financial manipulations that support them. It would use minimal military force only when the chances of success were good, aiming at isolating and neutralizing the Taliban regime rather than at immediately overthrowing it (and risking thereby a worsening of the sufferings of the Afghans)—unless it disintegrates through desertions and divisions. It would draw as much as possible on the expressed willingness of UN members to cooperate in actions against terrorism. But it would not let the present need for allies against it obliterate our efforts to combat human rights violations by regimes, for example, on Afghanistan's northern borders, whose repressiveness risks driving more of their victims into terrorism.

Such a policy would give diplomatic priority not only to coalition building but also to resuscitating the Israeli–Palestinian peace process. It would also show that, after the atrocities of September 11, we can listen both to the imperative of justice and to the views of others. It would avoid turning the lurid predictions of a "clash of civilizations" from a gloomy fantasy into a high risk. It could take advantage of the opportunity offered by the tragedy of September 11 to try to strengthen control over the most dangerous and elusive part of global civil society. But this should be done not only by states (in a porous world) or through interstate cooperation (always dependent on momentary circumstances) but also by international and regional agencies.

Some U.S. leaders have expressed verbal support for such a policy. Let us hope that they have the commitment, patience, and skill to make good on their words and will not plunge into military action that will kill innocent people. Let us also demand of them the intelligence and compassion to understand that beyond lining up allies against terror, the national interest means seeking partners in a quest for the many and differing solutions to the pursuit of life, liberty, and happiness in a bewildering world. We should now realize that we cannot safely enjoy these values at home if others, abroad, cannot hope for a share of them.

October 3, 2001

EPILOGUE

It is, of course, too early to predict the scope of victory in "America's new war." But it is not too early to point to some of the paradoxes and dilemmas that have marked its beginning and to wonder about its immediate and long-term effects.

America's war in Afghanistan was dictated by the need to react to the horrors of September 11 and by the felt obligation not to appease an implacable and murderous enemy—hence George W. Bush's choice of targets. One was bin Laden's al-Qaeda, and the other was the Taliban regime that had given him a base. This second objective was meant to show that harboring and supporting terrorism does not pay and that the punishment for doing so would be extremely severe. The problem with the first goal—capturing or killing bin Laden and dismantling his network—isn't only the difficulty of finding him and the scope and resilience of his organization but also that there is no good reason to believe that the elimination of bin Laden and the demise of al-Qaeda in Afghanistan would remove the threat that terrorism creates for the ordinary people it attacks all over the world. Obtaining a drastic reduction in terrorist acts would require a coherent effort to address at least the specific and often justified grievances that both drive humiliated and despairing people into terrorism and provide sympathy and support. Such a program would obviously have to take place over a long period, and its goals would never be completely achieved. The "crushing humiliation that has infected the third-world countries," the "feeling of impotence deriving from degradation," as the Turkish novelist Orhan Pamuk put it,[2] run so deep, and the remedies are so elusive, that one cannot have much hope of ultimate and definitive success.

This may be among the main reasons why the war shifted, during the first phase, from settling accounts with bin Laden to settling accounts with the Taliban. It thus soon moved from the uncharted terrain of war between a superpower and a private warrior-prophet to the familiar one of a war between states. Battering the Taliban seemed easier than getting rid of al-Qaeda. The desire for quick retribution led to a policy that aims at more than inflicting heavy losses on the military might of the Taliban. To discourage states from sponsoring terrorists, American officials concluded that the Taliban had to be removed from power. At first our adversary proved far tougher and far more resistant to bombing than we had thought. And our pounding resulted in civilian casualties and hence more anti-Americanism in a world where many of those who do not endorse terrorist mass murder are also repelled by the spectacle of a huge power beating on a small one, already devastated by thirty years of war and famine. When American strategy shifted from the bombing of the Taliban's rather feeble infrastructure to an attack on its frontline forces and used its sensors, its drones, and the information provided by it Special Forces to find appropriate targets and to coordinate its efforts with those of the Northern Alliance, the Taliban crumbled first in the north and soon in most of Afghanistan's provinces. The sense of liberation manifested in the cities the Taliban had ruled and oppressed mitigated the intensity of opposition to the United States in the Muslim world.

Leaving the Taliban battered but in place would have looked timid to much of the American public as well as to some of our allies and to some of the countries we wanted to understand that they had to choose between being with us or against us. It would also have resulted in preserving a safe haven for bin Laden's organization. However, getting rid of the Taliban raised two formidable problems: how much force would be required to do so, and what would replace it? Paradoxically, as Taliban resistance became concentrated in a few places, there was greater and greater need for American forces in Afghanistan and in neighboring countries, especially in order to help the Taliban's enemies wrest control from it in places where its popularity was greater than in the north. A complete collapse of the Taliban might still leave the possibility of guerrilla warfare in these regions—and perhaps in others as well, if the postwar scene turns bloody and chaotic, in which case American military involvement might have to persist or even increase.

One important factor in the Taliban's defeat has been the increasing ten-

sion between its Afghan members, many of whom clearly preferred to exter-
mination a defeat that left the future open, and the foreign members—largely
Arab, Pakistani, and Chechen—who were not welcome in a country in which
even opposed factions and ethnic groups of Afghans had old links and understandings. (This was brutally confirmed by the revolt of foreign members of
the Taliban captures at Mazar-e-Sharif and their massacre by their Northern
Alliance captors.) But since the speed of the war has been much greater than
the progress of negotiations toward a new regime, the United States found
itself in a quandary. Between the Taliban tyranny and the old feuding warlords who remembered, there were few visible local leaders (except a very old
ex-king), and the jockeying for power among factions became fierce. Even
the current transitional government cobbled together under American and
UN pressure might not last, especially if the Pashtuns decide they are under-
represented.

It will not be easy to find a tutorial force capable of preventing any new
government from following the murderous precedents of the pre-Taliban
years. The United States has shown little enthusiasm either for taking on that
task or for any kind of political trusteeship and peacekeeping by the United
Nations (as distinguished from relief and reconstruction work). The United
Nations, without the kind of standing force Sir Brian Urquhart has called
for,[3] has insufficient means even for relief, and the Afghan warlords prefer to
be left to themselves without any external control or constraint.

The biggest issue that the United States will face in the short term as a
result of its war in Afghanistan is raised by repeated statements of the president promising (or threatening) to pursue the war against states that support
terrorists throughout the world. Paradoxically, pressures for such escalation
could grow in either of two different developments. First, in Afghanistan
itself, a protracted guerrilla war could be compounded by a renewed factional
and ethnic war, so that U.S. escalation beyond Afghanistan would serve as a
diversion. Second, if there is lasting success in Afghanistan, the argument
that there is "no substitute for victory" could be interpreted to mean that victory against the Taliban needs to be extended and completed before our enemies in Iraq and other rogue states recover from the shock of that victory.

The administration seems still divided between those who see a need to
strike while it is succeeding militarily and would prefer to crush regimes that
support terrorism and those who would rather address the grievances that
feed or provide support for terrorism. (There is here, obviously, the complex
underlying issue of what would best ensure Israel's security. An all-out war
on terrorism favors the hard-liners in Israel; an attempt to deal with Muslim
and Arab grievances favors the Palestinians.) A policy of military attacks on
Iraq and other so-called terrorist states (even though some, like Syria and

Libya, are openly or silently supporting us against bin Laden) would vindicate the complaints of our critics and enemies about American brutality and hubris, especially if such a policy aims at overthrowing existing regimes. We would lose many of our allies in the Muslim world and practice what the French call *la politique de Gribouille*, after the hapless character who sought refuge from the rain by diving into a river.

When we think about the long term, we must distinguish between what is likely and what is desirable. What is likely is a mixture of good and not-so-good developments. On the one hand, despite the Bush administration's decision to scuttle the ABM treaty, the current rapprochement with Russia and the reduction of tensions with China may last, and the United States government may shelve more decisively its unilateralist and anti-UN inclinations, if only because international cooperation will be indispensable in the fight against terrorism as well as in the attempt to prevent the world economy from declining further. On the other hand, the events in Afghanistan, combined with the effects of September 11, will push terrorist networks toward dispersion and clandestinity. The asymmetry of power between them and modern states could turn out to be the terrorists' greatest asset and could make rooting them out extremely difficult.

In turn, antiterrorism at home is likely to slow down the "retreat of the state" in a world where the chief enemy is the terrorist who takes advantage of all the transnational facilities—open borders, open information and communications, and so on—that globalization has fostered, where supranational organizations are rare and international ones weak. We may instead find a "return of the state" in often unattractive guises: restrictions on internal liberties and on immigration and travel, increased powers for the police and the military, and a state obsessed with order and security rather than justice. How far this trend will go and how long it will last in the United States are major questions for Americans concerned with protecting their values. One of the casualties of this trend, abroad, could be further European integration, especially in the domain that remains the Achilles' heel of the European Union: common diplomacy and defense. Since September 11, the European nation-states, not the European Union, have been the actors, and Britain has returned to its old role of best ally of the United States.

What would be desirable? No one should doubt that the fight against global terrorism must continue. But it should take as its model and method—in the United States as well as abroad—a patient and shadowy policy involving police cooperation with friendly countries, improved intelligence, support for democratic forces, and, if need be, support for the U.S. Special Forces actions in hostile countries and regions. It also has to be accompanied by a long-term strategy aimed at addressing the reasonable complaints of the Third World.

We would help achieve the goal of protection against terrorism by linking it to the cause of human rights. After all, those rights can be attacked both by individuals and by states; freedom from terror is—or ought to be—a basic human right, and there ought to be a right of collective intervention that ranges from diplomatic pressure and sanctions to military action against extreme violations by terrorists. Such collective intervention could address cases of acute terrorism (state sponsored or by individuals) and instances of state crimes against humanity or genocide, such as those in Bosnia, Kosovo, and East Timor, to name only a few. Captured terrorists and murderous statesmen, future bin Ladens and future Milosevics, should be judged by the same international criminal court.

As part of this new kind of international law, one could think of a convention defining the conditions under which a collective intervention against terrorism could legitimately occur. Such intervention could punish or even try to topple a regime that sponsors and encourages terrorism against foreign people or against its own. An explicit authorization by the United Nations, showing broad support for such an action, would be necessary. The "return of the state" resulting from security concerns that I deplored previously would thus be counterbalanced by a reinforced defense of human rights.

More generally, if I had to summarize what is desirable, I would say this: an end of the old and tiresome battle between "realists" concerned only with the defense of a national interest defined by military and economic strength, suspicious of humanitarian moves, and distrustful of international agencies that don't serve our interests and "idealists" disturbed by the emphasis on and the effects of national power. Today idealism is often the best form of realism. We have, during and after the Cold War, collected allies whom we needed at the moment but whose internal and external policies in the long run created more grief than benefits for us. Saudi Arabia, Pakistan, and Egypt have supported Islamic fundamentalism in Afghanistan. Religious schools that teach hatred of the United States have been funded by the Saudis. Mubarak's regime has supported an anti-American press. Our support for Pakistan has encouraged Islamabad to help terrorism against India in Kashmir.

The most basic requirements of realism and the best protection against fundamentalisms can take the form of support for causes that have been too easily dismissed. These include not only the protection of human rights abroad but also aid for economic development given even to governments that are not democratic but are willing to push for economic and social reforms at home so as to narrow the gap between the rich and the poor, the powerful and the dispossessed. (The establishment of a genuine democracy in a country that has never experienced it takes time.) It is brutalization and misery that drive their victims into millennial and violent religious fantasies.

A "realist," however proud of American predominance and power, should understand that it is in the American national interest that the United States stop being the universal scapegoat—deemed responsible, for instance, for the failings of Arab, Islamic, or Third World societies. Some of this scapegoating is inevitable, the price of the success of the American economy and the diffusion of American culture. But some of the hostility can be avoided. In some cases, such as in the disputes over Palestine or Kashmir, it is American timidity that allows our critics to blame us for bloody stalemates that result in part from their own actions. In other cases, the United States will be safer and have more support and authority than it enjoys today if it follows a policy combining greater humility, greater attentiveness to the plight of others, more concern for doing what is just than for doing what is expedient, more determination to reduce our dependence on dubious allies (such as our dependence on Saudi oil), and more willingness to let other actors do more. We live in a world in which no single country, however rich and strong, can rule over the rest or even ensure its own security.

December 15, 2001

POSTSCRIPT

As of April 2006, despite the popular election of President Karzai, the Taliban has not been eliminated from Afghanistan. The priority went to Iraq.

NOTES

Chapter 14 was first published as "On the War," *New York Review of Books*, November 1, 2001, then reprinted in revised form in Robert B. Silvers and Barbara Epstein, eds., *Striking Terror* (New York: New York Review Press, 2002), and further revised here.

1. J. Bryan Hehir, "What Can and Should Be Done?," *America*, October 8, 2001.

2. See Ohan Pamuk, "The Anger of the Damned," in Silvers and Epstein, *Striking Terror*.

3. See Brian Urquhart, "For a UN Volunteer Force," *New York Review of Books*, June 10, 1993.

· *15* ·

Iraq February 2003: Instead of War

$\mathscr{W}$e know what the benefits of a war on Iraq would be: the ouster of a cruel tyrant and the elimination of his weapons of mass destruction. But we also know what the costs would be: prohibitive. The administration believes that the overthrow of Saddam Hussein could bring democracy to Iraq and, from there, spread like an oil slick to the rest of the Arab world. This is a fantasy. The confusion of our plans for Iraq itself—the frustration, divisions, and limitations of the Iraqi exiles—shows how difficult the introduction of democracy would be in a heterogeneous country that has never experienced it. After thirty years of repression, there could be violent settlements of account that U.S. forces, unprepared for such a task, would have to cope with, and a prolonged occupation and military rule would squander the goodwill we as liberators expect to prevail at first. Outside Iraq, Arab governments will try to contain the democratic oil slick in order to stay in power. Moreover, as long as we haven't decisively intervened to settle the Israeli–Palestinian conflict and suggest that it may have to wait until Arab regimes have changed, Arab suspicion of the United States will mount.

Indeed, American control of Iraq could make a huge contribution to Muslim terrorism and foster a xenophobic fundamentalism aimed at U.S. "imperialism" rather than a kind of democratic epidemic. Already the administration's obsession with Iraq and its bullying way of obtaining support have provoked considerable anti-American resentment abroad. The manipulation of the United Nations—through trying to buy votes and attacks on the "relevance" of the United Nations—and of our alliances with NATO countries, our efforts to split the European Union, and our disdain for public opinion abroad have tarnished the good image of the United States. Even more seriously, the Bush administration (already before 9/11) has recklessly attacked the very foundations of world order the United States had helped to put in place after 1945: the United Nations, international law, and the European Union have been the casualties of a team that has repudiated a distinction

155

we had wisely preserved throughout the Cold War, between leadership and dictation. This may result, in the long term, in something we had avoided so far: an anti-American ganging up of countries threatened by the growth of unchecked American power. And then there are, of course, all the economic costs of the war, of the need to rebuild Iraq so that our deliberate negligence of its needs does not further encourage all those who doubt American good intentions and observe how little the United States has done for Afghanistan after our military victory there.

Are these costs worth it? We have two main reasons to go to war. Both are shaky. Iraq is effectively defanged and incapable of constituting a real threat to us or to its neighbors as long as we operate freely in two no-fly zones covering half the country, as long as the Kurds have autonomy under Anglo-American protection, and as long as inspectors roam freely. Contrary to the administration's assertions and unlike in the fight against terrorists, containment can continue to work in the long run, especially if the no-fly zones and the inspections are maintained, if a tight naval blockade prevents military imports into Iraq, and if ground forces remain stationed at Iraq's borders. War is not necessary to render Iraq harmless to others.

The other, much more difficult issue is that of Saddam Hussein. Like preventive war, forcible regime change violates current international law. The exceptions to state sovereignty that, case by case, were made legitimate through the so-called humanitarian interventions in the 1990s have never involved "regime change" and had to be justified by the argument that the violation of human rights that provoked those interventions constituted a threat to international and regional security. This could have been an argument for intervening against Saddam Hussein's regime in 1991; the opportunity was missed, and since then Saddam Hussein has not committed mass crimes against humanity.

His remains a regime based on fear and terror. Sooner or later, states jealous of their sovereignty may realize that the observance of basic human rights (if not democracy) is itself a right that the subjects may claim. But this principle will need international support and not unilateral action to be established and a clear understanding of the differences between "ordinary" bad regimes and truly evil ones. Meanwhile, all those who sympathize with the plight of the Iraqi people yet do not want to increase their suffering through war and a turbulent postwar era can and should do all they can to make Saddam Hussein's position increasingly difficult. The International Criminal Court (which the administration so irrationally loathes) or a special criminal tribunal can try him for crimes against humanity, order a ban on travel by all top officials, deprive them of their fortunes abroad, and indicate that a recovery by Iraq of its full sovereignty will depend on its compliance with those decisions. Furthermore, we can provide covert assistance to groups of Iraqis willing to act against Saddam Hussein and overt aid if they try to overthrow him.

For these purposes, we could lead a "coalition of the willing" far bigger and less resentful than the one we're trying to force into supporting us for a risky and widely unpopular war. The democracy we say we champion should begin by recognizing that listening to what the publics say is not tantamount to appeasement and to inaction. Gaining more victories in the difficult war against terrorism is a far more widely shared goal and one that could be imperiled by American hubris in the war against Iraq.[1]

NOTES

Chapter 15 was published as "Are the Costs of Going to War Worth It?," *Boston Globe*, March 13, 2003.

1. On America's war, see Stanley Hoffmann, *America Goes Backward* (New York: New York Review of Books, 2004).

· 16 ·

France, the United States, and Iraq

$\mathscr{F}$rance's rift with the United States over Iraq has not ended despite various overtures from France and appeasing remarks from American officials. Even though the campaign of anti-French calumnies has ended, the damage to France's reputation in the United States remains, and the French position on Iraq is still widely misunderstood. As the exclusion of France and other opponents of the war from contracts for the reconstruction of the country has shown, those who, in Washington, considered that the French had doubly betrayed the United States—by opposing a war that the "senior ally" deemed in its national interest and by courting votes at the Security Council of the United Nations (as if the United States hadn't been seeking them too)—do not seem to be ready to forgive, even though their attempts to "punish" France did not have much success.

There are two stories here. One is that of the way French dissent was treated in Washington. In the days of General de Gaulle, his attempt to dissuade the Johnson administration from getting into a quagmire in Vietnam and failing as badly as the French had when they spent eight bloody years (1946–1954) fighting Vietnamese nationalism was interpreted by American officials as evidence of the general's malevolence and anti-Americanism. His suggestions for a settlement were dismissed—and eight years of American war followed despite the original conviction in Washington that the Americans would be welcome as protectors against communism, untainted by colonialism. But there was no general assault on France. De Gaulle's position in France, in Europe, and in much of the Third World was just too strong, and the general's support of the United States during the Cuban missile crisis had been impressive.

This time, despite France's support of and active participation in the war against the Taliban after September 11, there was no such restraint in Washington. Indeed, there was an extremely well-orchestrated campaign of innuendoes, distortions, and lies aimed not only at discrediting French arguments

159

but at France herself. When the French ambassador, a patient man, finally listed the biggest lies (for instance, about French material interests in Iraq or recent weapons shipments to Iraq) and sent the list to the White House, the campaign stopped. What was said about French fundamental unwillingness to support any war against Saddam Hussein was false. What was not said was that the French had informed the United States of the forces they would contribute if there was evidence of the terminal unwillingness of Saddam to get rid of his remaining weapons of mass destruction. Nor was it said that, shortly before the war began, the French had made a compromise offer that would have allowed the United States to interpret the unanimous (and therefore ambiguous) resolution 1441 of November 2002 as a basis for war and the French (and their supporters) to disagree, but without a divisive vote in the Security Council on a second resolution—the famous second resolution that Bush had promised to Blair, that would oblige all members of the Security Council to show whether they were "with us or against us." The French had predicted that the United States would not win in the Council unless it made concessions, and Washington had, at the end, withdrawn the resolution anyhow for lack of enough votes. The Bush administration also made much of a "hardening" of the French position in mid-January 2003, without revealing that the U.S. representative at the United Nations had just informed his French counterpart that the United States had decided to go to war very soon—at a moment when the French still hoped for a prolongation of UN inspections. Colin Powell himself, in mid-March, interpreted a statement by Chirac asserting that France would not support the second resolution drafted by the United Sates "under any circumstances" as showing that France would never go to war. Washington was so furious at the French for having rallied enough support on the Security Council to deprive the United States of the legitimation it was seeking from the United Nations that it encouraged a boycott of French products in the United States and stated that it would ignore Germany, remain friendly with Russia (both of which had sided with France), and punish the French.

The second, and ultimately more important, story is that of the French position itself. France disagreed with the American case for reasons, some of which it held in common with American critics of the neoconservative push for war. They did not believe that Iraq, weakened by its defeat in 1991 and by seven years of UN inspections, posed a "clear and present danger" for the United States and that deterrence of Iraqi aggression against its neighbors or Israel was no longer a valid policy (the United States had deterred the Soviets, a far more powerful adversary than Iraq, for forty years). The French (like General Brent Scowcroft) feared that war against Iraq would both deprive the war on terrorism of attention and resources and attract terrorists to Iraq.

Above all, the French emphasized the importance of international law and of such institutions as the United Nations, NATO, and the European Union in an interdependent world where no power can, by itself, get its own way, a position dismissed by the hard-liners in the Bush administration who had only contempt for international norms, the United Nations, and established alliances and proclaimed the virtues of unilateralism and of "coalitions of the (handpicked) willing" fished out of such alliances.

The French preference for a return and toughening of UN inspections over immediate war had three components. One was faith in the ability of these inspections (which did indeed discover, just before the war began, Iraqi missiles that exceeded the limits fixed in 1991—and got the regime of Saddam Hussein to destroy them). The French had full confidence in Hans Blitz, whom Washington tried to discredit despite his obvious objectivity and toughness.

A second component was France's reluctance to wage a war for regime change. The French had no more enthusiasm for Saddam Hussein than anyone else, although they (along with the United States) had provided him with help at the time of his war against Iran. But on the one hand, they thought that removing a government from power should not be done by one country or a small group of countries without broader legitimacy, a formula for world chaos. In addition, there was no recent evidence of spectacular violations of human rights (of the kind Saddam Hussein had inflicted on rebellious Kurds and Shiites in 1991), and there was little chance that the United Nations would endorse such a move—too many skeletons rattled in too many members' closets, including Russia and China. On the other hand, they thought that the American objective of democratizing Iraq (and to use Iraq as a lever for spreading democracy all over the Middle East) was far too simple-minded, that the "liberated" Iraqis would be resentful of foreign occupation, and that, indeed, the American habit of both discounting the importance of nationalism abroad and equating democracy and moderation was unrealistic (they remembered the democratic elections in Algeria in 1991 that gave a majority to the Islamists). Chirac, in his youth, fought in the Algerian war and saw the strength of Arab nationalism.

Third, the French—with five or six million Muslims in France and long experience of terrorism on French soil—were eager to avoid provoking a real "clash of civilizations" between the Muslim world and the West. They thought that an attack on an Arab country that could not be justified in terms of self-defense (unlike the war on the Taliban) or in terms of complicity with terrorism would only fuel anti-American hatreds and increase, especially among the young and the poor, the influence of Islamist extremists both in the Muslim world and in France (the rise of anti-Semitic incidents in France, committed mainly by Arab immigrants, has deeply alarmed Chirac). The foreign minister, Dominique de Villepin, a passionate believer in the complementarity of cultures (and a man born in Morocco), has been particularly worried about further turmoil in the Middle East, the spread of terrorism across borders there, and a rise of anti-Western feelings. There is no doubt that for the French, priority ought to have been given to a settlement of the Israeli–Palestinian conflict and that the American priority of the war against Iraq and of the war on terrorism could only help the politics of Ariel Sharon.

Of course, the story of the Iraqi adventure is not over, but so far—despite the capture of Saddam Hussein and the return of "sovereignty" to Iraq—it seems that the French have been more right than the Bush administration. Nor have the French been isolated despite the best efforts of Washington to sideline NATO (where the French have a veto) and to divide the European Union. In Europe, the Franco–German alliance is tighter than ever and more determined to push ahead for a stronger European defense system with all those other members of the European Union that are willing to take part in such an enterprise. At this point, it is the British who appear isolated—devoid of real influence in Washington; weakened, on the European continent, in their effort to make sure that the developing common European diplomacy and defense does not go too far in seeking autonomy from Washington; and hurt by the lengths to which Blair has gone in aligning himself with Bush. In many countries of the developing world, including in the Middle East, the French position has been popular—not to mention with many of the opponents of the war in the United States, particularly in New England.

Having predicted the troubles that would afflict a foreign occupation of Iraq, the French wasted no time in proposing a radical shift in policy. Having, with both good logic and solid evidence, concluded that it was the occupation itself that provoked resistance and became the target of discontents, they have suggested replacing the "logic of security" with a "logic of sovereignty." They do not deny, needless to say, the seriousness of insecurity and the trouble it causes for the political and material reconstruction of the country. But they believe that the way of dealing with it is to restore as swiftly as possible Iraqi sovereignty, to put the occupation forces under U.S. military command at the service of the Iraqis while they reform their institutions, and to grant to the United Nations—with its long experience in peacekeeping and in nation building—a general supervising role both over the military operations and over the political transition. They are clearly concerned that the members of any Iraqi temporary authority entrusted with Iraqi sovereignty be both capable of coping with the immense ethnic, religious, and political tensions of the country and as immune as possible from the charge of being stooges of the American occupiers.

Washington's reaction was, at first, predictably derisive and hostile—the French plan, according to Colin Powell and Condoleezza Rice, was thoroughly unrealistic. After the escalation of attacks on American and other targets in Iraq, the United States abruptly changed course and moved forward an "Irakization" that would, in fact, rapidly transfer authority to an Iraqi government without waiting for a general election and new constitution. Differences with French proposals remain: the speed promised by Washington was still not as great as Villepin had argued for, the length of the military occupation of Iraq is a bone of contention, and a genuine increase in the role of the United Nations is still anathema to the Bush administration. The way in which Saddam will be tried is another potential cause of disagreement. But the fact that the Security Council had agreed unanimously in October 2003 to the American draft resolution outlining, even in rather vague terms, a transformation of the occupation showed that the French were quite capable of pragmatism once the direction set was no longer the opposite of what they deemed the right one.

Differences between France and the United States in foreign affairs will continue. They have many origins. In international politics, the United States seeks to preserve and extend its hegemony (and will undoubtedly continue to do so even if it should rediscover the necessity of multilateralism as the way of making hegemony effective and acceptable). The French, who do not mean by "multipolarity" a return to the balance-of-power politics of the eighteenth and nineteenth centuries, as Americans seem to believe, think that American might and hubris need to be restrained by other powers and that in fact it is only in the military area that the world is unipolar; as my friend and colleague Joseph Nye has pointed out, economic power is not an American monopoly, and what he calls soft power—the power to attract, to persuade, and to influence—is very widely distributed (and the Bush administration has reduced America's soft power drastically). French ambitions for the European Union are not aimed at making it a rival of the United States (or the euro a rival of the dollar) but, quite simply, at making it a force of its own and not a satellite, often alongside the United States.

A more fundamental source of irritation is the fact that the United States and France are the two democracies whose revolutionary heritage has convinced them that they are exceptional by having universally valid values. These are not identical (the main difference resides in the French experience of and attachment to a strong state, in the importance the French give to economic and social rights, and in French dislike of uncontrolled capitalism); also, the French don't have the means to propagate these values by force if necessary. But Americans are irritated by the pretension of (as John F. Kennedy said) a country the size of Texas to "grandeur" and universal relevance. A new area in which a difference in values has recently appeared concerns sovereignty: in the United States, not only on the right, a kind of legal exceptionalism reluctant to accept the superiority of international norms is still pervasive, whereas in France, for so long a champion of national sovereignty, the notion of shared or pooled sovereignty has become the basis of European integration and the essence of a new world order.

A third source of American annoyance has to do with the French style in foreign affairs (very well analyzed by Charles Cogan in a book published by the Institute of Peace).[1] The French believe in being assertive, forceful, and articulate in their defense of what they deem right. The contrast with British (but not Blairish) understatement or German contemporary mildness could not be greater. The man who is largely responsible for this style is General de Gaulle. It was both an expression of his formidable personality and a major part of his pedagogy aimed at restoring French pride and influence after the decadence of the interwar period and the disastrous years of occupation by and official collaboration with the Nazis. The recent debate on French decline is not very significant—it is largely the outcry of a few intellectuals who want faster economic and social reforms that would unfetter the economy for more free enterprise and fewer social protections than would probably be tolerated by the beneficiaries of the welfare state. These critics also want France to follow not only the American social model but also the American lead in world affairs. What is important is not the fear of decline, which has been present ever since France's defeat by Prussia in 1971, but the self-confidence of political elites and bureaucrats who have absorbed, consciously or not, the message of de Gaulle: "Be yourselves."[2]

There are, of course, serious internal problems. Reforming the educational system and social security remains difficult, given the opposition of the people who would be affected. The left is leaderless and resembles the current U.S. Democratic Party. Above all, the integration of the Muslim population remains difficult and devisive—even within the government and its majority.

None of this should worry Americans. Their popularity as a people remains high in France, where distinguishing between a nation and its government is a product of France's own turbulent history. The Chirac administration, during the recent storm, deliberately refrained from attacking American motives and policies in the way in which the Bush administration savaged France's. Not every critic of U.S. actions is anti-American, any more than critics of Sharon's moves are all anti-Semitic. And sometimes, it is the sharpest critics who are foresighted and right.[3]

NOTES

Chapter 16 was published as "France, the United States, and Iraq," *The Nation*, February 16, 2004.

1. Charles Cogan, *French Negotiating Behavior* (Washington, D.C.: U.S. Institute of Peace Press, 2003).

2. See Stanley Hoffmann, "France: Two Obsessions for One Century," *A Century's Journey*, ed. Robert A. Pastor (New York: Basic Books, 1999), 63–90.

3. See also my preface to Dominique de Villepin, *Toward a New World* (New York: Melville House, 2004).

· 17 ·

Out of Iraq

I. THE TRAP

 $\mathscr{T}$ he war in Iraq has become a costly trap from which the United States should extricate itself soon—the Republican administration that insists on "staying the course," on denouncing the insurgents as desperadoes, and on reassuring the public that things are improving just as almost 2,000 American soldiers have died and attacks have sharply increased. Those who had put their hopes in a change of administration in Washington have had several reasons for being frustrated and disappointed.

First, the Democratic team seemed anxious not to upset voters who have been persuaded by the administration that the "war on terror" depends on the American "liberation" of Iraq and do not want to hear about the limits on American power. John Edwards talked of ultimate victory, and John Kerry crippled his campaign by his all-too-calculated contradictions, especially when he stated that he would have voted for the congressional resolution that granted the power to initiate war to the president even if he had known in October 2002 what is known now. He should have noted instead, as Senator Hilary Clinton did, that had we known then what we know now, there would have been no resolution and no vote.

The two Democratic candidates have been critical of the ways in which the Bush administration invaded Iraq and bungled the occupation. But they could have put forward much earlier arguments that Kerry only began to make in late September 2004:

1. Saddam's regime did not present a clear and present danger to the United States.
2. No proof of collusion against the United States between Saddam and al-Qaeda has ever been shown.
3. In fact, the switch from the war on terrorism, which led to the over-

throw of the Taliban in Afghanistan, to the war in Iraq was a highly imprudent diversion of resources and a contribution to—indeed a godsend for—terrorism, a classic case of self-fulfilling prophecy.

4. The lofty goal of liberation of the Iraqis cannot be achieved by imposing a regime of exiles through military force, in circumstances drastically different from those of 1945 Germany and Japan.

5. The awarding of lucrative contracts to American companies alone has thrown a deep shadow over the idealistic language of the administration.

6. The willful decision to limit the size of American forces in Iraq (for reasons that were never made entirely clear) was an unexpected boon to insurgents since the U.S. forces could not deal with the acute burdens that were inevitable in a partly devastated country.

7. American expectations that the occupation would be popular were based on a mix of ignorance, hubris, and misinformation provided by exiles such as Ahmed Chalabi.

8. A genuine concern with liberation would have required close U.S. collaboration with internal factions, restraint in the use of destructive tactics, prevention of looting or from disenfranchisement, and scrupulous respect for international obligations, especially toward prisoners.

9. During most of the period that went from the summer of 2002 to that of 2004, the Bush administration—and especially the civilians in charge of the Pentagon—treated Congress as a minor nuisance and evidently thought the public could easily be deceived. It is still doing its best to fool the voters.

Instead of presenting a convincing argument, the positions of the Kerry campaign on Iraq suffered from a variety of flaws and unconfronted questions:

1. Kerry has repeatedly claimed that he would do a better job than Bush in rallying other countries to a genuine coalition that would ensure security in Iraq. This is wishful thinking. Muslim countries have shown no enthusiasm for helping Iraqi authorities as long as the Coalition is still under U.S. control. Those NATO countries that favored the Coalition are already in it (or, in Spain's case, were), and, except for the United Kingdom, they provide very little by way of military force. France and Germany are unlikely to join. The French don't want to give the Muslim world the impression that the "West" is opposed to "Islam." Aware of the insurgents' attacks on the United

States and its protégés, most states are not likely to share the human and financial costs of a counterinsurgency war, certainly not as long as it is waged under American command. Whether NATO will show any eagerness for training large amounts of Iraqi security forces or guarding Iraq's borders is still not clear. No doubt, many governments would have been better disposed toward a President Kerry than toward President Bush. But decisions touching on war and peace tend to be based on realities on the ground and at home, not on whether one leader is more agreeable than another.

2. Kerry was largely silent about the relations between American-led forces in Iraq and the interim government headed by Iyad Allawi and also the transitional government that emerged from the assembly elected at the end of January 2005. Would the American-led forces continue to decide on military operations by themselves even if these governments objected to them?

3. The hope that Iraqi security forces can be recruited and trained effectively so far has turned out to be illusory. Training is not all; training and a good salary may be better, but ultimately motivation is essential, and the fear of being killed or wounded by insurgents and only tepidly supported by the population may well cause newly trained police and troops to fade away, as many have already done.

The facts are that the number of attacks on American and other forces and installations has multiplied by five since Bush stood under a sign announcing "Mission Accomplished" and proclaimed the "end of major combat operations" in Iraq, that a number of cities in the Sunni triangle and elsewhere are not under the control of the "Coalition" and of the Iraqi interim government, and that the United States and the provisional Iraqi government now face a deep dilemma. If they leave insurgents in control, whether in Sunni territory or in Sadr City in Baghdad, more Iraqi insurgents and foreign jihadists will flock to these places, some with increasingly potent weapons. If attempts are made to regain control of the cities and districts where hostile forces seem to operate with impunity, the number of Iraqi dead and wounded will rise, fewer Iraqi civilians will side with the Americans, and more will resent their heavy weapons and their air strikes against fellow Iraqis (even if they might dislike the insurgents or wish that the latter had chosen other places to fight in). To dismantle and disarm of private militias would require either a large-scale American military operation or willingness on the part of Iraqi authorities to appear as the submissive clients of the American occupiers. This seems likely to encourage the rebellions. Isn't this what has happened in cases as diverse as French Indochina, Vietnam, and Algeria?

Raymond Aron's advice to the Prince's would-be counselor was that he should put himself in the Prince's place and should not look at things from the perspective of the radical critic, the idealist, the perfectionist, or the enemy. Fine, as long as one remembers that Aron himself, a columnist for the conservative daily *Le Figaro*, had early concluded (and wrote accordingly, but not in *Le Figaro*) that the only way for the French to deal with Algeria was to grant it independence—a notion that neither the right nor most of the left found palatable at the time. Aron's lesson was that there are times when tendencies to temporize and hope for incremental improvements can lead to disaster.

At present, there are many who believe that the United States has to "stay the course." Its credibility is thought to be at stake, especially after it failed to support the insurrections against Saddam Hussein that the United States itself encouraged the Kurds and the Shiites to undertake in 1991. Moreover, civilian supporters of the war in the Pentagon continue to hold out hopes for building a democracy in Iraq that would somehow survive. They therefore believe that the United States must not only help the provisional government defeat the insurgents but also stay in Iraq as long as any new government needs protection.

Such hopes are being demolished by the realities of Iraqi hostility to the United States and its protégés. The spread of terrorism makes it difficult to distinguish either the jihadists from outside the country or the postwar followers of Osama bin Laden in Iraq from other Iraqis opposed to the occupation. Thus, the administration's "war on terror" is achieving the very connections between the Iraqis and members of al-Qaeda that Bush falsely told the public justified the war. As a recent study convincingly argues, the prolonged occupation is "an open invitation for a steady build-up of grassroots Muslin anger"[1] and a breeding ground for terrorism. Much of the insurgency, moreover, has been aimed not only at American forces but also at oil pipelines and ordinary technicians, foreign private contractors, and Iraqis working for and with the Americans. It may well be that many Iraqis currently opposed to the occupation will be increasingly revolted by the killings of fellow Iraqis by the insurgents. In that case, an Iraqi policy aimed at defeating insurgents may become popular or at least accepted. But as long as such a policy depends on intervention by U.S. forces, it is unlikely to crush the rebellion. Although the United States is increasing its efforts to train security forces, as the *Financial Times* commented, they "cannot stand alongside a US military that daily rains thousands of tons of projectiles and high explosives on their compatriots."[2]

There are therefore good reasons for calling for an end of the occupation. As in Palestine, the occupation is the main cause of the current troubles.

This certainly does not mean that they will end if we leave, but whatever we do to try to resolve the internal conflicts is likely to backfire. Continuing U.S. military control, direct or indirect, will feed anti-Americanism (as in post-1965 South Vietnam) and provide a training ground for terrorism, both indigenous and from other countries. American interests would be better served by a shift of U.S. resources toward two objectives. The first is the fight against al-Qaeda and its allies throughout the world, which have become more diversified and decentralized. They continue to receive financial and other support from powerful groups in officially pro-American states, such as Saudi Arabia and Pakistan. They are not easily defeated by high-powered military operations, and they continue to recruit members from extremist madrasas, whether in Pakistan or in other Muslim countries.

The second objective would be a much larger program aimed at rebuilding the economic infrastructure of Iraq and at establishing new institutions there, but only with the help of other states experienced in state building. The departure of American and British forces would make it easier for countries that have not supported the war to provide assistance, including police training, under UN auspices. The United States, for its part, should make available the rest of the $18 billion appropriated by Congress for reconstruction in Iraq, of which no more than $1 billion has so far been spent. The study I mentioned earlier is persuasive in arguing that "a permanent military garrison in Iraq" would "impose enormous costs and a host of new headaches for the American taxpayers and the military alike" and that the American military presence in Iraq contributes "to a worsening perception of the United States by a growing number of Muslims" (and, I would add, non-Muslims).[3] In its struggle against terrorism, the United States should give priority to threats posed by Islamic jihadists (the most dangerous for U.S. and Western interests), and it should devote far more attention to a permanent solution to the Palestinian problem, along the lines almost agreed on at Taba in 2001 and in the Geneva Accords negotiated by independent Palestinians and Israelis.

II. AS OF OCTOBER 2004

What would such an exit strategy mean, concretely? It would require a statement by the Coalition of its intention to withdraw its forces by a certain date, for example, within six months of the election of a new assembly and the government that emanates from it. If elections take place in January 2005, a phased withdrawal should be completed by the end of June. While the interim government is in place, the United States should take measures that have genuine political and symbolic significance: the U.S. Embassy would reduce its scale of operations, formal U.S. advisers would be gradually withdrawn, and the United States would make commitments not to launch military operations unless they are requested by the elected Iraqi government.

The United States should leave the preparation and supervision of the coming elections to the United Nations, which could cancel or replace the decisions made by the election commissions set up by Paul Bremer. Only the certifiable criminals of the Baath army and bureaucracy ought to be excluded from voting, as should terrorists condemned for their actions. It is particularly important that the United States allow the Iraqis to decide on the nature of their future government and their new permanent constitution, in which such issues as Kurdish claims to autonomy will have to be resolved. During this period, the training of Iraqi security forces may have to remain a Coalition task, but it will be more successful if it is monitored and supervised by the United Nations.

After the elections, the withdrawal of Coalition forces would begin. They would be replaced by Iraqis and by the forces of any country—including the United States and the United Kingdom—acceptable to the new Iraqi government that agrees to participate in an international peacemaking and peacekeeping force. That force would be established with the consent of the new Iraqi government and placed under the control of the United Nations. The command should be Iraqi. The new government would have the right to renegotiate the contracts awarded by the Coalition and to decide on a permanent status for the oil industry. No foreign bases would be established in Iraq.

Such a policy could present more difficulties than opportunities for anti-American insurgents and terrorists. They could no longer argue that Iraq is an American imperial outpost with a government chosen by Washington. If they continue their attacks and if it can be shown that a large number among them are from outside Iraq, they would risk unifying Iraq's political and security forces against them. Successful counterinsurgency requires popular support, and foreign occupation inhibits such support. Conversely, the longer the occupation forces remain in Iraq, the more difficult it will be for Americans to extricate themselves; they are likely to get caught up in conflicts among political factions, tribal leaders, religious groups, and ethnic forces eager to either oppose or court the occupiers.

Such a plan should not depend on the elections of January 2005. Sunni Iraq may be in too turbulent a condition for its citizens to be able or willing to participate. It should be clear that no election that leaves out a large part of the group that was dominant under Saddam Hussein would have much validity or authority. Moreover, an election excluding the Sunni region would leave two large groups in contention: a Kurdish minority that is practically self-governing—and will resist any constitutional regime other than a loose federation—and a Shiite majority whose leaders are reluctant to grant the Kurds autonomous status and to compromise their claims to majority rule.

The plan I suggest here would explicitly transfer to the United Nations the power to negotiate with the Iraqi insurgents the conditions under which they would participate in the elections. Attempts at reconquering dissident strongholds by armed force—which would have to be largely American—would not only lead to more Iraqi casualties and "collateral damage" but also leave a significant part of the population in a sullen and angry mood of defeat and humiliation.

A policy that seeks accommodation with the anti-American insurgency is not a policy of weakness: it is with one's enemies, not with one's supporters (and former collaborators), that one has to make peace, as de Gaulle understood in Algeria. Given the lack of confidence of these enemies both in the United States and in the interim government, the burden of negotiation will have to fall on the United Nations, whose mandate needs to be made far more precise and comprehensive than in the resolution of June 2004. If the United States decides it must prepare for elections by using strong force against its foes, it may establish a "peace of the graveyards" as a prelude to voting. On the other hand, if the United States decides to postpone the elections for any considerable period, this would only prolong the agony of suppressing the insurgents who are causing the delay. It thus seems crucial that the United Nations have as much authority as possible to organize the elections.

It may also be that UN efforts will fail and that the secretary-general will conclude that no safe and valid elections can be held by the end of January 2005. Should this happen, the United States should transfer the control of security to the UN-sponsored and commanded security force I have described. It should begin by withdrawing its own forces and keep to the deadline of the end of June 2005 or to a deadline close to it.

No doubt such a course entails risks. A breakup of the country can by no means be ruled out. Although an elected Iraqi government would be in a strong position to ask other countries, especially in the Muslim world, to provide the forces needed by the United Nations, it may find those countries unwilling to risk their soldiers' lives. Conflict over a new constitution could lead to a civil war or to foreign interventions, say, by Iran helping Iraqi Shiite clerics or by Turkey trying to prevent Kurdish secession. Such risks partly explained why the first Bush administration was reluctant to intervene in the domestic affairs of Iraq after its victory of 1991. Preventing a bloody disintegration of Iraq and preventing a takeover of Iraq by extremist Islamic terrorists if new Iraqi security forces prove to be inadequate should be left to international diplomacy by the United Nations and regional organizations as well as to international peacemaking forces provided by them and by individual countries. Both the European Union and other countries, especially moderate Arab ones, have pragmatic incentives to support such a plan. Prolonged civil conflict could threaten not only oil supplies from Iraq but also the stability of Saudi Arabia, with the world's largest oil reserves.

Such an American policy would mean giving up some of the goals the Bush administration announced when it decided to invade Iraq. It would mean abandoning the hope of transforming the entire Arab world, beginning with Iraq, and thus changing the balance of forces between Sharon's Israel and its enemies. It would mean recognizing that change in countries such as Syria, Iran, and Saudi Arabia will be, at best, slow and gradual and that democracy cannot be implanted surgically in countries that have no experience or preparation for it, although this does not mean denying support for forces of reform and progress. It would mean giving up the less-talked-about but central U.S. aim of turning Iraq itself into a U.S.-dominated satellite, with American bases, American companies in charge of its oil, and a compliant regime.

There are excellent reasons for repudiating this anachronistic attempt to create an extension of America's empire. Americans will be able to argue that they helped Iraq decisively by eliminating Saddam (at a heavy cost in international support and prestige) and gave Iraq back to its people and that it is now up to the Iraqis to make a success of their new situation with the help of the international community whenever it is needed. The best course for the United States is to avoid being trapped in the vicious circle of counterinsurgency warfare and to shift resources toward aid for reconstruction and development—which has been scandalously lagging so far—as well as to take part in genuinely international peacemaking and peacekeeping if the Iraqis call for American participation. It is neither ignoble nor cowardly for a nation to recognize that it has overreached itself and that the time has come to give up an attempt at remolding a country that—apart from its exiles—had not asked the United States to take it over (partly because when anti-Saddam rebellions had broken out before, we did nothing to help) and to concentrate instead on repairing some of the damage the war has done.

But Iraq is not the only stake. Remaining trapped among equally unsavory choices would weigh heavily on U.S. foreign policy in general. The strategy of withdrawal outlined here would aim at reconnecting the United States with moderate Arab opinion at a time when U.S. policy seems increasingly to consider Arabs and Muslims as potential terrorists. That policy encourages extremism and anti-Americanism by actions that range from unpunished torture in Iraqi prisons to the recent revocation of the visa of a leading Islamic thinker—Tariq Ramadan—who had been invited to teach at Notre Dame

University. The United States should be making it clear that the necessary war on terrorism does not mean giving carte blanche to the domination of Palestinians by Ariel Sharon or the Chechens by Vladimir Putin. Withdrawal from Iraq would also make more possible a reconciliation with friends and allies shocked by Washington's recent unilateralism and repudiation of international obligations and thus do much to restore—not to reduce—American credibility and "soft power" in the world. Recognizing the limits of America's vast military power might, paradoxically, do more than anything else to increase American influence in the world.

Withdrawal from Iraq, combined with a new effort by the United States, the United Nations, the European Union, and Russia to end the Israeli occupation of Palestinian lands and to create a livable Palestinian state, would mark a return to reality, to good sense, and to a moral politics.

III. AS OF AUGUST 2005

The preceding analysis and the proposals that followed have been largely vindicated in the past ten months. My main error was a failure to point out clearly that the insurrection had become largely a Sunni phenomenon and thus led to an incipient civil war even more than to a direct clash between insurgents and Americans. Nevertheless, the attacks on Shiites and Kurds were aimed not only at preventing the domination of a new Iraq by a coalition of Shiites and Kurds but also at weakening Iraqi security forces trained and largely controlled by the American occupiers.

I see no reason to change my recommendations. As the assembly elected in January 2005 finally succeeded in voting on a constitution—and if the Iraqi population accepts it—we should leave within six months of the new elections that will follow. We have further compromised our position in Iraq by a heavy-handed effort at serving as the brokers of a compromise. Washington realized that without the participation of the Sunni representatives in the bargaining on the constitution, it would lack both legitimacy and effectiveness. But the bargaining has revealed and even increased the depth and multiplicity of the lines of fracture in Iraqi society, not only the lines that separate the three main ethnic and religious groups but also those that divide the secularists from the Islamists and those that split the Shiites along political lines (i.e., the populist Moqtada al-Sadr versus his adversaries). For the United States to get into the business of trying to erase these lines is an impossible task. Moreover, it would only serve to inflame further Sunni suspicions, to create anti-American resentment among Shiites, to feed al-Sadr's hostility, and so on. The way in which the constitutional process has moved will have done nothing to weaken the insurgents.

An Iraqi government that knows it cannot count much longer on walking with American crutches might be in a far better position to appeal to Muslim and other countries for help against the insurgents and to make serious efforts at splitting the Sunni insurgents from the al-Qaeda and foreign ones, even at the cost of watering down whatever provisions for loose federalism and Islamic supremacy we finally included in the constitution in order to obtain Shiite and (in the case of federalism) Kurdish consent. No longer under American supervision and left largely to its own devices, a new Iraqi government would at last be able to concentrate its efforts on what really matters to the public and what could indeed more effectively reduce the insurrection than the building up (and massacres) of security forces: material reconstruction, providing the public with the basic necessities of life, and ridding the country of its many militias and gangs.

The argument that we must "stay the course" because civil war or the breakup of the country would otherwise occur neglects the obvious fact that under the American watch an incipient civil war has already broken out and that if the components of that fractured and fractious society want to separate, we can do very little to prevent them. Even if American forces continue to stay and to struggle, Iranian influence in much of the Shiite land will manifest itself, and Kurdish desire for full autonomy and control of its oil resources and of its main cities will persist. We cannot build other people's nations, especially not when it isn't clear that we are dealing with a single nation.

An American withdrawal would not be a desertion. We would still have to participate—indeed, better than we have so far—in the country's reconstruction. We have paid heavily, in blood and money, for a war that has no purely military solution and in whose political solution we can play only a counterproductive role. Once again, out of sheer ignorance and semi-imperial, semi-idealistic hubris, we bit off far more than we could chew. We have done for Iraq all we could have done—and some of it has been bungled, some of it has been brutal, and little of it has contributed to America's popularity and influence in the world. It is time for the Iraqis whom we have helped put in power to take charge. The longer we stay, the more we offer targets and pretexts for the insurgents, the more they will say—and show—that the Iraqis they fight are our stooges, the more terrorists we breed, and the less able we are to concentrate on the other problems in the Middle East: helping, without heavy and merely verbal hectoring, the frail shoots of democracy grow; prodding our clients toward political opening in their own long-term interest; and concentrating our efforts (along with our partners) on reviving the road map at a crucial moment when Sharon makes it increasingly obvious that he accepts only a Palestinian "state" that is no more than a Bantustan and that no respectable, even ultramoderate, Palestinian could ever endorse.

I have as few illusions about being heard as I had in 2004. But it is doubly my duty to insist and persist. As a political analyst, my role consists in stating what my analysis of the problem suggests. As a contributor to the study of the ethics of international relations, I cannot but continue to condemn the shocking aspects of a war launched under false pretenses and without international legitimacy and to doubt that those who launched it and misplanned its aftermath are the best qualified to repair by themselves the damage they have done.

NOTES

Chapter 17 is a revised version of my article "Out of Iraq," *New York Review of Books*, October 21, 2004.

1. Christopher Preble, *Exiting Iraq: Why the US Must End the Military Occupation and Renew the War against Al Qaeda* (Washington, D.C.: Cato Institute, 2004), 30.

2. "Time to Consider Iraq Withdrawal," editorial in the *Financial Times*, September 10, 2004.

3. Preble, *Exiting Iraq*, 17.

U.S.–European Relations: Past and Future

I.

The closest of America's postwar alliances has been with the West Europeans. Their closeness was shaped during World War II. In this sinister period, both the United States and the Soviet Union undertook, each one in its own way, to restore a continent that had been overrun by Nazi Germany and found itself in dire condition in 1945. Moreover, already during the war and even more in the period that immediately followed it, the United States found that it had to supplement in a decisive way Britain's waning power. Reading the correspondence between President Roosevelt and Sir Winston Churchill is quite edifying in this respect. In the postwar situation, the United States was indeed indispensable for Europe's economic reconstruction, which it handled with considerable skill, in particular by insisting on cooperation among the West Europeans. Above all, the United States undertook to protect Western Europe from the looming Soviet peril, and, in order to do so, it accepted to draft and participate in an Atlantic alliance treaty that clearly was one of those foreign entanglements America's founding fathers had warned against. Out of that treaty came the organization of NATO. It never eliminated the divergences among its members: over decolonization, over German rearmament, and a little later over détente, over the Vietnam war, and, insofar as U.S.–French relations were concerned, over the degree of military integration France was willing to accept. Despite all those difficulties, the alliance fulfilled its function; it was not seriously damaged by General de Gaulle's decision to withdraw France from the integrated military structures of the alliance, especially as he was keeping his forces in Germany and as he remained an ally of the United States in the North Atlantic Treaty itself. In the 1980s, NATO survived one more crisis, this time over the deployment of American missiles in Germany.

Despite some dire predictions, the alliance, having lost its main enemy, nevertheless survived. It was useful to both the United States and the West Europeans as a kind of reassurance policy in case of difficulties with Russia. It survived also because it became a tool of management of the relations between its members on the one hand and the newly liberated Central and East European countries and Russia on the other. Then in the 1990s, the alliance had to face a real problem of civil war within the disintegrating Yugoslavia. Divisions of course continued, especially over the Yugoslav wars, but despite their original preference for an arrangement that would have made of Eastern Europe and Russia partners but not members of NATO, the European members more or less grudgingly accepted the American plan for NATO expansion, especially as it was managed in a way that took into account Russian susceptibilities. Another contentious issue was that of the European Union's "military ambitions," the desire of some of its members to increase the military capabilities of the European Union so that the latter would cease being primarily an economic and monetary enterprise.

The remarkable thing is that, from crisis to crisis, the alliance survived and found ways, if not of pleasing everyone, at least of keeping very diverse countries together. In a sense, the "Atlantic community" rested on two myths. One was the absence of any necessary conflict between European integration and the Atlantic community—a myth that served both to try to contain de Gaulle's ambitions for a generally autonomous "European Europe" and to reassure Atlanticists on both sides of the ocean that the task of European integration could be seen as a subset of the Atlantic community. The second myth was that Europe remained, for the United States, the most crucial diplomatic and strategic theater, one with which the United States was linked not only by vital economic and security interests but also by the link of a common culture and common values.

A school of thought that had for many years a hegemonic position in the academic study of international relations, neorealism, had predicted that the collapse of Soviet power and of the Soviet threat would operate as a dissolvent of the alliance and that American unipolar hegemony would incite the Europeans to try to balance American might. This has not happened. Neither the older school of thought, realism, nor Marxist theories of imperialism provide any explanation for the kind of preponderance exerted by the United States, a reluctant imperialist often more interested in wielding economic power (on behalf, mainly, of free trade rather than as a mercantilist) than in using military might and better at what Joseph Nye has termed "soft power" (the power of persuasion and the influence derived from its attraction on and imitation by others) than at the application of traditional hard power. Realism and theories of imperialism do not explain why the principal alliance of the United States links North America with the main economic rival of Washington.

The reasons for the survival of the alliance in the 1990s are, as usual, multiple. There are traditional factors, such as common vital interests—in facing a chaotic and uncertain Russia, still a major nuclear power but not yet a democracy; in trying to restore stability to this perennial powder keg, the Balkans, where each conflict risks involving peripheral states; and in seeking to pacify the Middle East by resolving the Israeli–Arab conflict, by deterring Iraq and the hard-liners in Iran, and by combating terrorism. Equally vital was the common interest in a growing world economy. Other factors are more original. The United States and the Europeans are the most interconnected partners in economic globalization—American direct investment in Europe is higher than in Asia, and transatlantic mergers have become daily happenings. Common values explain a great deal about the allies' solidarity in the Gulf War and their reactions to the Yugoslav dramas. The United States, during the Clinton years, began to accept the idea of a modicum of European military autonomy within NATO (through combined joint task forces). As for the Europeans, they have been too busy deepening the European Union's integration to engage in deliberate power balancing—the European Union itself, with its single market and currency, is a remarkable combination of balancing (by increasing Europe's wealth and economic clout) and cooperation.

In retrospect, the 1990s appear like a somewhat amorphous transition period. The Atlantic alliance had played a quite remarkable role during the Gulf War since this time the alliance functioned far from Europe without any major dissent even from France, which had been the most keen in limiting the scope of NATO to Europe and the Mediterranean. British and French forces played a significant role in the first Gulf War. The defeat of Saddam Hussein led in Washington and elsewhere to the dream of this revival of the original conception of the United Nations, the "new world order" mentioned several times by the first President Bush. The original United Nations was meant to be dominated by a Security Council that had to make all the important decisions in matters of war and threats of war and whose resolutions could be, under chapter VII of the UN Charter, actual decisions, and of course Roosevelt's dream had been one in which the five permanent powers on the Security Council (or rather the "Big Four" plus France, on England's insistence) would be in effect the arbiters of war and peace. However, this was not to be. The United Nations never managed to have the forces and the military structure that the Charter had envisaged, and, in economic matters, antagonisms between the developing countries and the richer ones made discussions far more contentious than they had ever been expected to be. With the end of the Gulf War, the Atlantic allies found themselves, with some relief, in a world in which no major enemy could dictate their common diplomatic and strategic agenda. NATO then became a field for U.S.–European relations. These encompassed rivalry and cooperation. Rivalry dominated the approaches to Eastern Europe; the Europeans wanted—or perhaps rather felt that they could not prevent—the eventual entry of Central and East European states into the European Union (Mitterrand had tried such a policy in 1991, but the scheme presented at a meeting in Prague—which invited the newly liberated countries to become members of a confederation because they were not ripe for full membership and was a confederation in which Russia would participate but not the United States—turned into a resounding fiasco.) However, since the European Union was still primarily an economic operation, the host of economic differences between the two halves of Europe and the fact that membership in the European Union required the adoption by the new applicants of an enormous mass of EU regulations that had been adopted over the years meant that accession could not be easy or fast. This allowed the United States to extend the protection of NATO to several Central and East European countries quite swiftly and deftly enough not to antagonize President Yeltsin. In this respect, the United States won the race with the West Europeans. Cooperation prevailed in the Balkan crisis, at least after 1995, when NATO played a considerable role in the military intervention against Yugoslavia and provided the necessary legitimacy to the war against Milosevic in defense of the inhabitants of Kosovo.

Meanwhile, the sum of difficulties the Europeans had encountered with the Americans in the Bosnia and Kosovo conflicts—the evidence provided by these conflicts of the huge technological gap between the U.S. military establishment and those of the Europeans—led to a greater European desire for reinforcing military cooperation. When Tony Blair in 1998, at Saint-Malo, decided to follow this trend, even though Britain had usually been much more protective of NATO's military preeminence, it looked like a major shift. In fact, it probably was both an indication of Britain's need to assure the continental Europeans of its desire for full participation despite the British refusal to accept the euro at that time and also a way of making sure that the renewed strategic cooperation within the European Union would not go so far as to become an emancipated rival to NATO.

On the whole, in this post–Cold War era, some very familiar features persisted. The Europeans often complained about American hubris and bravado; statements (often by Madeleine Albright) about the "indispensable nation" that "sees farther" set European teeth on the edge, especially when they seemed to neglect European contributions, for instance, to the forces deployed in Bosnia and Kosovo, to the reconstruction of these regions, or to the reunification of Germany (former officials of the Bush administration often presented it as an achievement of 2 + 4 in which the 2 were the United States and the Federal Republic!). The Europeans have complained also about the risk and loss aversion of America's military and political leaders. As for American officials, they kept deploring the divisions among the Europeans and the institutional complexity of the European Union (was it that much more complex than the decision-making process in Washington?) and the tendency of the Europeans to behave as free riders unwilling to share the burden fairly with the United States (to which the Europeans reply that it isn't only the burden but also the decisions that need to be shared).

In fact, the Europeans have often enjoyed the luxury of criticizing American policies in parts of the world in which Europe has been very inactive, and Americans have often accused the Europeans of being incompetent and impotent while hesitating to encourage them to shape up lest they emancipate themselves from America's grip. After all, as a brilliant young Italian scholar of alliances, Marco Cesa, has pointed out, alliances are not just instruments of common protection against a foe. They are also a tool that allows the dominant partner to control its allies, to thwart coalitions among them, and to monopolize key public goods (e.g., security)—which is what NATO has allowed the United States to do. Alliances are also a tool that gives to the smaller partners a way of influencing the senior power—but this, in the post-1989 unipolar era, has turned out to be more difficult for the Europeans, hence their discontent. Indeed, they were beginning to face two serious trends in the United States.

One was unilateralism—in two quite different forms. One is the unilateralism of diktats, of imposed decisions in agencies dominated by the United States, such as the International Monetary Fund (IMF), NATO, or the Security Council (where the United States has often acted to limit or weaken the mandates of the United Nations or of UN-sponsored forces in Yugoslavia or Africa). The other form is the unilateral refusal of many kinds of collective or internationalist responsibilities (funds for the United Nations, rejection of treaties, and so on) and the unilateral imposition of American preferences and practices by executive or legislative fiat. Thus, a major retreat from reciprocity was proceeding.

Indeed, a second peril is the fading of the kind of "internationalist" consensus that prevailed, not always and everywhere but quite widely during the Cold War (although it broke down over Vietnam and weakened over détente). In the realm of economic affairs, the free trade–open markets coalition was increasingly challenged by an antiglobalization backlash that threw together defenders of the environment, protectionists, labor leaders worried about the effects of open borders and institutions like the World Trade Organization (WTO) and North American Free Trade Agreement on the quality of work and the wages and benefits of workers in the United States. Defenders of global human rights, champions of sovereignty, and critics of capitalism were the bedfellows of Seattle when the WTO met there.

In the political-strategic realm, postwar internationalism remained popular in the public but increasingly lacked political spokesmen of eloquence and prestige. Among many Republicans, one found an antimultilateralist nationalism, a blend of resentment at the alleged free riding of foreigners and of aggressive confidence in American power. For these people, American unipolarity is the best possible structure for the international system, and U.S. foreign policy should be one of free hands—as well as aimed at preventing rivals from challenging what M. Védrine calls the American "hyperpower." Among most Democrats and some Republicans, the dominant mood was a bit more internationalist, but the United States was seen as the necessary and indisputable leader of the world: when America leads, others will follow, and the world itself tended to be seen in traditional terms, that is, in terms only of the dangers created by potential rising powers and by rogue states endowed with weapons of mass destruction. This is a view that not all other states, aware of the diversity of sources of trouble, were willing to endorse. This particular brand of muscular and selective internationalism lacked any enthusiasm for international or regional institutions that the United States does not control.

II.

At this point, President George W. Bush was elected, in rather extraordinary circumstances. At first, during the election campaign, he said very little about foreign policy except that America's foreign policy would be "humble" and that there would be a return to the wise precepts of realism, which meant coping only with threats to the national interest of the United States; in other words, there would be no altruistic nation building and no deep involvement in hopeless situations (as one realized quite quickly, after the Clinton fiasco at Camp David, Bush wanted no continuing entanglement in the Palestinian–Israeli tragedy).

The real turning point came, of course, on September 11, 2001. It is still difficult to evaluate fully the violence and depth of the shock a country that had never in recent times experienced war and heavy casualties on its own soil experienced on September 11. Two years later, the citizens' preoccupation with security remains as anxious as immediately after the terrorist attack. September 11 provided a whole new rationale for President Bush's foreign policy and for his domestic policy as well. It was a global war against terrorism, which he declared without much consideration for the arguments of those who, like Sir Michael Howard and Jacques Chirac, warned him that the fight against terrorism was something quite different from a war among states not only because it gave one the illusion of a possible and decisive victory but also because the methods needed in a war against terrorist gangs required essentially police methods and police cooperation rather than the mobilization of armies.

Whereas the containment rationale that had prevailed from 1947 until the fall of the Soviet Union had turned out to be quite effective, on the whole, as a national doctrine capable of rallying allies abroad, the new American rationale proved to be divisive. The Europeans were more than willing to participate in a fight against al-Qaeda and other terrorist organizations, but they did not see in this issue the central problem in international relations. Other issues, such as the conflicts in the Near East, in the Far East, or over Kashmir; the proliferation of weapons of mass destruction; the economic issues of world disease and poverty so often mentioned by Tony Blair; the environmental problems of the earth—all this was seen as at least as perilous for world stability and for the future. Insofar as the president's presentation of this new war suggested a heavy emphasis on the use of force, the Europeans were suspicious, given their growing aversion to the militarization of international relations.

As for the United States, it became quickly apparent that the war on terrorism was an exceedingly broad tent indeed. On this change of priorities was grafted a whole new approach to international relations by the administration. It amounted to a rejection of the restraints so long accepted by American diplomacy on American independence. The new doctrinaires were above all "sovereignists" and had made explicit and effective their hostility to a variety of treaties, ranging from the comprehensive test ban and the ABM treaty to the Kyoto Protocol on the environment and above all to the International Criminal Court, on which the United States practically declared war as if it were a terrorist organization, with sanctions attached against allies that dared to support the court. This comprehensive new approach meant not only a rehabilitation of the national interest over more international interests but also an extension of the national interest to threats in the whole world, going as far as leading to some restrictions on the very globalization of which the United States had been and remains a champion, for instance, through the imposition of restrictions on students and foreigners traveling to the United States, and implying a much tougher attitude in economic negotiations. It meant also war against countries that harbored, equipped, and supported terrorist gangs; this led of course to the invasion of Afghanistan, endorsed immediately by the NATO members because the behavior of the Taliban in sheltering and helping al-Qaeda seemed to provide the United States and its allies with a perfect case of self-defense. Next, it meant the replacement of the prudent policies of containment, aimed above all at preventing war, with an embrace of preventive war, seen as necessary not only against terrorists, who were indeed difficult if not impossible to deter, but also against rogue states hostile to the United States, eager to build arsenals of weapons of mass destruction and linked to terrorism. Above all, it meant an enthusiastic embrace of unipolarity and unilateralism. The new attitude toward members of the United Nations (President Bush kept referring to the United States *and* the United Nations, as if the United States was not a very important member of the organization) was one of suspicion, and America's own allies were told that if one was not on America's side, one was against it. What this meant, especially in the eyes of the neoconservatives who were in control of the Pentagon and of the vice president's office, was that institutions—even alliances—that did not fully support the United States in its war on terrorism would be sidelined and replaced with "coalitions of the willing," in other words, ad hoc groupings, case by case, for which these institutions would serve as a kind of pond within which the United States could fish out those fish that could be, so to speak, drafted for the coalition. It was up to the United States to pick and choose its clients, just as it was up to the United States to pick, in the mass of international norms and agreements, those that it deemed necessary to maintain international order.

This was not the only graft on the fight against terrorists. The biggest was Iraq, which had been a sore point for many of the members of the Bush administration for many years. Many of them who had been in or around the administration of Bush the father had been very bitter about the decision made by him and his main advisers not to overthrow the Saddam Hussein regime at the end of the Gulf War and not to come to the rescue of the Shiites and Kurds who had revolted and been massacred by Saddam's remaining forces. Dick Cheney, who was then the secretary of defense and had seemingly gone along with this, obviously had belated second thoughts. As for Colin Powell, who as head of the Joint Chiefs of Staff had vigorously pushed for an early end to the war, arguing that nothing would be worse than engaging the American army in civil conflicts in Iraq, he was thus seen with great suspicion by his rivals in the new administration. The whole strategy of Iraq's enemies in Washington consisted in their persuading the president that Iraq deserved to be made a test case in the war on terrorism because of the weapons of mass destruction that Saddam could not but possess, especially after the UN inspectors withdrew from Iraq in 1998, and because of possible links to terror organizations. Moreover, many of the neoconservatives, who were anything but conservative, had developed a radical dream of using a war against and the overthrow of Saddam Hussein as a lever to change the whole complexion of the Middle East. The idea was to push for democracy in states that did not have it and to use this threat of democratization as a way of putting pressure on several of America's old Arab allies whose attitudes toward terrorism were highly ambivalent, such as Egypt, Saudi Arabia, and Pakistan. One of the benefits this grand operation would have, in the eyes of many of its advocates, was to establish moderate governments in the Arab world, willing to accept a settlement of the Palestinian issue more favorable to Israel than what Arab states had accepted before. The president gradually came to endorse this conception, and the battle between the more moderate State Department and the neoconservatives was in effect settled. It continued over issues of procedure in which Colin Powell, in his preference for obtaining a UN legitimation, had the full support of Tony Blair.

I will not go into details of the period of UN bargaining from September 2002 to March 2003 but will look briefly at the first effects of the victory of the American and British forces. President Bush's popularity rose to new heights because victory was swift and casualties were low; this popularity had already been bolstered by the American public's acceptance of the main arguments of the president concerning the threat represented for world and American security by Saddam's weapons of mass destruction and the horrors of his regime, and they had also swallowed whole the very dubious argument about the connection between Saddam Hussein's Iraq and al-Qaeda (particularly concerning the hijackers of planes on September 11, not one of whom, in fact, was an Iraqi). It is quite remarkable that the failure to find weapons of mass destruction did not deeply affect the president's standing in the eyes of the American public and that, unlike in Britain, no thorough investigation arose of the intelligence that had been provided to the government and of the possible degree to which members of the administration itself might have "sexed up" these reports. If one remembers that the main reasons given for refusing to extend the inspections by the UN inspectors were the bad Iraqi climate in the summer and therefore the need to act very quickly against such dangers, one realizes that the administration had never been serious about letting the UN inspectors persist in their tasks or even about the possibility of subordinating an invasion to a clear-cut resolution by the Security Council. Europe was badly split by this whole episode. The United States was successful in obtaining the approval of a number of governments from the present European Union and from the governments of the countries that had asked for and obtained their admission for 2004. The result was not only a division between what that great phrasemaker Secretary of Defense Rumsfeld had called the old and the new Europe but also a split between all of the publics in continental Europe, east and west, and several of their governments. While the European Union was divided, NATO was sidelined. The slightly absurd clash over an alleged Turkish request for military aid in case of an attack from Saddam Hussein—a request that was not presented by the new Turkish government itself—made it clear that it would be difficult for the United States to obtain unanimity within NATO, and, just as the offer of NATO's services for Afghanistan had been rejected in 2001, the United States left it aside in the case of Iraq. The United Kingdom found itself in a most uncomfortable position, having inspired at least one of the two letters of support of European governments to the United States and rather unfairly put all the blame for the failure to obtain a second resolution at the United Nations on the French. In other words, the casualties were international institutions.

III.

One interesting aspect of American foreign policy in the first administration of George W. Bush has been the rise of U.S. dogmatism as compared with European empiricism. Most European governments have made it clear that not all terrorists, hideous as their methods are, can be lumped together. Their grievances have many different causes, their targets have very different ranges, some of the causes of terrorism are religious, others are intensely secular and parochial, and declaring a global war on terrorism risks both fomenting more terrorists and creating an unholy alliance between very different types of terrorism. In particular, if the priority in world affairs is the eradication of terrorism or a solution of the Palestinian problem or indeed of the Kashmir problem, is likely to remain elusive. Even though President Bush, under pressure from Tony Blair, other European countries, and Colin Powell, returned to the Palestinian conflict by drafting his road map, the emphasis he put on a priority of the dismantling of Palestinian terrorism—which would mean a civil war among Palestinians—and his consent to major Israeli settlements on the West Bank contributed to reducing the gains that one could have expected from that initiative. It has seemed for a while that U.S. diplomacy was now in the hands of rather gleeful neoimperialists who believe in diplomacy by threat and hope for the crumbling under such threat of the hostile policies or even the regimes of countries such as Syria or Iran or North Korea. The price that has had to be paid so far has been a precipitous decline in the prestige of the United States, which seems to have abandoned the practice of what Joseph Nye has called soft power, for a policy that relies primarily on force and the threat of force. It has also been a slow erosion of the forces of Washington's allies in Iraq.

The difficulties encountered by the United States in Iraq, due in large part to an astonishing lack of preparation for the aftermath of Saddam Hussein's collapse, have not yet turned American public opinion decisively against the war itself, but they have nevertheless awakened many anxieties. A tenacious insurgency in Iraq, a return of Taliban terrorism in Afghanistan, rising casualties, and rising costs are worrying the public and even more the members of Congress, already disturbed by a huge deficit that results in part from George W. Bush's tax cuts. It is therefore not surprising that this turn of events somehow strengthened the rather weak position of Colin Powell and the State Department and persuaded the president that, given the choices available in Iraq, the least risky was an appeal to more countries, including more European countries, to send forces to supplement the so-called coalition. But a huge gap remained between Americans still rather bound by the evident reluctance of the neoconservatives and of the president himself to appear eating humble pie and to endorse a transfer of supreme authority (if not military command, which nobody had actually suggested) to the United Nations and a number of governments, including France and Germany, that had been hostile to the American-led war and did not see why they should contribute forces and money to a war that had been waged rather deliberately against their advice and against a reluctant United Nations. To American legislators and pundits, it may seem that sharing losses and costs is the right thing to do for America's allies and potential partners, but why it should appear in this light to the latter is not a question one often found discussed in Washington.

After November 2004, there has been a new, softer tone toward the Europeans in Condoleezza Rice's Department of State, but it is not clear that there is much change in substance, except in the rather grudging American support of the "EU3"—France, Germany, and Britain—in their attempt to find a diplomatic solution with Iran. Nevertheless, what is striking is the absence of any attempt, even in these somewhat difficult moments for the administration, to return to the old institutional game, to go to NATO and to a European Union in the middle of an institutional reform aimed at, among other things, strengthening its foreign and defense policy. Nor has Tony Blair made much of an effort at restoring bridges blown up between the United Kingdom on the one hand and France and Germany on the other. While the embarrassments of Iraq may have curtailed the ambitions of those who had already been talking about exporting the same kind of strategy to countries such as Iran and Syria (or even North Korea, which the administration has, somewhat reluctantly, also chosen to approach in a more multilateral way), it is not at all clear at this point how deeply the Iraq adventure will affect the tone and substance of American foreign policy and in particular its relations with Europe. The one thing one can perhaps predict with a certain degree of certainty is that the central importance of Europe for the United States will remain under a cloud. Many people in Washington—and not only among the neoconservatives—see in the prospects of a Europe with greater defense ambitions altogether a pipe dream, a waste of money, and a source of irritation, and they see in the economic and monetary strength of Europe a potential threat to American economic predominance. They have been comforted by the failure of the referendum on the European constitution in France and in Holland and by the bitter split between Chirac and Blair not only over Iraq but also about the internal priorities of the European Union.

The days of relative harmony between the United States and the European Union have not returned. The EU crisis of 2005 makes hasty predictions about a shift in world power, away from the United States and toward the European Union, seem a bit absurd and comforts American suprematists; but the truth is that both sides are in mediocre shape—for the greatest benefit of rising Asian powers and of terrorists. The truth is also that major disagreements persist. For instance, none may be more divisive than the divergence between the United States and the Europeans on what constitutes a threat. The Europeans have been in favor of both Clinton's and George W. Bush's attempts at "engaging" the Chinese and of their support for democracy, a free market, and nuclear arms reductions in Russia. But the Europeans share neither the American priority of fighting terrorism nor the American phobia of rogue states. They find it hard to believe that small states whose leaders know they'd be wiped out if they used weapons of mass destruction against the United States or its allies constitute a serious menace. In this connection, American plans for limited antinuclear defenses, at the expense of the ABM treaty, have been particularly open to criticism. Once more, the allies were not consulted. The technology isn't ready. The alleged North Korean threat isn't credible. The scheme throws other states such as Russia, China, and the Europeans together in criticism of the United States and seems like a symbol of a certain kind of disengagement since it would protect the United States only (and if it should expand in such a way as to be able to protect the allies, it could be seen, as in the mid-1980s, by America's rivals in Moscow and Beijing as a threat to the effectiveness of their nuclear forces and as an attempt at moving away, at their expense, from the commonly accepted condition of mutual vulnerability. This would kill arms control and rekindle the arms race).

Assuming some progress in European efforts toward a common security policy, what would happen if the United States, in NATO, refused to share critical assets with the EU force (especially during the probably long period during which the European Union would try to narrow the gap in military technology with the United States)? Conversely, the United States wants to keep forces in Europe not only as a deterrent against a resurgent Russia—something the Europeans agree with—but also because Europe is a staging area for forces to be sent to the Middle East or the Far East—areas where the Europeans don't see as many looming threats as the United States.

Another realm of conflicts is economic and cultural. While the Atlantic governments have a consensus on the benefits of globalization and a joint interest in keeping their financial systems sound and their economies growing—a global depression would be a global disaster—the Europeans do not see eye to eye with the United States on a variety of issues. What makes the disagreements particularly sharp is that interests and values get intertwined. European agricultural protectionism is both an issue of economic interest—the defense of European products and farmers against an onslaught of cheaper American goods—and an issue of culture, in the sense of a way of life, even as the number of farmers in western Europe declines (but Europe will enlarge in the east, where peasants still abound); the quarrel over genetically modified products is typical in this respect. Cultural issues will continue to be divisive. The United States tends to look at films and television programs as tradable goods that should circulate freely; the European Union wants a European cinema and European television programs, even watched by a minority of spectators, to survive. The United States does not want to recognize copyrights not recorded on its soil, is eager to deliver patents for the exploitation of the genome, and is hostile to any restrictions on the Internet. These positions seem, to the Europeans, characteristic of America's drive to commercialize all things and to spread its influence through the market. The Americans do not appear to mind uniformity through globalization since the single brand would be American. The Europeans insist on diversity, on the protection of local cultures, on the distinction between a market economy and a market society. This will not make the task of the WTO easy. A comparable mix of political, economic, and cultural reasons explains the greater European concern with aid to developing countries at a time when the U.S. contribution to it remains very small—another example of a difference in the evaluation of threats.

The management of differences and conflicts will require a great deal of wisdom on both sides of the Atlantic. On the American side, the fact that the United States believes it sits on top of the hierarchy of power in every dimension of power—military, economic, and "soft"—breeds a vast amount of complacency. Monopoly, said de Gaulle, appears natural to whoever enjoys one. And yet the very complexity of global society makes it unmanageable by a single power, however great, and risks making it both violent and chaotic if left unmanaged and ungoverned. The United States will, in circumstances far less clear-cut than in the 1950s, have to relearn internationalism, nonover-bearing cooperation, the merits of international norms and regimes, the way of being *primus inter pares*, but no more.

As for the Europeans, their slow emancipation from a dependence that has lasted more than half a century should be seen as necessary—at a time when the hegemon shows signs of battle fatigue, assistance fatigue, and compassion fatigue—and welcome—for a single power has no monopoly on wisdom, and the United States in particular could learn a great deal from European societies that are no less attached to freedom but less unconcerned with social injustice. On the other hand, a Europe with the ambition of being a complete power will need to play a greater role in international institutions as well as in parts of the world where it has either been shut out by the United States (the Middle East) or only too happy to leave the headaches to the United States (Asia). Europeans and Americans alike will need to make bigger and longer efforts to rebuild failed states.

Strange as it may seem, the United States and Europe have no adequate forum for comparing, coordinating, and discussing their strategies. NATO has, despite various attempts, never transcended its military functions. The WTO, the IMF, and the World Bank deal with economic issues. The G8 includes more than the transatlantic partners, and is more a show than a serious agency. An informal transatlantic council in which the United States and the European Union would review their approaches and policies as equals would be most helpful—as long as the United States does not behave as big brother and the European Union does not see it as a cage.[1]

NOTES

Chapter 18 incorporates elements from "U.S.–European Relations," *International Affairs* 79, no. 5 (October 2003).

1. A briefer discussion of the "crisis in transatlantic relations" can be found in my essay in Gustav Lindstrom, ed., *Shift or Rift* (Paris: EU Institute for Security Studies, 2003), 13–20.

· 19 ·

The European Sisyphus, Once More

I. EUROPE'S TASKS

In the 1990s and the first years of the twenty-first century, the European Union was fully engaged in five connected and difficult enterprises—all of which had repercussions on the transatlantic relationship. The first one (chronologically) was the reform of the Byzantine institutional system of the European Union, aimed at completing the design left unfinished by the Amsterdam treaty of 1997. While it was a reform of modest proportions, decisions about the size of the Commission, weighted voting in the Council, and the extension of majority rule were not insignificant, especially as a first step toward making the European Union more manageable before the number of its members increased. The discussions tended to pit the smaller states against the larger ones—and to "smoke out" the enthusiasm (or lack of it) for more majority-rule decisions among the major states. The Nice treaty of 2001 was widely seen as disappointing, and one writer referred to "a Europe of bits and pieces."[1]

The second one was the launching of the European Monetary Union. Everybody agreed that the single currency, once in effect, would lead to greater cooperation among the states that accepted the euro. But two big questions remained. How much economic coordination would actually take place, and how much autonomy would each participant want to preserve over fiscal policy, labor policy and practices, and social security arrangements? In addition, would the independence of the European Central Bank be complete in practice? In the United States, the Federal Reserve operates in the relatively simple environment of a single state, where a broad consensus on the Fed's independence exists. The European Central Bank has had eleven countries in its orbit and had to face difficult decisions when some of them got into trouble with the requirements of the "stability pact" demanded by Germany. The degree of coordination has remained low; France and Germany

193

did not meet the stability pact's demands. The struggle for some kind of political supervision of the Bank is far from over—indeed, it hasn't even begun. Nevertheless, the euro has shown considerable strength vis-à-vis the dollar.

The third task is in many ways the most ambitious and difficult: the development of a common defense and foreign policy. The impetus was created by the experience—bitter for the Europeans—of the Yugoslav wars, where the gap between U.S. and European capabilities was humiliating, and by the "conversion" of Tony Blair to the idea of a common defense instead of perpetual and exclusive reliance on NATO. The obstacles have remained huge. In diplomacy, the major European powers continue to have their *chasses gardées* and habits of independence. In defense, a common security policy that would make possible European military interventions in areas the United States might deem not worth American losses requires a drastic reorganization of national armed forces (especially in Germany), a harmonization of armaments, and increases in expenses for technological research and development. This has not taken place. Moreover, even before Iraq, there was no full Franco-British agreement on the degree of autonomy from (as opposed to within) NATO the new defense system should have—and it was probably wise not to raise this issue too soon as a matter of principle. This is, of course, the undertaking that American officials have considered with the greatest amount of skepticism and more than a small dose of hostility, for should it succeed, it would change the balance of power and influence within and perhaps the structure of NATO, intangible so far.

The fourth task was enlargement (which logically entails some kind of common understanding of the limits of Europe). This too is a formidable and risky undertaking. A Europe of twenty-seven states will be extraordinarily heterogeneous and will inevitably resemble that *Europe à la carte* that the European federalists fear and dislike. The new members were able to meet the preconditions for joining the European Monetary Union and adopting the euro. But many of them show very little enthusiasm for a common diplomacy and defense. They want to join because, as one of their diplomats put it, they are eager to share in the good life, but for their lives, that is, their physical security, they prefer to rely on NATO—especially if they are near Russia. Having alienated their sovereignty for fifty years, they are not eager to sacrifice too much of it. Having, as they see it, regained their freedom thanks to American containment of the Soviet Union, they see in the United States their chief protector and have no great desire to take part in an attempt to "balance" American might. As for current members of the European Union, their commitment to enlargement is a matter of inevitability and reason (what justification would there be for leaving those countries out? In addition, membership would be likely to consolidate their democratic institutions, one hopes) more than a matter of enthusiasm, given the many economic points of dispute and the fear of immigration from the east or from Turkey in a Union that guarantees the free circulation of the members' citizens.

The fifth task was deciding on the final institutional nature of the European Union. Interestingly, the debate began even though the first task (the modest institutional reform described previously) wasn't yet finished and enlargement hadn't yet occurred. Those who, like Joshka Fischer and Jacques Chirac, spoke early seemed to agree on the need for what the latter has called a *noyau dur*, a hard core of countries willing to go farther than the others. Britain, as long as it hasn't joined the European Monetary Union, remains hostile to the idea—as are all those current and future members who fear being relegated to a second-class position. The enlarged European Union, in this conception, would be above all a vast free-trade single market with a common agricultural policy, whereas the *noyau dur* would have a common currency, diplomacy, and defense. A second issue, not any less prickly, was the institutional setup of the hard core. Here, the divide separates federalists who don't believe that a common diplomacy and defense can be effective if all decisions have to be made by unanimity or even a qualified majority and intergovernmentalists who resist going beyond the *pooling* of sovereignty all the way to its *transfer* to a federal executive and legislature. It was not easy to finesse an issue that carries so much freight (what happens to national identity in a federal *noyau dur*? What happens to the dream of a "complete European power" in a predominantly intergovernmental one? The French, it seems, wanted it nonfederal but effective, which may not be a very Cartesian stance). The European Convention on the Future of Europe, composed of national officials and national and European parliamentarians, succeeded in producing, in 2003, a "constitutional treaty" that streamlined and reformed the institutions of the European Union but left many issues unresolved. It was more a statement of how far the members were willing to go—not very—than a potentially permanent framework. Unsurprisingly, it dropped the idea of the *noyau dur*.

Even before 2005, several developments were disturbing: the difficulty of obtaining popular approval of EU treaties and of obtaining substantial results at recent EU summits; the malaise about the "democratic deficit," which reflects unease not only about the preponderance of the executive over parliaments—a phenomenon that is pervasive within European states—but also about the behavior of the European Council as energetic defender of national interests; about the more "European" Commission's relative marginalization; and about the importance of nondemocratically selected institutions such as the European Courts and the European Bank: technocracy over democracy. Three particularly worrisome cases have been the way in which the current EU enlargement proceeded—many EU governments were reluctant, and their lack of enthusiasm cooled the ardor of several of the new applicants; the difficulties of the Convention (there were limits to the consensus method); and of course the spectacular post–Iraq invasion crisis of the attempt at establishing a common foreign and security policy.

II. THE CONSTITUTIONAL TREATY'S CRISIS AND THE CRISIS OF THE EUROPEAN UNION

The process of ratifying the Constitutional Treaty the Convention had drafted, under the leadership of Valéry Giscard d'Estaing, has hit an unexpected, major roadblock: the rejection of the text by the French and Dutch electorates. Each state had a choice between ratification by parliamentary approval and ratification by referendum if its own Constitution allowed for one. Even before the French fiasco of May 29, 2005, one could ask whether the Convention and a new Constitution were the best way for an enlarged Union to proceed. It could be counterproductive if it made it more difficult to move ahead in the pragmatic way that had been followed in the past: by accretion, adaptation, and flexibility (the common law rather than the Roman way). Moreover, if the purpose of the Convention was to make the European Union more effective and to reinforce democracy, the latter aim would require in the present Europe of nations a greater participation of the representatives of the different *demoi* in the decision-making process of the European Union. If one wants to push toward a future European *demos* despite the multiple languages and cultures, one needs to do much more than a Constitution can do in order to create a European public space, genuine European parliamentary elections, and a single executive composed of members functioning in a dual capacity—as delegates of their nations and as European statesmen. Would this have been acceptable to the new members and to the smaller of the old ones?

The crisis provoked by the rejection of the text by the French—the nation that was at the origin of the whole process of European integration—showed once again that proceeding by referendum means playing Russian roulette. The Maastricht treaty, which created the Monetary Union, barely obtained a popular majority in France in 1992, partly because many voters who disliked President Mitterrand voted no—certainly not because they wanted no common currency. For a considerable negative vote to appear, all that is needed is a momentary coalition of dissenters, often moved by considerations quite unrelated to the question asked. In 2005, in France, dissatisfaction with the government of President Chirac and the state of the economy were major factors. The European Union became the scapegoat for a variety of discontents, and the target of fears about the effects of globalization on French social policies (even though these remain in the national, not the EU domain) and on those of the European Union's competition policy on French public enterprises. Those who, on the far right, thought that the Constitution would further reduce French sovereignty, became the bedfellows of those, on the far left, who complained that the European Union was not doing enough to help and protect the poor, the unemployed, "les petits." In Holland, grievances against immigrants were targeted on the European Union's Schengen agreements about the circulation of foreigners. The Turkish application for membership in the European Union became a reason for voting no, even though it was not related to the Constitution. Many French voters also resented the fact that the enlargement of the European Union in 2004—a major transformation—was not submitted to them and was thus, in their eyes, one more fait accompli.

Maybe many of those converging yet contradictory phantasms were created by ignorance. But many who read the text and tried to inform themselves were turned off by its excessive length and by the complexity of its provisions. Part 3, which is the longest and lists all the common policies of the Union, had provisions that could not fail to offend or annoy a motley mass of pressure groups and individuals. Inserting it in the Constitution was a mistake, made by the intergovernmental conference that reviewed the Convention's text. These provisions should, at best, have been annexes—although the number of protocols and declarations was already huge. The single "merit" of including part 3 was that it could be revised only by unanimity and thus perpetuated past deals among governments.

The fiasco has the merit of highlighting six major problems for the future of the European Union. The first—and perhaps most fundamental—is the relationship between the political elites and the publics. The process of European integration, ever since 1950, has been led by the elites—governments, parliamentarians, and academics. The crisis of 2005 may well mark the end of "a purely aristocratic logic of integration," and it shows "the difficulty of translating the democratic aspiration at a European level in a paradigm that isn't that of the national scheme."[2] The attempt at creating a "European public"—not a European nation, since that is most unlikely, but a "demos of demoi," a people of nations, in Kalypso Nicolaidis's conception—has not gone very far. The European Parliament has—until recently—been too devoid of power, and above all elections to it, which take place in the national framework and offer the electorates choices among purely national slates of candidates, are consultations about the domestic politics of the member states: they do little to foster transnational concerns. There is, as Nicolaidis points out, a need "to reenforce a participatory dynamic, and to put it in the service of a representative democracy, not just direct democracy"—which is both risky and likely, at best, to produce high levels of abstentions. If the European Union is to develop into a "community of others," a triumph of "radical pluralism," an "orchestration of diversity rather than a forger of harmony," all three of its major institutions—the Council, the Commission, and the Parliament—have to find more ways of bringing together more than transnational interest groups but also people of different walks of life as well as countries and particularly the young (and also the immigrants). Some programs exist (Erasmus, in higher education), but many more are needed. And the representatives of civil societies need to be included in future constitutional exercises. One could also think of a second chamber, consultative or legislative, composed of representatives of trans-European interests.

A second issue rudely put forward by the crisis of 2005 is that of the economic and social orientation of the Union. Having helped dismantle the wall of protectionism that separated European countries in matters of trade and investment and helped remove or lower the barriers between them and other countries, the European Union appears to many of its members as a servant of economic liberalism and thus of globalization, an agent of the endless destructions that capitalism effects in the quest for more efficiency and aggregate prosperity. Social protection is, especially in periods of recession, a target and victim of this quest—and it remains primarily in the national domain. It is a matter of redressing the balance. The text of the Constitution attributed to the Union a remarkable number of powers in various "social" domains, including that of ensuring the coordination of national employment policies and that of defining the main orientations of economic policies, to be coordinated by the members. It would not be an attack on the independence of the Central Bank if, as the French have often suggested, a council in charge of such coordination was established among the euro countries.

A third issue is a hardy perennial—cooperation (largely intergovernmental) versus integration. The latter obviously requires strong central institutions and a shrinking of the domain of required unanimity. The Constitution tried, rather skillfully, to find a middle way. It certainly did not go as far as federalists would have liked, if only because they are in power nowhere. But, by making of the Commission something more like a government and of the Council a rather original, if not fully convincing, mix of supergovernment and second chamber of state representatives, it did reduce further the purely intergovernmental aspects of the European Union. The risk it thus took was considerable, given the resistance to more integration by many of the new members (the Czechs, for instance), keen on preserving a recently regained sovereignty, as well as the Scandinavians and the British, who were determined to prevent majority rule in many areas of domestic (as well as foreign) policy. This is an issue that can only be solved in one of three ways: it can be finessed by compromises, as in the past; or, if these turn out impossible, by the creation of a hard core of states willing to get more integrated, surrounded by a less integrated periphery; or else by a resort to "reenforced cooperations" among those EU members who want to move faster than others in given domains. All three come at a heavy price, especially the second.

A fourth issue is another perennial: as always, the deepest root of the malaise is the unwillingness of the EU nations to tackle directly the key issue: what is Europe for? (*L'Europe: pour quoi faire?*) There is agreement on the welfare function, but it demands the right combination of financial stability and economic growth. This in turn requires a more effective European executive with a policy of noninflationary growth (which could make the issue of subsidies to the poorer members and regions less contentious); but for such a policy, Europeans depend on the state of the U.S. economy as well as on the willingness of their peoples to accept some limitations on the European welfare state model. There is agreement in particular on the external part of the welfare function: the defense and promotion of the European Union's economic interests in the world. Here, however, the spectacular clash between Chirac and Blair about the common agricultural policy showed the limits of consensus. It was a clash between the leader of a nonagricultural country, eager to provide developing countries with more opportunities to export their resources, and the leader of a nation deeply attached to what is left of its rural past, even if this attachment limits the development of poor countries.

Moreover, on the idea of a Europe that would be a "full power," with a common foreign policy and defense, there really is no agreement at all. The new members, for obvious reasons, turn to the United States for their security not only because of America's enormous might but perhaps also because they have not yet liquidated intra-European suspicions that the western Europeans have overcome in the past sixty years. In several countries of the "old" Europe of the European Union, the budgetary costs of a significant defense effort seem prohibitive or not worth it since the United States can in any case do so much more, and several of the smaller members like the idea of Europe as a peaceful and somewhat curative civilian power. Add to this the "revolt" of the smaller states and of the European middle powers (Spain and Italy) against the Franco-German leadership of the European Union (but without it, there would have been no motor at all). Finally, add the factor of the United Kingdom as Hamlet, oscillating from St. Malo to the Bush "coalition." As a result, the common diplomacy attempt has so far only been a choice between mutual exasperation and a rhetoric of incantation and deploration. In the Arab–Israeli conflict and in Iraq, internal divisions of the European Union have combined with American reluctance to limit the influence of the European Union. The Constitution would have given the European Union a genuine and powerful foreign minister, member of both the Commission and the Council.

Things are not much better in the realm of security. Counterterrorism policy is hampered by the European Union's lack of powers of investigation and prosecution. The ambitious common action plan of December 2003 on "a secure Europe in a better world" stresses preventive engagement and "effective multilateralism"—"ambitious goals which will stay unfulfilled if the current gap between ends and means is allowed to persist."[3] For the time being, it is mainly in ex-Yugoslavia that the European Union is showing its military muscles. Ultimately, in the realm of diplomacy and defense, it may well be that the European Union will have to proceed with "reenforced coordinations" or else with a fluctuating membership à la carte.

A fifth issue was raised by the constitutional debate of 2005—a corollary of the fourth. What are the limits of Europe? It certainly cannot be a Europe "de l'Atlantique à l'Oural"! But those who believe that the larger the European Union becomes, the more it risks becoming primarily a free-trade zone, and the more difficult it will be to develop further integration policies, are likely to be very reluctant to go beyond the admission—not too soon—of Balkan applicants. Those who think in rather grandiose terms of Europe as a potential superpower in world affairs see no reason not to admit countries such as Ukraine or a democratic Belarus if they desire to become members. Turkey is a big bone of contention both among the elites and in the publics, for a variety of reasons, good and bad: its size, its stage of development, continuing suspicions about the role of its army and its degree of secularism, the fear of more Turkish immigration (even though a Europe with a falling birthrate needs immigrants), the presence of such a large Islamic state in "Judeo-Christian" Europe, and so on. In my opinion, a categorical definition of who can be in Europe and who cannot is likely to be unhelpful, and decisions ought to be made case by case—within the limits of common sense. Historically, the borders of Europe have fluctuated.

Finally, last but not least, the 2004 enlargement, the debate on the Constitution, and the French "defection" have raised a crucial problem. Any international enterprise requires a "motor": states that initiate change, propose new solutions, and try to rally their partners. For many years, it was the

Franco-German team. In a Europe of twenty-five or twenty-seven members, this team remains important, but it does not suffice. Rather than a series of ad hoc "motors"—a perfect guarantee for a return to balancing and counter-balancing tactics that would do great harm to the need for continuity, mutual confidence, and cooperation—one could think in terms of an informal or even formal "directory" in which France and Germany would be joined by Britain, Spain, Italy, Poland, and two smaller countries so as to attenuate the clash between the greater and the weaker powers. Seven, of course, is a heavier and clumsier mechanism than the Paris–Bonn axis. But there have been tensions between France and Germany, and their power of attraction and persuasion is not what it used to be. Britain's participation in this directorate raises many problems. The United Kingdom is not in "Euro-land," it remains an obstacle to ideas of greater institutional centralization and majority rule, and it is recurrently tempted by the idea of putting the United States first and the European Union second. But any development of joint diplomatic and security policies requires its participation. In addition, Blair's priorities for Europe's future deserve to be taken seriously; they are ambitious and challenging.

These are the problems the crisis of 2005 has raised. It will take at least two years until the fog lifts (if it does) over the constitutional issue. If four-fifths of the twenty-five members ratify the text, the Council will have to decide what to do next. If—as is likely—the negative fifth comprises both France and Britain, Holland, and one Scandinavian and one or two eastern European states, the present constitutional treaty will have to be abandoned. If the momentum toward ratification revives and Britain then decides to proceed by parliamentary vote, the treaty will still need to be revised and cans of worms reopened. But the one merit of the crisis is that it provides to European elites and electorates alike a time for reflection that should allow them to measure what is at stake, how much has been achieved in the past fifty-five years, how much the European Union is enhancing the power of each member, and what dangers they would face if the most constructive enterprise in a treacherous world were to disintegrate or even just stop moving forward.

NOTES

1. Deirdre Curtin, "The Constitutional Structure of the Union: A Europe of Bits and Pieces," *Common Market Law Review* 30 (1993): 17.

2. Kalypso Nicolaidis, "UE: Un Moment Tocquevillien," *Politique étrangère* 3 (2005): 497–509, at 498.

3. Jean-Yves Haine, "ESDP and NATO," in *EU Security and Defense Policy*, ed. Nicole Gnesotto, preface by Javier Solana (Paris: Institute for Security Policies, 2004), 52–53.

·20·

The Foreign Policy the United States Needs

I.

$\mathcal{D}$uring the Cold War Americans believed that in order to eliminate risks of nuclear war, a policy of edgy coexistence with the Soviet Union was worth pursuing. Few believed that America should prepare for a military showdown with Moscow. In the debates between doves and hawks, everyone assumed there would be a very long contest with the Communist world.

The rapid collapse of the Soviet Union left the United States as the only superpower, or so it seemed. George H. W. Bush talked about a new world order in which the "real world" of American supremacy and the formal world of the UN Charter would somehow merge. But Bush Senior was soon gone, and Clinton had no large international vision. This may have been a blessing, and relations improved with allies, including France and Germany, which had occasionally been miffed by shrill official statements about the United States as the "indispensable nation" endowed with greater foresight than others.

People such as Dick Cheney and Donald Rumsfeld, who had long thought it time to proclaim U.S. hegemony, were enraged by Clinton's failure to do so. When George W. Bush came to power, September 11 provided what seemed an unchallengeable opportunity for a drastic change in strategy and in diplomacy. The "war against terrorism" was now seen as a kind of World War II reborn, yet it was without a clear enemy and without allies comparable to Stalin's Soviet Union or even Churchill's British Empire. A brief era of American triumphalism—or imperialism—led to, but did not survive, the disaster in Iraq and the fall in American popularity and influence abroad that the war provoked.

The United States is back to debating what to do next, but the setting of this debate is quite different from that of the past. In addition to the familiar world of interstate conflicts, some of the most horrible wars of recent years have been internal, and some of the most spectacular acts of violence have been committed by private groups of terrorists not allied to any state. More than a few of the members of the United Nations—Zimbabwe, Somalia, Uzbekistan—are "failed" or murderous states whose inhabitants live in a nightmare of chaos and violence. The "realists," i.e., those who believe national interests are fundamental, must now take into account the United Nations, which for all its flaws serves to certify legitimacy, as the current administration discovered when it defied the predominant opinion of the Security Council in attacking Iraq.

It is also a world in which globalization—partly under American leadership—erodes effective sovereignty of states (although least for the United States) and creates a world economy that offers a very complex combination of permanent competition—especially for oil—and incentives to cooperate, not only for states but for private interests. There is now a transnational society that includes multinational corporations, nongovernmental organizations, criminals, and terrorists. This global economy, with its unprecedented combination of private and state capitalisms, can be immensely destructive, as when it eliminated millions of jobs in developed countries. It deepens inequality at home and abroad. It lacks an adequate network of regulatory agencies and what international governance exists is stronger for economic relations through such organizations as the IMF and WTO than for political ones. So far, violence between states competing in the global economy has been limited, but in the contest for energy sources military force is already being used, for example in Nigeria, and could well increase. This, then, is the kind of world in which the "sole superpower" (as well as the largest source of global warming) must act: a world that is anything but flat.

America is now being widely criticized as a new empire. Toward the end of World War II De Gaulle wrote about FDR's will to power, a will that soon took the form of an American-controlled network of unequal alliances, military bases abroad, and economic dominance. The harshest criticisms of U.S. imperial aims were made against Bush after 2001: the United States and much of the rest of the world fell out over America's new unilateralism and its refusal to accept the International Criminal Court, the Kyoto Protocol, and arms control generally. Most nations were appalled by America's flaunting of its dominance; its use of preventive war, particularly the invasion of Iraq, was widely seen as proof of a will to reshape and dominate the Arab world.[1] America's new mixture of patriotism and religiosity annoyed many secularists at home and abroad, and the American way of fighting terrorism by bombing and torturing Iraqis and mistreating Afghans shocked many previously well-disposed allies.

Another category of criticisms concerns the American belief that globalization should come only in the orthodox form of American free-market and pro-business policies. Many Europeans see this as a denial of the state's responsibility to provide social justice, public services, and safety nets for the poor, the unemployed, and workers. Other sources of dismay were America's reluctance to include in international agreements provisions for standards of health or workers' rights, or to accept codes of conduct for multinational corporations, as well as the connections between American corporations and American political agencies—not only in occupied Iraq.

The most flagrant and widely deplored contradiction is between America's self-image as a force for democracy and human rights and a reality in which many rights at home are sharply limited, the death penalty continues along with the torture of "enemy combatants," and the United States repudiates the international laws of war. Abroad, U.S. support of dictators and its failure to protect victims of genocide in Rwanda and Darfur[2] have contributed greatly to anti-Americanism. Foreigners can observe for themselves, on the one hand, the weakness of public services throughout the United States, the cult of low taxes, and the distrust of any redistributive role for government and, on the other hand, the formidable apparatus of American military and intelligence services throughout the world and in the United States itself. The strength of America's destructive power and the lack of American interest in nation-building and development abroad have become all too evident.

Anti-Americanism is also fostered by various American illusions: "all human beings want what we want—freedom," to paraphrase George W. Bush; hence democratization should be easy.[3] Democratization has become confused with elections, and the legal institutions and protection of rights needed for a workable democracy are neglected. America sometimes downplays or denies its own nationalism in its rhetoric, and yet America has asserted its sovereignty more forcefully than any other advanced nation in recent history (including Mrs. Thatcher's Britain). Most other countries are more affected and limited by U.S. policies than the United States is by anyone else's. Therefore most countries are very uneasy about a world in which the United States is the single superpower.

Thus, while the mighty United States faces a huge number of problems that affect other nations as well—including global warming and the depletion of natural resources—at the same time it distrusts or attacks global institutions such as the International Criminal Court that could be of some help. It shows little understanding of the pride, fears, and humiliations of others, and has damaged its "soft power"—the power of influencing others through persuasion and example—by its policies in Iraq, its recent abuses in Abu Ghraib and Guantánamo, and its restrictions on foreigners eager to come to the United States.

II.

Several recent books have tried to go beyond such failures of the Bush foreign policy, particularly the war in Iraq and the violence committed in carrying it on.[4]

Francis Fukuyama's *America at the Crossroads: Democracy, Power, and the Neoconservative Legacy*[5] might have been called "Goodbye to Neoconservatism," which has dominated the Bush administration. He describes neoconservatism as a doctrine with four components: (1) "a belief that the internal character of regimes matters and that foreign policy must reflect the deepest values of liberal democratic societies," (2) a belief that American power "has been and could be used for moral purposes," (3) "a distrust of ambitious social engineering projects," and (4) "a skepticism about the legitimacy and effectiveness of international law and institutions to achieve either security or justice." He discusses how these aims have been contradicted by American support for dictatorship in the Transcaucasus and by the failure of the United States to provide adequate aid for people in Darfur or for the eradication of AIDS in Africa. He now calls for "multi-multilateralism," involving "new institutional forms," public and private, national and international, mainly aimed at meeting the economic needs of the global economy. He thinks such multilateral relations will be more efficient than treaty-based formal institutions such as the United Nations and its specialized agencies.

Since he believes this multilateralism is necessary, he criticizes America's attachment to absolute sovereignty. He also denounces the negative effects of American economic and political domination, which "rests on a belief in American exceptionalism that most non-Americans simply find not credible." Nor is it tenable, since "it presupposes an extremely high level of competence" that we do not have and a domestic political system with greater attention to, and willingness to finance, foreign policy goals than the American one. Moreover, "although political reform in the Arab world is desirable, the United States has virtually no credibility or moral authority in the region."

Fukuyama believes that U.S. power is most effective when it is latent and not seen (he mentions, for example, recent relations with India and other parts of East Asia), and most important when it is used to shape international institutions. He is obviously very far from his former neoconservative allies. Success in promoting democracy abroad depends on the past historical experience of a country, on the willingness of its government to organize free elections and thus "permit some degree of freedom for the groups that are part of civil society to organize" (as in Serbia or Ukraine), and on the political will within a society to overcome "bad governance, weak institutions, political corruption." His model for an "engine of institutional reform" is the European Union's process of admitting new members, which requires them to sat-isfy democratic requirements before being allowed to join the EU.

Why did Fukuyama, in view of his emphasis on multilateral institutions, ever sympathize with neoconservatism in the first place? The "realistic Wil-sonianism" he now embraces, along with his condemnation of excessive use of American force and threats abroad, is obviously very far from the neocon-servatives' credo. Also, how could he fail, as he does, to emphasize a crucial element in neoconservative doctrines—imperial ambition and pride? It has served to connect the neoconservatives and the apostles of brute force, like Cheney and Rumsfeld, who don't take seriously the democratic proselytizing of the neoconservatives. The imperial nationalism of both groups reminds one of that of the French Revolution, which wanted both to export the "prin-ciples of 1789" and to expand French rule of other countries. In neoconserva-tive thought, the idea of expanding hegemony was as important as that of encouraging democracy. The neoconservatives failed to understand the diffi-culties of both.

Stephen M. Walt's *Taming American Power: The Global Response to U.S. Primacy*[6] is no less critical of the Bush administration's record than Fukuya-ma's book. Walt and his former colleague John Mearsheimer were prescient opponents of the invasion of Iraq. His book is, however, primarily an incisive analysis of how the world's other countries have responded to American supremacy and tried to limit it. His chapter on "the roots of resentment" is particularly impressive. It is not only American power and official policies that are resented but also, in varying parts of the world, American political values, cultural products, and the activities of "U.S. corporations, founda-tions, media organizations, and various nongovernmental organizations." He writes that "the combination of a universalist political philosophy and a strong evangelical streak" is "bound to be alarming to other countries, includ-ing some of our fellow democracies." Walt deplores Americans' failure to understand foreign hostility. American leaders and much of the public, he charges, suffer from "historical amnesia," fostered by "U.S. textbooks and public rhetoric" that portray America's international role as "uniformly noble, principled, and benevolent."

Walt finds that while there have been few formal alliances to contain the United States, other countries resort to "soft balancing," defined as "the conscious coordination of diplomatic action in order to obtain outcomes con-trary to U.S. preferences." The refusal of the main European countries to back the war in Iraq is the most obvious example. At the moment, Venezuela, Bolivia, and Cuba have formed an alliance against American power in the Caribbean and Latin America, and to one degree or another, Brazil, Argen-tina, and Mexico are resisting American economic and diplomatic pressures.

Some states, he writes, are also mobilizing their domestic resources in ways that limit U.S. capacity to pressure them. Such a strategy can emphasize conventional military power, as can be seen in the growing strength of Chinese military forces. It can also take the form of terrorism and building weapons of mass destruction, both apparently aims of the current regime in Iran. The United States should try to discourage other nations from taking such measures, Walt argues, by seeking "to convince most states that they have little to fear from U.S. power unless they take actions that directly threaten vital U.S. interests." He believes a principal task of U.S. policy is to persuade other nations that its "privileged position is legitimate," which requires that the United States respect established international law and procedures—something it has failed to do before and throughout the war in Iraq.

Some nations, Walt believes, have collaborated with the United States for protection against threats, such as Lebanon and Jordan, which wanted U.S. help against the threat of Syria. Some foreign leaders "bond" with Bush—Blair being a cautionary example. He also mentions the efforts of foreign powers to influence Congress and the administration, the most flagrant case being the Israel lobby, the subject of his taboo-breaking essay with John Mearsheimer in the *London Review of Books* and of Michael Massing's recent article in the *New York Review of Books*.[7]

Writing as a traditional realist, Walt argues that America's national interest demands that it try to achieve a just peace between Israel and the Palestinians. If that fails because of Israel's unwillingness to grant the Palestinians a workable state, the United States should continue to support Israel's existence but no longer act as if Israel's interests and U.S. interests were identical. Instead, the United States should end its excessive military and economic support of Israel.

Moreover, he argues, large U.S. forces are no longer needed in Europe and only air and naval bases are needed in Asia. The United States should avoid preventive war, intervene in the Middle East only with the participation of others, and withdraw from military engagements, if they become necessary, after a "threat has been thwarted." The United States should also deemphasize its nuclear weapons programs so as to decrease "other states' incentives to get nuclear weapons of their own." Bush, by putting North Korea and Iran in the "axis of evil," only ensured that they would act more aggressively.

Similar conclusions are reached by John Brady Kiesling, for nineteen years a career foreign service officer with wide experience in the Near East and in Greece; he resigned publicly—with a strong letter explaining his decision to Colin Powell—when he became convinced that the Bush administration was determined to invade Iraq.[8] His *Diplomacy Lessons: Realism for an*

Unloved Superpower[9] provides the invaluable perspective of someone who has seen American foreign policy from the inside. What we learn from his lively, often witty, and incisive report is invaluable. The Bush administration hoped that some Greek leaders and much of the public would support its invasion of Iraq in view of past U.S. aid to Greece and collaboration with its military. In fact, he writes, the Iraq war was unpopular throughout Greece and U.S. standing there suffered because of it. American success depends "on respecting domestic politics in other states as well as our own. Those politics ultimately compel America to embrace the rule of law . . . as the basic principle of effective diplomacy."

Notwithstanding the advice of Kiesling and others, the administration simply did not understand that a Greek politician who supported the war would be in trouble. He also argues that "when the United States promotes local and regional security and prosperity, even to the short-run benefit of tyrannical regimes, it creates the soil in which democracy can grow." This happened in Taiwan, where U.S. protection helped to allow democratic forces eventually to take power.

Kiesling gives his own account of conflict between two types of foreign service officers: U.S. diplomats "whose playing field is the foreign country in which they are posted," and those he calls bureaucrats, such as the Bush administration's champions of "elf-aggrandizement and political fantasy at home, whose job is reinforcing the prevailing inclination of the chief policymakers. Lurking in some obscure or less obscure university is all the intellectual underpinning required for any fatuous scheme." He mentions the neoconservatives who, in the months before the Iraq war, introduced Professor Bernard Lewis to Dick Cheney.

Successful counterterrorism, Kiesling writes, requires respect for the lives of innocents. Iraqis, for instance, see dozens of their innocent fellow citizens being sacrificed again and again in American bombing attacks that often are unsuccessful against terrorists in any case. Yet their dismay and anger are not understood. Kiesling's condemnation of torture is eloquent: "The U.S. war on terrorism is at heart a war to strengthen the rule of law in societies whose citizens are themselves often helpless victims of illegitimate violence." The use of torture by the United States only makes a mockery of attempts to sustain the rule of law. As a working diplomat, he was appalled by bureaucrats who "took the word of their president that preemption of terrorism required unilateral violence and the death of innocent civilians."

Kiesling argues that U.S. insistence on expanding its own nuclear arsenal destroys any effective nonproliferation strategy. He finds secret intelligence operations often damage U.S. interests—for instance, when the CIA backed corrupt warlords in Afghanistan. "Secrecy's role in the U.S. government is to keep senior officials from learning from their mistakes." The "war on terror-ism" for Kiesling has been a "failed reprise" of the moral clarity of the Cold War. It has turned the most powerful nation into the most frightened one. He hopes for a political leadership "brave enough" to bring into the open the "hidden environmental, social, and other costs" of the American way of life. He writes in the tradition of George Kennan when he argues that while Americans may argue that their security depends on the spread of morality and justice abroad, they should first practice both at home.

III.

What would be the outline of a decent and effective American foreign policy? The first prerequisite, in my view, is to improve America's own economic and moral condition, a change that would be well-received abroad. This would mean a return to the rule of law and the protection of civil liberties, and an end to efforts to escape from the obligations of international law in the fight against terrorism. The United States should accept, despite its flaws, the Kyoto Protocol on global warming and try to improve it, and it should sign the International Criminal Court treaty. Accepting both would undo some of the damage of recent years.

The United States also needs a fiscal policy that would take seriously the reduction of America's deficit and debt, and therefore of American depen-dence on foreign countries that are willing to subsidize the United States by buying its debt in exchange for what we provide in return—security for Japan, access to U.S. markets in the case of China. Otherwise the United States will remain, in Charles Maier's words, an empire of consumption.[10] Greater investment at home in technological and educational progress is indispens-able. A serious effort, including a tax on carbon emissions, to reduce the con-sumption of oil in favor of new sources of energy is essential for several reasons: to preserve the global environment from global warming and other dangers, to escape from dependence on corrupt and tyrannical regimes in the Middle East and elsewhere, and to protect against the temptation to seize control of oil production in, say, Iraq as an insurance against possible trouble in Saudi Arabia.

A second prerequisite is a willingness to break dramatically with the for-eign policies of both Republicans and Democrats. Throughout the postwar era, and especially after the fall of communism, these policies have oscillated from multilateralism to imperialism, but they have assumed, as Walt does, that the world could only benefit from American primacy, seen as both a fact of power and a condition of world security and prosperity. Even Democratic critics of neoconservative hubris and critical commentators such as Walt have not put in doubt the need for the United States to set the course for its partners and for the world. Nor have the merits of the United States being the world's only superpower been seriously questioned, except on the isolationist fringe and among the libertarians of the Cato Institute. These deeply ingrained views, by now as ritualized as the late thoughts of Mao, need to be changed. They do not correspond with the realities of power.

The United States has an undeniable, overwhelming superiority in raw military might and in the capacity to project it. But as soon as we turn to other kinds of power—"hard" economic power, which is the power to reward, or bribe, and to coerce; "soft power"; and what I would call "building power," the power to help others construct their institutions—we see that we live in an increasingly multipolar world. This has become all the clearer in view of the recovery of Japan, the spectacular rise of China and India, and the growth of the EU, notwithstanding the current sluggishness of the European economy.

Global economic competition is now a clash of varieties of capitalisms, each one expressing a specific, mainly national, conception. And in recent years the United States has lost ground, whether in its influence in international economic organizations such as the World Trade Organization or in its generally inadequate efforts to help nations like East Timor, Sri Lanka, and Haiti to build badly needed national institutions. This is the result of many factors: the war in Iraq, the war on terrorism, and the U.S. ideological hostility to "nation-building," a view that is overtly expressed by the U.S. military and is generally supported by the conservative American preference for the market.

In fact, if we switch from a consideration of the ingredients of power to whether it can actually be deployed, we find that much American military power is practically unusable because of international risks (as with nuclear weapons) and domestic opposition both to the draft and to protracted wars with high casualties. Finally, even when U.S. military power can be used, it is often ineffective or worse, as is shown by U.S. failures to anticipate political problems in Iraq and to protect the population there from insurgent and sectarian violence. Military power, in short, can serve as a deterrent, but America should avoid using it to destroy cities, people, and regimes. For the most part, only soft power and the power of state-building and of promoting economic development, can have beneficial results.

Even if America's power were as enormous as U.S. politicians assert, there is a huge difference between American hegemony now and past empires. Nineteenth-century Britain had much less military power than the United States today, but it had much more ability to get things done within its empire than the United States in today's world. Hence the need for shifting from a policy of primacy (however cautious and considerate, as in Walt's analysis) to a genuine policy of partnership based on reciprocity and compromise. No doubt a world of 191 UN members and thousands of nongovernmental organizations requires leadership but this can be exerted by more than one nation (as has usually been the case in the EU), and that one nation should not always be the United States. The leader, or group of leaders, needs to work by means of persuasion and diplomacy, not command. The world political system too needs a degree of democratization.[11]

A true partnership is particularly necessary concerning several major issues. The first, and most urgent, is the Middle East. Two conflicts there have bred terrorism, jihadism, and hatred of the West, particularly of America. First, the Israeli–Palestinian conflict has been scandalously neglected since the fiasco of Camp David in 2000, despite the "road map" that has remained largely fictional. By now it should be clear that the occupation has long been the root of the trouble. It does not justify Arab terrorism aimed at civilians, but it goes a long way toward explaining it. Cutting off aid to the Palestinians because they voted for Hamas was exactly the wrong thing to do: it was punishment for exercising democratic choice. A unilateral "solution" imposed by Israel is no solution at all, only a recipe for continuing war.

The United States and its partners—the so-called Quartet—need to work hard for a two-state solution close to the one almost reached at Taba in early 2001. Then and now, a settlement would require that the Palestinians give up, in practice, the right of return to Israel, but it would provide them with a workable state that is not truncated or walled-in and has financial support. In arriving at such a settlement, Hamas—obviously divided between extremity and moderation—could be legitimately pressured to recognize Israel explicitly and to condemn terrorism unequivocally. In the immediate future, what is needed is a cease-fire based on a Palestinian declaration renouncing rocket attacks on Israel, and an Israeli declaration renouncing incursions and air strikes in Gaza. Moreover, the Palestinians would release the Israeli corporal held by their gunmen, Hezbollah would release the soldiers captured during its cross-border attack, and the Israelis would release the Palestinian officials they have seized.[12] To achieve these outcomes, as war spreads in Lebanon, would require far more active American participation than has been the case so far. The destruction of Hamas by disproportionate Israeli reprisals would have the same effects as destruction of the Palestinian Authority by Sharon earlier: it would escalate violence, further radicalize the Palestinians and much of the Arab world, and encourage further attacks on American passivity or "complicity."

In dealing with Iraq, what I proposed in the *New York Review of Books* two years ago seems all the more necessary[13]—a deliberately and carefully planned American withdrawal that would force the feuding politicians and the conflicting ethnic and religious factions to confront the reality of civil war and continued killing, and to try to find a political solution to the insurgency and to sectarian conflict. As long as American forces stay there, they both exacerbate the discord and terror and provide Iraqis with an alibi for ceaseless haggling. If the Iraqis want peace and unity as much as the American champions of "staying the course" assert, it is up to them to act accordingly. The argument about how much good we could still do by staying is, to put it mildly, undermined by how little we have done to provide protection and essential services to a population that the U.S. invasion exposed to bitter violence and hardships. We need to pull out completely, leaving behind no imperial residues. Whatever protection (of Sunnis, for example) will be needed should be entrusted to UN peacekeeping forces to whose creation and support we should be prepared to contribute both money and weapons. We should also get out of Afghanistan soon: our presence has not deterred a Taliban revival or the emergence of an opium economy dominated by the Taliban and warlords; non-American NATO forces should be supplemented by non-European forces under UN command.

Secondly, what is needed for the United States is—as Walt suggests—a drastic long-term policy of demilitarization carried out in collaboration with foreign partners. It should begin at home. The U.S. military and domestic security budget exceeds $550 billion and amounts to almost 20 percent of U.S. expenditures. It seems more like a program of public works than one of national security, and the American economy has other badly neglected domestic needs. Our military budget is more likely to be a provocation than a deterrent to America's current rivalry with China. A reduction of 50 percent in military expenditures would allow the United States to take better care of its poor, to establish a decent health care system, to improve education, and to invest in conversion to more efficient fuels. It would also liberate funds for urgently needed nation-building, health care, and development in Asia, Africa, and Latin America. This drastic change ought to be part of a plan that would aim, globally and regionally, at reductions in the nuclear arsenals of the established powers and at a new policy against nuclear proliferation.

This policy would include security guarantees to powers such as North Korea and Iran that have plausible fears of attack provoked by the hostility of their neighbors and the United States. The guarantees would entail nonaggression pacts, the reduction or departure of American forces near these countries' borders, and the kinds of arms control agreements that were worked out in the later phases of the Cold War between the United States and the Soviet Union. Such agreements would reassert the right of all signers of the nonproliferation treaty to nuclear energy for civilian uses—a right many more states may want to use so they would not have to depend on foreign oil supplies. It would offer them a range of choices, including the transfer of uranium enrichment activities to foreign suppliers that already have them. If a country insists on enriching nuclear fuel itself, it should come under strong international pressures to accept a very strict and intrusive inspection regime.

General rules are needed to prevent ad hoc deals, such as the new U.S.–Indian agreement accepting India's nuclear weapons programs. Nevertheless, a serious recent study of nuclear proliferation concludes that U.S. policy should be "more flexible, not less," and take into account the preferences of states for different "levels of commitment" and different kinds of non-proliferation schemes.[14] A policy of demilitarization would aim not only at putting an end to preventive war—which the 2006 U.S. National Security Strategy statement still supports[15]—but at ultimately eliminating most weapons of mass destruction and, in the meantime, at narrowing the gap between those who possess them and those who do not.

Thirdly, as for the United Nations, any useful changes in its structure are being blocked by the unholy combination of John Bolton and a number of developing countries, such as Brazil, India, Egypt, and South Africa, that are suspicious of the UN Secretariat's potential power. They are now opposing the reform plan endorsed by Kofi Annan. But in view of the poverty and instability of many states, the United Nations is in great need of more funds, more military forces, and more efficient and authoritative governance. It will be essential to reinforce existing international and regional organizations and to establish new ones in economic matters now unregulated (such as capital movements), as well as measures to ensure their accountability to the people they serve.

Another component of a new policy would be an effort, in association with other states, to consolidate the progress made in such states as East Timor, Georgia, and Uganda, and to rescue failed states such as Zimbabwe, the Central African Republic, Haiti, and Chad, which have been disastrous for their citizens and for other states, not only because, in most cases, of extremely bad leaders but because, as Lawrence Freedman has put it, of "sudden population movements, environmental disasters, [and] local conflicts being exported through expatriate communities."[16]

A new policy should also provide for a concentrated effort to protect human rights: while democracy cannot and should not be imposed from the outside, widespread violations of human rights, as in Darfur today, should be, along with defense against aggression, the only legitimate cause for collective armed intervention, preferably through forces put at the disposal of the

Security Council. Removing genocidal regimes should be legitimate if authorized by the United Nations or, if the United Nations is paralyzed, by an association of genuine democracies.[17]

Most challenging of all is the need to form a new "partnership" of advanced countries for the economic development of the underdeveloped ones. For many reasons—political, economic, and philosophical disagreements—this will be difficult to organize; the attempt to eliminate absolute poverty and to prevent the poor from succumbing to epidemics would be a worthy first step. At the same time national and international action to prevent the destruction and mass migration expected from global warming should become an urgent priority. An issue that threatens all countries, it requires energetic, diverse, and imaginative measures for the curtailment of CO_2 emissions. A revised and strengthened version of the Kyoto Protocol would be a beginning.[18] Most other problems shrink in comparison to this one.

These proposals may appear utopian. Yet striving to realize them would make for a safer world; they would not abandon or damage any of America's main interests; they would allow regional disputes to be dealt with primarily by the members of the regions, and with the assistance of international and regional agencies. The United States would not be the only "indispensable nation" or the nation that knows best what the real interests of others are. There is always a danger when dependent nations gain autonomy, but autonomy is the condition of responsibility. A world in which several large or middle-sized powers would have a larger say than they do now does not mean a return to the balance of power mechanisms of the eighteenth and nineteenth centuries in which war decided disputes. Competition has to continue, but—as Kant speculated—it should be constrained by the ever-increasing costs of war and by the benefits (as well as the dangers) of interdependence. As Kiesling puts it, "Morality and self-interest are inseparable, provided we persuade our politicians to take a long enough view of these interests. In the long run, security cannot be purchased at the expense of justice."

July 13, 2006

NOTES

Chapter 20 was published in *New York Review of Books*, August 10, 2006.

1. I have discussed many of these issues in *Gulliver Unbound: The Imperial Temptation and the War in Iraq* (Lanham, MD: Rowman and Littlefield, 2004) and *America Goes Backward* (New York Review of Books, 2004).

2. Samantha Power, in *"A Problem from Hell": America and the Age of Genocide* (New York: Basic Books, 2002) and in her subsequent writings about Darfur, has been an elo-

216   Chapter 20

quent voice against America's failure to protect the victims of genocide. So has Nicholas Kristof on Darfur.

3. My analysis of the "American style" in *Gulliver's Troubles: Or, the Setting of American Foreign Policy* (New York: McGraw-Hill, 1968) remains, alas, valid almost forty years later.

4. The most recent is Richard Falk, Irene Gendzier, and Robert Jay Lifton, eds., *Crimes of War: Iraq* (New York: Nation Books, 2006).

5. Francis Fukuyama, *America at the Crossroads: Democracy, Power, and the Neoconservative Legacy* (New Haven, CT: Yale University Press, 2006).

6. Stephen M. Walt, *Taming American Power: The Global Response to U.S. Primacy* (New York: Norton, 2005).

7. John Mearsheimer, "The Israel Lobby and US Foreign Policy," *London Review of Books* (March 23, 2006); Michael Massing, "The Storm Over the Israel Lobby," *New York Review of Books* (June 8, 2006).

8. John Brady Kiesling, "Iraq: A Letter of Resignation," *New York Review of Books* (April 10, 2003).

9. John Brady Kiesling, *Diplomacy Lessons: Realism for an Unloved Superpower* (Washington, D.C.: Potomac Books, 2006).

10. Charles Maier, *Among Empires: American Ascendancy and Its Predecessors* (Harvard University Press, 2006), chapter 6—a thoughtful and erudite exploration. See also the review by Robert Skidelsky, *New York Review of Books* (July 13, 2006).

11. See Dominique de Villepin's remarks in *Le Requin et la mouette* (Paris: Plon, 2004).

12. See Gareth Evans and Robert Malley, "A Proposal to Curb the Escalating Tensions in Gaza," *Financial Times* (July 6, 2006).

13. See Stanley Hoffmann, "Out of Iraq," *New York Review of Books*, October 21, 2004.

14. Jacques E. C. Hymans, *The Psychology of Nuclear Proliferation* (Cambridge: Cambridge University Press, 2006), 220–21. His arguments against the adoption by the foes of nuclear proliferation of a principle of a "duty to prevent" it by force if necessary are convincing.

15. See *The National Security Strategy of the United States* 4 (March 2006). Henry Kissinger has commented that "if each nation claims the right to define its pre-emptive rights, the absence of any rules would spell international chaos" (*International Herald Tribune*, April 13, 2006).

16. Lawrence Freedman, *The Transformation of Strategic Affairs*, Adelphi Paper 379 (Routledge/ International Institute for Strategic Studies, 2006), p. 32.

17. I have suggested such an association in *Gulliver Unbound*, and Fukuyama makes a similar proposal in *America at the Crossroads*. "Regime change" requires, however, remembering Auguste Comte's precept: "one can only destroy what one can replace"; it is the replacement of a genocidal regime that is the most difficult task.

18. In addition to Al Gore's movie and book, *An Inconvenient Truth* (Emmaus, PA: Rodale Press, 2006), see Tim Flannery, *The Weather Makers* (New York: Atlantic Monthly Press, 2005), and Elizabeth Kolbert, *Field Notes from a Catastrophe* (New York: Bloomsbury, 2006), all reviewed by James Hansen in *New York Review of Books*, July 13, 2006.

Index

tember 11, 36; Shklar on, 37–38; of
state of nature, 31, 35; Thucydides on,
31; war and, 32–33; of WMD, 34, 36
foreign policy, 2, 11–12, 134; in Europe,
194; UN and, 110
foreign policy, U.S., 3–4, 5, 111, 115, 136,
174, 184, 189; after September 11,
184–85; anti-Americanism from, 142,
205; break with Republican and Demo-
crat, 210–11; building power and not
just military power in, 211; bureaucrat's
fantasy in, 209; under Bush, G. W., 1,
122, 123, 184–85, 188; civil liberties,
fiscal policy, and, 210, 214–15; Cold
War, 204; collaboration, against mutual
threats, 208; counterterrorism, torture,
and, 209; decent and effective, 210–16;
demilitarization of, 213–14; democratization, nationalism, and, 205; distrust
of global institutions by, 205–6; failure
of, 204–10; global capitalistic competition and, 211; globalization and, 204–5;
Iraq, 189, 212–13; Israel, Palestinians,
and, 208, 212; neoconservativism and,
206–7; past hegemonies, power, and,
211–12; policy of partnership in major
issues for, 212, 215; in states, 143;
tyrannical regimes supported by, 209,
214; UN and, 214; U.S. power in, 113
France, 31, 34, 57, 203; on anti-Americanism, 161–62; Constitutional Treaty and,
196; EU and, 162, 163, 200; globalization and, 197; international affairs in,
164; on international law, 161; on Iraq,
160; on Iraqi sovereignty, 162–63; on
Iraq, U.S. v., 159–64; NATO and, 162;
Security Council influence on, 160; on
state sovereignty, 163–64; on Taliban
war, 159; on United Nation inspections
for WMD, 161; U.S. boycott of, 160
Freedman, Lawrence, 214
free market: capitalism in, 44–45; in EU,
195; ideology of, 22; in states, 46–47
French Revolution, 207

Friedman, Thomas, 10–11, 12, 13, 16, 27,
142
Fukuyama, Francis, 10, 206–7

General Assembly of United Nations, 48,
50, 107
genocide: intervention against, 92, 153;
UN on, 92, 107
Germany, 2, 203
globalization: anarchical society in, 16; cultural, 12–13; economic, 12, 15, 18, 24,
60, 111, 153, 181; effects of, 39, 75; EU
and, 198; France and, 197; Friedman
on, 10–11, 12, 13, 16, 142; hegemon
affected by, 135; international politics
and, 14–16; international relations and,
2, 5; NGOs in, 13; peace in, 16; political, 13, 111–12; social justice v., 205;
state fragmentation v., 9, 204; in states,
45; terrorism and, 7, 15, 16, 17–18, 25,
152; U.S.-European relations and, 191;
U.S. influencing, 13, 18, 108, 138–39,
148, 185, 204–5
global politics, conflicts in, 86–87
global society, 14, 16, 18; anarchical society
v., 76; capitalism and, 49–50; complexity of, 191–92; control attempts in, 149;
democracy in, 41; fear in, 31–41;
Hobbes on, 35; idealism in, 25; individ-
uals/states in, 96, 143–44; institutions
and, 19; Kant on, 47; liberalism in, 37,
41; terrorism in, 9, 17, 122; violence
and, 12
global warming, 204, 210, 215
Great Britain, 2, 32; on U.S. ally, 152
Great Powers, 56, 128
Greece, 209
Gulf War, 128; collective security and, 99;
in U.S.-European relations, 181

Hamas, 212
Hassner, Pierre, 17, 21–23, 22, 124
hegemony: dispute of, 133; globalization
affect on, 135; hostilities in, 135; insti-

222 *Index*

About the Author

Stanley Hoffmann is the Paul and Catherine Buttenwieser University Professor at Harvard University, where he has taught since 1955. His main areas of interest are international relations (including U.S. foreign policy and the ethics of international relations) and French political and intellectual history. His major books are *In Search of France* (co-author, 1965); *Gulliver's Troubles* (1968); *Decline or Renewal: France since the 1930s* (1974); *Duties Beyond Borders* (1981); and *Gulliver Unbound* (2004). He is currently working on a book on the French political community from the Old Regime to the present.